MW01288853

My Amish Roots

Stoltzfus Family Stories 1624 - 2010

Shawn Smucker

The painting on the front cover, "Tree of Life," is used by permission of Freiman Stoltzfus. To view his work, please go to: freimanstoltzfus.com

Acknowledgments

It is impossible to write any book alone, but especially a book like this. So many people have given me their suggestions, input, stories, and time.

First of all, I would like to thank Sam Beiler. Without his encouragement (in many forms) this book would not have come into existence. This was one of my first projects when I began writing full time in 2009, and without it I would probably be doing something besides writing. Thanks, Sam.

Thank you Amos and Hannah Stoltzfus for so many stories, so many chicken salad sandwiches, and for letting me borrow that priceless journal for a few weeks.

Thanks to Lloyd and Annie for the hot dogs, and for not minding when I showed up unannounced.

Thank you to all of Grandma's brothers and sisters, for letting me crash your sibling hangouts even though the younger generations are (normally) prohibited.

Thank you Grandma for telling me so much about yourself, your parents, and your grandparents. I am proud to be part of our family.

Thanks to the children of Henner and Naomi Blank who spent the evening answering my questions and sharing such wonderful stories with me.

Thanks to Paul Kurtz and Zach Stoltzfus from the Nicholas Stoltzfus Homestead for the valuable information and encouragement.

Thanks to Cody Hall, for helping me design the cover.

Thanks to Freiman for allowing me to use one of his beautiful paintings on the cover of this book. Your talent is unbelievable, and I'm proud to share common ancestors with you.

Thanks to Mom and Dad for introducing me to good books and letting me read them long after I should have been asleep.

To Maile,
for believing in me enough to go just about anywhere,
from the palm trees of Florida
to our little cottage in England
to the laughter and tears in Virginia,
and even into the darkness
of my parent's basement for four months.

You are the reason I write.

)

Introduction

PART ONE: SPRING AND THE OLD WORLD

PART TWO: FIVE SONS

PART THREE: FOUR DAUGHTERS

Introduction
Uncovering Fertile Ground

Who am I?

In Lancaster I could answer that question, "Samuel's Eli's Merrill's Shawn." In the rolling hills and fertile fields of this place you are the period to your great-grandfather's, grandfather's and father's existence. By the time you are born, your identity is already etched into the community's mind of stone, and whether or not that is an honorable lineage has, at least for the first half of your life, less to do with your own character than that of the three generations (of men) that came before you.

If those three names cannot clear up my identity for a fellow Lancaster County native, I'll ask them if they've heard of Squirrel Stoltzfus. Nicknames also help to identify us here, since so many generations have the same first and last names. My great-grandfather on my mother's side was known to crack walnuts with his teeth, so he picked up the nickname Squirrel. It's always amazed me how many people will know my family tree as soon as I tell them I'm one of the Squirrels.

"Oh, yes," they say. "Those Stoltzfuses."

My last name is Smucker, but I am also a Beiler, a Glick, and a Stoltzfus. I am the 10th generation of my family to live in Pennsylvania since Nicholas Stoltzfus arrived in 1766 with nothing but his family and a large storage chest. For nearly 250 years, we have been born here, lived here, farmed here, raised children here, started businesses here, grew old here.

Died here.

Who am I?

I never thought about that question when I was young. In fact, I have only a few memories from my early years: standing in a Springfield, Missouri, hospital cafeteria at the age of 2 ½, eyeing up the gum ball machine, waiting for my sister to enter the world; seeing my first road runner while riding with my dad on his motorcycle down a wild, dusty road in Laredo, Texas at the age of 4; sitting on my dad's lap as I drove the car home from our Mesquite, Texas church when I was 5.

Then, as if a switch was flipped, as if God said, "Let there be light," my memories began, and the initial point in this timeline is moving back to Lancaster, PA: moving "home". At the age of five, the majority of my life had been spent outside of Lancaster County, yet I got the sense from my parents, and the sudden emergence of cousins and aunts and uncles and grandparents, that I had indeed arrived home.

Sometimes I wonder if this homecoming in my early years helped to reinforce the strong bond I have with this place. Just at the age when my mind began retaining memories, I traded Texas heat for Pennsylvania snow storms, Spanish for Pennsylvania Dutch, and homes in those faraway places where my mother must have felt very lonely for a community that welcomed us back with shoo-fly pies and open arms.

Thirteen years after that homecoming, after going to the same school from 1st grade through my senior year and spending nearly every holiday with the same folks, I left Lancaster County for Messiah College. Not a monumental move by any standards, at least not when distance is the factor. But once I hit the turnpike and traveled west, everything seemed different. A world existed outside of Lancaster County that I did not know. Inexplicably, when people asked, "Who are you?" they only wanted to know your name – the name's of your father and grandfather and great-grandfather meant nothing to them.

When I left, I had no idea that I wouldn't live in Lancaster again for 15 years. How could I? That day (apparently Dad cried the whole way home), when mom and dad dropped me at my dorm, formed a bigger turning point for me than any 18 year old could capably understand. It sent me on a 15-year trajectory away from home. And back again.

In college, I met Maile. We got married, and once again trade-offs were made. We gave up the woods and winters of Messiah College for the sand and humidity of Jacksonville, Florida. After two years there, it was off to England, where the trees seemed so old that I thought, under the right conditions, they could tell me stories about the dragons that roamed there a thousand years ago.

During our time in England, my great-grandmother Katie Stoltzfus died. Stories were lost. Events, people, happenings that she saw were gone forever. Memories vanished with her last exhale, in the same way that the molecules of her last breath were dispersed around the room, then around the house, and finally out into the spring air where they rose into eternity.

The tragedy is that this happens every day, every minute, every second. Stories are lost. Stories are not like buried treasure – they cannot be dug up again. There are no maps with red "X"s, stuffed in bottles and thrown into the ocean which, when washed up on some distant shore, lead us to the location of lost stories.

We spent four years in England, after which Maile and I moved back to the States. Virginia this time: the suburbs. At some point during our life in Virginia I remember thinking, "I might go the rest of my life and never live in Lancaster County again." This thought gave me a somber feeling, as if a realization was setting in that I would never again see a particular old friend face to face. It was hard to imagine my four children growing up without the same surroundings, without the same hills and creeks and cornfields that had served as the backdrop for my childhood.

Would they visit "Amish country" as tourists? Would they ever answer the question, "Who are you?" with the response "I am Eli's Merrill's Shawn's"? Would they ever meet someone and explain their heritage with the inexplicable reply, "I'm a Squirrel"?

The thought that they would not associate themselves with their Anabaptist heritage saddened me. I felt so close to those roots; it meant so much to me. But an unforeseen turn of events brought us back "home," rather suddenly, and the thing I never thought would happen was suddenly staring me in the face: we lived in Lancaster County.

Old roads I hadn't driven on for years flew underneath me again: the kids shouted, "Go faster, Dad" as we careened down the same narrow country lanes from my childhood. The school I attended, the house where I grew up, the creek I fished in, the ball fields I played on: they swirled around me, each emanating their own ghosts and memories.

Yet the spirits of my past were not the only ones wandering these lonely cornfields.

I began hearing stories, just whispers at first, but then louder. Stories about my great-grandparents, my great-great grandparents. Fascinating stories of chance or fate or God, without which I literally would not exist. The early deaths of spouses that led to my great-great grandparents marrying. The survival of children who became my ancestors, in an age when 20% of children died before they reached the age of ten.

The more I dug, the more interesting it became. All of the ancestors I traced, from my grandparents back, had been Amish. At least as far back as the 1700s. It's a strange thing, having Amish roots yet never having lived in that community.

Stranger yet, I started seeing pieces of my own story in these men and women whose lives, while taking place so long ago, led to mine: the women's love for family and community; the men's relationship with the physical landscape of Lancaster and their passion for stories. I began to wonder if, at the end of this journey into history, I might find a key that would unlock a particular part of myself, a part that would otherwise remain hidden, forever.

I'm sharing this with you because I've learned through this process that we are not isolated beings. We have not been born into this world as only a piece of matter unto ourselves. We are connected. There are parts of us that go back hundreds of years and will continue hundreds of years into the future. Maybe it's your love of the cold. Maybe it's your sweet tooth. Maybe it's the way you have two cowlicks on your head. Maybe it's the way you stutter when you get excited. Maybe it's the way your body is shaped or your mind works.

Maybe it's the way you will die.

I think the beautiful part about knowing our family history is that sometimes the things we don't like about ourselves become explained, perhaps even cherished, when we see the root. I never thought twice about my bushy eyebrows, but now that I know they go back to my great-great-grandfather Amos King, I'm kind of happy about them.

So who am I?

Who are you?

I attended a Natalie Merchant concert recently. Towards the end of the show, she said that she had read, many years before, that commercial developers had covered up some of the most fertile ground in the world, here in Lancaster, with strip malls and shopping centers and parking lots. She found this to be one of the saddest stories in the world.

As each of my ancestors leaves this world and their memories and stories are lost or forgotten, it is as if another acre of fertile ground is covered with concrete. I feel an urgency to exhume these stories before the dump trucks and excavators and heavy pieces of machinery move in and level the hills, haul away the debris of demolished farmhouses, and begin pouring pavement.

These are the stories I was able to salvage, before the blasting begins.

PART ONE:
SPRING AND THE OLD WORLD

1624 – 1774

Paul Steltzefuss
m. Margarethe Eberhardt
|
John Adam Steltzfuss
m. Catherine Lerch
|
Christoph Steltzfuss
m. Anna Margarette Schwimmer
|
Christoph Stoltzfuess
m. Catherina Bergmann
|
Nicholas Stoltzfus

Chapter One
Her Last Breath, Or a Spring Breeze

May is a wet time in England: the earth is a saturated sponge, and the trees and tall hedgerows are such a deep green that they almost look black at dusk. But during the four years that we lived there, so much of that English countryside reminded me of Lancaster, PA: the ancient forests, the winding roads, and the fields that rose and fell, more like mountainous ocean waves than actual land that you could walk on.

As spring faded into British summer, the sun began to set rather late in the evening: I remember when the last parts of a sunset could still be seen at eleven o'clock. We rarely saw the night in those days – we were asleep before the sky went black, and by the time we woke up the next morning, sunlight blazed through our window.

There is something to be said for an existence formed entirely of light. There is a particular kind of energy that only sunshine can create. But I found myself missing the shadows, the stars, and the peace and stillness of a walk along a creek that reflects the dark sky. I've always been rather fond of the night.

On one of those not-yet-dark, not-yet-summer nights, my mom called. The five-hour time difference meant my wife and I were nearly asleep.

Calls at that time of the night were never made just to talk about your day.

"Hello?" I answered the phone, probably sounding very groggy, probably trying very hard not to sound groggy.

"Shawn?"

"Hey, Mom. What's wrong? Everything okay?"

"Were you sleeping? I'm sorry."

"No, it's okay. What's up?"

"I had to call. We're all a little sad," her voice caught, stumbled over itself, then continued in a somber tone. "Mummi[1] died this evening."

Mummi was what we called my great-grandmother.

"Oh, wow, I'm sorry, Mom. How's Grandma?"

"She's okay. You know. She's sad, too, but it was time."

A huge yawn engulfed my face for a moment.

"So where are you right now?" I asked.

"We're home, but we're going back over to Lloyd and Debbie's. That's where she was when she died."

I was quiet, just thinking. I remembered the last time I had seen my great-grandmother, at my grandmother's house, sitting hunched over in an armchair. I had walked over to her, sat down beside her in the neighboring armchair and asked a few questions. She had asked me about England, what it was like to live there. Her mind was as sharp as mine, but her eyes seemed lost in a misty shadow, sort of like those long hours of British dusk, and I had to lean in and talk loudly so that she could hear me. It takes some getting used to, shouting at someone whose face is only a few inches away from your own. But she loved to talk, and if she heard you, her mind was sharp enough to follow along with any conversation.

"I'll let you get back to sleep," my mom said.

"Okay, Mom. Call me tomorrow. Tell Grandma we're thinking about her."

"Good night."

"Bye."

---

[1] We always pronounced the term for my great-grandmother as "mummy," but that seemed strange to write. Some suggested that the proper spelling would be "mommy," but that didn't feel right either. So I went with Mummi.

I told Maile what had happened – one of those late-night conversations where neither of you can keep your eyelids pried open. We didn't talk long.

But after Maile fell asleep, I lay there, suddenly awake: it was almost as if I could feel the English spring fading with that particular sunset. I imagined, for a moment, flying out of the house, up through the May sky and that last ounce of sunlight, flying west, away from London. I pictured flying over the west coast of England where white-capped waves dash against prehistoric rocks, seeing Ireland all misty and green to the north, then continuing a few thousand miles over the Atlantic. The east coast of the United States came into view, and I flew south down the coast to Philadelphia. The skyscrapers rose up around me like a forest of concrete and steel.

Then, I went west.

Go west, young man.

The city streets morphed into suburbs, the suburbs flattened into cornfields in the spring when the foot-high stalks flap wildly in even the slightest breeze. The sun rose. Then, in my imagination, I saw Lancaster County: so many of its small towns formed by the crossing of two back roads; rows and rows of horse fences and the patchwork quilt of fields, tobacco and soybeans and ankle-high hayfields already mown once.

I pictured her white hair, her ivory skin, the way she smiled. I wondered what her last few days had been like.

My great-grandmother Katie Stoltzfus, referred to as "Mummi" by most of us, was a seventh-generation descendent of Nicholas Stoltzfus. He was the first Stoltzfus to arrive in America, 229 years before I write this. Mummi's energy and presence had spanned over a third of that time period. But it was May, 2005, and three days before she died, she had rested quietly in the house of her youngest son and his wife.

Relatives later told me that her eyes remained closed most of the time during her last days, her lips a flat timeline nearing its end. Everything around her faded, just as she was fading away from those around her. She lay on her back, her white hair gleaming against the new nightgown purchased by her granddaughters. The sheets lifted up under her arms. Her transparent hands rested at her side.

In the years leading up to that day, Katie's eyesight had irresistibly dimmed until most of the world was a blurry mix of darkness and light. Her hearing, too, had been turned down, so that we had to lean in and speak loudly, slowly. But in her last days, even these senses had become unnecessary. It wasn't on the perception of her vision, or the sharpness of her hearing that her life continued – it was on the strength of her heart, a heart that refused to stop beating.

So she lay there, waiting, and her family gathered.

Meanwhile, outside of the house, life pushed up from the fields. New things grew by the day, carpeting the flat areas in green. Summer approached, and spring prepared to fade. May in Lancaster is inevitably a green time, a new time, stopping for nothing. Not even the impending death of someone who had seen nearly 100 months of May.

You could have heard the singing from outside the house, they tell me, with the tiniest pearls forming in the recesses of the storyteller's eyes. The voices were beautiful, they say. Sometimes they sang quietly, so that she could rest. Sometimes they sang in boisterous tones, as if their singing were some kind of defiance against death and darkness. They were the voices of her family: sad and joyful, mourning and celebratory. They were the voices of her family, singing.

The family ate meals brought by friends or pizza delivered to their door. And, while they ate, they brought up all the old stories, the memories that Mummi had passed down to them throughout her 96 years. Sometimes the stories would end in raucous laughter, and there would be coughing and sputtering. "Do you remember the time…?" someone would begin, and even though everyone had heard that story a thousand times, they leaned forward, as if hearing it for the first.

At other times the stories would die down quietly, like the soft dimming of a light, and the entire group of them (some combination of her seven children with their spouses and children and grandchildren) would sit quietly in that particular memory, their heads bowed as if in prayer, letting the story soak in through their skin. In those moments of silence, mortality was not just pondered – it was grasped. The presence of the silence between stories served as a tangible reminder that some day, if all went well, each of them would be lying on a bed in a back room while their descendants told stories, laughed, cried, and waited for them to pass on. The circle of life could be felt in that silence.

If the silence lasted long enough, the seeds of songs would sprout. One voice would start, humming the tune. Someone who remembered the words would join. The silence in the spaces between stories usually led to mournful songs, the kind that long for death to come quickly so that paradise can be ushered in, the great end to all parting.

I like to imagine a stranger from a faraway place driving through the Lancaster countryside those days, marveling at the beauty of spring. I like to imagine that he heard the voices of my family singing during Mummi's last days. I like to imagine that he had to pull off the road and listen, and that he wiped his eyes because of the impending loss of someone who must have been so special.

My aunt Kate arrived from California the Tuesday before Mummi died – she was the oldest granddaughter. My great-grandmother Katie and my aunt Kate: these cycles and repetitions of life can slip by us, unnoticed, if we do not pay attention. There was a barely audible bedside exchange between the two, the passing of a tiny ember nearly extinguished. Kate sat beside Mummi's bed for hours at a time and took her in, like a breath: the sheets, the nightie, the old hands. Kate, only one year into her fifties, reached over and held one of Katie's nearly century-old hands – light as a piece of paper. Light as a story.

For two days they held vigil. The family waited. During that time, Kate heard all the stories of Mummi's decline.

She heard about how Mummi, staying with her daughter Priscilla, had been visited by two of her married daughters and their husbands. At one point Mummi joined them in the living room, the five of them talking, shouting for Mummi's benefit. Whenever she entered the room, they made adjustments for her convenience – her three daughters sat closer to her chair, and her two sons-in-law moved to the sofa.

At some point during the visit, Mummi got a confused look on her wrinkled face.

"Who is that third man on the sofa?" she asked.

The sisters looked at each other, bemused.

"What are you talking about ,Mummi?"

"Who is that third man on the sofa, between Amos and Lloyd?" she asked again.

Her daughter Priscilla leaned toward her and made sure that Mummi could hear her.

"Mummi, there's only two men on the sofa."

Mummi frowned, then stood up quickly (or as fast as she could) and walked away, her cane thump-thumping its own persistent rhythm.

"Well, I see three," she said, agitated, disappearing into her room.

This wasn't the last time that Mummi would claim to see, or talk to, people who couldn't possibly have been there, or people from her life who had passed away many years before.

It was also during those last weeks that Mummi asked Grandma why the horse-and-buggies were already lining up in the driveway. Why were they coming to view her? Panic began catching on to the edges of her voice. She wasn't dead yet. Did they know that? Did all of those people coming for her funeral realize that she wasn't dead yet?

Grandma did her best to reassure her that no one was coming to view her, that no one thought she was already dead, that no one would bury her while she was alive. These were sad days, when Mummi began to confuse her dreams with reality, when 96 years of life began to intermingle with 96 years of memory, like two tangled threads. She could be heard having conversations with her husband, Samuel Stoltzfus, who we had always called "Daughty." He had died 21 years before.

My Aunt Kate took turns sitting with Mummi. She entered the small room, settled in beside Mummi's bed and then reached over and held her hand. Tuesday turned to Wednesday. Wednesday turned to Thursday. The hospice employees couldn't understand how or why she was still hanging on. Her body had slowly begun shutting down, the way the lights go out in a skyscraper as the last person leaves each story. But her heart would not stop beating. Like a metronome set for eternity, it kept on: tick-tock, tick-tock, tick-tock.

Then, Friday, May 6, 2005.

Mummi was alone while everyone got something to eat in the kitchen, so Kate walked quietly into her dimly lit room. She could see Mummi's barely visible breathing. She sat in the chair and took Mummi's hand. Mummi's oldest son Amos came into the room and sat on the other side of the bed. Then Mummi's oldest daughter, Annie, came in and joined them. Oldest son, oldest daughter, oldest granddaughter.

They could hear people laughing and singing in the kitchen. Life going on even while death was preparing to enter the house.

"You know," Amos said, "I've heard that it's best to keep things kind of quiet when someone is dying. Mummi loved her family so much. Maybe it's hard for her to let go when everyone is around and we're all talking."

Kate nodded.

"That makes sense," she said. The three of them stopped talking for a moment and became deliberately still. Then Kate lifted Mummi's hand and placed it gently across her stomach. She had always held Mummi's hand when she sat by her bed, but in that moment, she decided to let go.

Less than a minute later, the softest exhale, like the last breath of wind on the last day of spring.

"That was it," Amos said quietly, fascination and sadness lining his voice. "She's gone."

"Are you sure?" Kate asked, leaning in slowly and looking intently at Mummi. "How can you tell?"

"I just know it," Amos said, his voice cracking. "That was her last breath."

A stillness swept into the room, but it wasn't an empty feeling. There was no despair. Only peace mingled with a kind of melancholy, like a sigh.

Or a spring breeze.

Chapter Two
The Limping Herdsman

Katie Stoltzfus died, and the world barely stopped to notice. There were no television news stories covering her life well lived; there were no lengthy newspaper articles heralding her existence. I was in England at the time, unable to make it home, and the days before and after Mummi's passing began to swirl together, like the colors of a child's painting. Sometimes I forgot that she had died, but the realization would eventually come, stark and sudden.

Our stories do not end with our death – they continue on, long into the future. Whether or not we have children, our influence on those around us shapes the future of the world in small and large ways. Our stories do not begin with our birth – so much comes before. So many sacrifices are required to lead to our existence. So many choices and accidental omissions.

The earliest traceable beginning of Mummi's story, which is also my story, began in Germany, four hundred years ago, a story in which I am the 13th generation. European wars, journeys spanning continents and oceans, deaths and unlikely survivors: so many things had to happen. It began with a herdsman named Paul Steltzefuss.

The limping herdsman prodded the stragglers with his wooden staff. A few of the younger men walked in the midst of the cattle, shouting them along, laughing to each other. The oldest man rode a horse, slumped forward, a dark cloak draped down over his shoulders, covering half of the animal. His staff dragged along the ground – he was nearly asleep.

Approximately fifteen to twenty cattle, directed by five men, funneled on to the muddy road that ran through the main street of the forest village. Hut-like houses lined the narrow thoroughfare. Tall trees mingled with the drab structures. Mountains rose in the distance: sheer cliffs of slate-brown and a muted green, a grim contrast against the steel-gray sky.

The herdsman had driven the cattle through the surrounding hillsides that day, occasionally grazing them along the river. The muddy ground at water level sucked around the animals' hooves. The men wandered, always close by. The river ran straight through the hills, below the village, then was pushed aside by the mountains.

The lone herdsman limping at the back of the pack stopped for a minute as the rest of the men and cattle were welcomed into town. His clothes were brown and off-white, and his hat had a wide, floppy brim that allowed the rain to drip away from him. His face hid in the shadow.

Wood smoke rose from the huts as the village prepared for an evening meal. The herdsman limped the rest of the way into town, leaning heavily on the staff. He sat at his small dwelling and tried to rub the ache out of his leg. The sky began to dim as night fell. Stars traced their path across the void. All was quiet in the small village, save the barking of dogs at invisible animals, but rumors of war infiltrated the villagers' sleep. The children had nightmares of being led away in shackles. Adults dreamed that their village was on fire, woke with a start, and listened carefully for the approach of some far-away army.

But the next morning all was well, and the herdsmen took the cattle out again.

This image comes from Pieter Bruegel the Elder's painting, "Return of the Herd." Bruegel lived in the mid-1500s in Northern Europe, just before my ancestor Paul would have been born. He was known for his paintings of peasant life and proverbial images. Even though it is very unlikely, I can imagine that my great-great-great-great-great-great-great-

19

great-great-great-great-grandfather Paul Steltzefuss is the herdsman at the back of the painting, the portly fellow with a limp, watching the young men from the village run among the long-horned cattle.

During the 1600s, perhaps when Paul Steltzefuss was about my age, a struggle for power by surrounding countries collided in Germany. Frederick V accepted the Bohemian throne and was crowned in Prague in November 1619, in blatant disregard for Ferdinand II, recently chosen as the Holy Roman Emperor. Technically, due to that election, Frederick owed the new emperor his allegiance, but by accepting the Bohemian crown, Frederick was challenging the rule of the Holy Roman Empire.

Ferdinand organized a powerful army, aimed at squashing the forces of Protestant Frederick. This army was pulled from surrounding duchies and strategic partners: Maximilian the first contributed most of the force and was promised the lands and positions of Frederick, should he be defeated. Frederick, in the mean time, received no practical support from the surrounding Protestant nations.

A one hour battle at White Mountain decided it: the armies, organized by Maximilian and Ferdinand, marched on Prague, and Frederick's Protestant army crumbled. Nearly one year to the day after being crowned, Frederick fled Prague, his family in tow. Frederick's wife, Elizabeth, was the daughter of James I of England, and their one-year reign led to them being referred to as the Winter King and Queen. A century later their grandson would become king of England: George I.

The emperor Ferdinand II and Maximilian I gained a lot of resources and riches with the victory. But the two seemed highly suspicious of each other – at that point Ferdinand controlled Bohemia, and Maximilian held part of Austria to keep Ferdinand in check but also as a deposit until Ferdinand repaid all of his war debt. [2]

Thus began Ferdinand's oppression of Bohemia, modern-day Germany, bringing him an enormous fortune.

---

[2] http://www.historyworld.net/wrldhis/PlainTextHistories.asp?ParagraphID=idd#ixzzz0tzvuiDFr

These are the contrasts that stories present to us: there is the broad, all-encompassing importance of a war, and then there is a detail so small as to at first seem insignificant. A gravestone with a date etched into its mossy surface; a crumbling stonewall; the last name of a peasant man.

But in the 16th century a man's name conveyed much more meaning than it does today, and the name of my ancestor, Paul Steltzefuss, literally means "stilt-leg" or "stilt-foot." The theories as to how exactly he received this name are endless: perhaps he was a traveling clown? a worker who wore stilts? The simplest explanation is most often the answer, and in this case, Paul probably got his last name due to a severe limp. His last name could very well be translated peg leg, if we apply the vernacular of our day.

Stoutness runs in the Stoltzfus side of our family, and I've always struggled, off and on, with a sciatic issue that gives me a severe limp for weeks at a time – perhaps it's a gift from my ancestor Paul. How interesting, if he had the same nerve pain that I have, and that's how he got his name?

He is listed in the town registry as a herdsman, so his profession at that particular time would have been attending to the various livestock of the town. Did he get his limp when an animal from the herd stepped on his foot and broke it, or was he relegated to watching the herd because he was born with a disease like MS or polio? Or did a birth defect cause his limp?

Whatever the case, the time during which Paul was alive was a time of radical and violent change. Nations were on the move, and their boundaries in constant flux. Kings gathered fortunes. Wars were fought. In the midst of these kings and nations waging war all around him, oblivious to the decisions being made by Ferdinand and Frederick and Maximilian, Paul Steltzefuss was one of the millions of poor peasants and shepherds and farmers trying to scratch together enough food to get through the day. I can imagine him wandering the hills with the herd, slowly meandering through the woods and the fields and walking along the streams and rivers.

Then Paul, as men have done in every generation, spotted a woman he wanted to marry. It is doubtful that she had money, as peasants generally found a marriage partner from among their own ranks. But however they met, and whatever the courtship, in 1624 Paul Steltzefuss married

Margarethe Eberhardt, the earliest known matriarch of the Stoltzfus family. Yet we know nothing about her personality: what was she like? Quiet or boisterous, large or small, kind or cruel? Which of her traits would we recognize in the matriarchs of our Stoltzfus families today?

Around that time, the Anabaptist followers of Jakob Amman began moving from Switzerland into the Alsace and other northern destinations, the Duchy of Zweibrucken in Germany being just one. Amman had recently led the split from the Mennonites – his followers would eventually be referred to as Amish.

Ironically, the Anabaptists, while known today for their stringent pacifism, were, in those early times of their history, often associated with violence and upheaval because of the Muntzer rebellion during which Anabaptist Thomas Muntzer led the peasants of Bad Frankenhausen in an unsuccessful uprising against the local lords. But even in the 1600s, this was mainly a misrepresentation, as the Anabaptist community, nearly as a whole, had embraced the non-violent example of Menno Simons and others. This attitude of non-violence would eventually be exemplified in *The Martyr's Mirror*, and the spread of those stories solidified these values within the Anabaptist community.

But why mention this northern migration of the Anabaptists when Paul Steltzefuss was anything but an Anabaptist? Because their movement across the landscape would have a huge role in determining the future of Paul Steltzefuss's descendants for hundreds of years to come.

We know little else about Paul Steltzefuss. We don't know how the war impacted him or exactly how close the battles came to him. I imagine him traveling slowly around the hillsides on the outskirts of his village, tending the animals, watching for threats, listening for the clash of swords off in the distance.

I wonder what his dreams were. What were his aspirations?

The 30 Years War would be remembered as a period of chaos and upheaval that took the lives of nearly 3 million Germans. It was a violent time. Somehow, not only did Paul Steltzefuss and Margarethe survive, they also had a son. Their bloodline continued. Their heritage was passed down.

Chapter Three
Sewing Her Own Funeral Gown

Like all Amish after they die, my great-grandmother, Mummi, was given a viewing before her funeral. It was held at her son Samuel's house, where she had stayed one out of every six or seven months, as she made her way around to live with her children in her later years.

Mummi was laid in her room. As is customary for Amish viewings, they removed all the furniture and pictures, so that when her family came into view her body, the only thing in the room was the coffin, and a gas lantern either hanging from the ceiling or resting on a small side table. There was one window.

When my mom arrived to view her grandmother, it was mostly dark out. The gas lantern hissed persistently, as if fighting against not just the darkness but death itself. My grandmother escorted my mom into the room to view Mummi – this also is how things are done. A family member of the deceased always takes you in – no one goes into the room unaccompanied.

Mummi had been placed in an Amish-made coffin. The wood was stained dark, and the inside had a white lining. Her hair was white as a field of lilies. This is what everyone seems to remember the most about

Mummi as she lay in her coffin: the perfect whiteness, so much of it in that dimly lit room. Her hair, the coffin's lining, the light: these were not the only white things in the room. Her gown was also white.

She had made that gown herself.

This making of one's own funeral gown is another Amish tradition. At some point during the previous years, while she could still see, my great-grandmother made her own funeral gown. I can imagine her working on it, late at night, when she knew she would not be interrupted. I wonder what she thought about as she placed each stitch: I imagine her patiently threading the needle, a reminder that someday she would no longer be here. Each tiny pull on the thread represented one day in her life, each portion finished was like an event or a time period. A sleeve for her childhood. A seam for her marriage.

When it was completed, she put it away. Done was done. She laid the white gown in a box and stored it under her bed. That was it. She was ready.

My mom looked at great-grandmother lying in the coffin. Over the white funeral gown she also wore an organdy white cape and apron, the very same one she had worn on her wedding day. Organdy is a plain-woven, sheer, stiff cotton fabric. My grandma noticed that Mummi had altered it in later years to fit her – her body had changed from her wedding day, as all do.

I don't know if Mummi ever did this, but I imagine her standing in front of a mirror, altering her wedding cape and apron, not having worn them for 60 or 70 years. I wonder if she thought about the difference between the young girl who had first worn that cape and apron, looking forward to life, and the 90 year-old woman reflecting on a life. Probably not. Mummi seemed very matter-of-fact. I don't know if she would have given much value to melancholy reflections.

Something about making your own funeral clothes sounds very peaceful to me: acknowledging the inevitability of death, planning for it, staring it in the face for a moment, but then placing that realization under the bed, going about your everyday life, knowing there is little to be done about it.

When Amish people die unexpectedly, sometimes it is left to the living to make their funeral clothes. My aunt remembers visiting some

24

relatives the day after a loved one died. The daughters sat in a circle in the living room. They would cry, and they would sew, and then they would graciously allow someone else to have a turn.

"I'll do this sleeve," one of them would say through tears. It was an honor for them to make the clothes their loved-one would be buried in, and still they passed the garment graciously, giving everyone a turn.

My great-grandmother's viewing was held all day. The churchwomen made food for the meals. Family and friends came and went, visiting with the immediate family. They were taken into see Mummi. They were brought back out. And so the day went.

Finally, well after dark, the family made their way around the house. They pulled down all the green window curtains, as if to say to everyone, "Thank you for coming. The viewing is over." The front door is pulled tight. Then, as if on cue, everyone in the house got down on his or her knees to pray.

My mom was still there. She was no longer Amish at the time, but her Amish cousins and Amish aunts and uncles surrounded her. One of the preachers from the church read the prayer, speaking in Pennsylvania Dutch, but my mom couldn't focus on what he was saying. She could only think one thing.

"I still feel like I'm Amish."

Her parents, my grandparents, had left the Amish when she was a little girl. But not before the lifestyle had seeped into her blood: the plain clothes, the horse and buggy rides, the winter evenings playing games under gas lanterns. Kneeling there, on the floor, she knew that it was still in her, somewhere.

It went on for three or four minutes, the preacher's voice praying in that sing-song way with heavy Germanic accents that generate from the back of the throat. Those languages, both Pennsylvania Dutch and High German, sound rich and deep to me, solemn, like a freshly plowed field at dusk.

The sound of the prayer reached throughout the house, even into the back bedroom, empty save for Mummi's body lying in her coffin. Her dying day had come and gone, as had her viewing. The cool evening crept in around the doors. The window in her room was dark.

Approximately 400 years before my great-grandmother Katie Stoltzfus's viewing, John Adam Steltzfuss was born, the son of herdsman peasant Paul Steltzefuss. He most likely became very comfortable around animals, knowledgeable in their ways and ailments. Like most young boys he probably adored his father and wanted to be just like him, at least for a time. But, also like most boys, at some point he started wanting to attain more than his father had. He wanted to go further in the world.

Somehow John managed to receive an education and become a teacher in the town of Bad Frankenhausen, Germany, the very same town in which Anabaptist Thomas Muntzer had led The Rebellion. It is difficult to know if the civilians of Bad Frankenhausen still considered the Anabaptists a violent sect due to their involvement in The Rebellion – after all, over a century had passed. But whether or not they were viewed as potential anarchists, they were certainly still viewed as outsiders with heretical theological viewpoints. Because of this, many basic rights, such as owning land or marrying outside of their sect, were still denied them.

It is very likely that John Adam Steltzfuss would have had a negative view of Anabaptists, something I find extremely ironic since we now know him as the great-grandfather of Nicholas Stoltzfus, one of the most prolific progenitors of Anabaptists ever. I wonder if John Adam Steltzfuss viewed the Anabaptists of those days with skepticism or fear, disdain or loathing. I wonder if he knew any of them personally. It seems unlikely.

But whatever his relationship with that small sect, John married Catherine Lerch and continued his studies until receiving a degree in divinity, eventually accepting a Lutheran pastorate at St. John the Baptist Church in Rottleben, Germany. Being a Lutheran pastor makes it even more likely that John would have held strong anti-Anabaptist sentiments – the Lutheran church instigated much of the persecution against the Amish and the Mennonites in those times.

John and Catherine had a son: Christoph Gottlieb Steltzfuss.

Christoph married Anna Margarette Schwimmer and followed in his father's footsteps, joining him as a minister at St. John the Baptist.

Christoph and Anna had a son, also named Christoph, but Christoph Sr.[3] only lived to the age of 36. This means Christoph Jr., was 16-18 years old, at the oldest, when his father died. His grandfather, most likely, was no longer alive. Perhaps this explains why, unlike the two previous generations, Christoph Jr. did not enter the ministry but instead took up a trade.

Christoph Stolzfuess Jr. worked as a wig maker and provided his craft for various dignitaries in western Germany. Way back in 1624 – ironically, the same year that Christoph Jr.'s great-grandfather Paul Steltzefuss married Margarethe – King Louis the VIII went prematurely bald and had an extravagant wig made. These decorative wigs became all the rage throughout Europe, worn by all upper class men. By the mid-1700s even the middle classes wore them.

Christoph Jr. was the first businessman in a long line of Stoltzfus businessmen. He was also probably seen as a bit of a rebel since he did not follow in his father and grandfather's footsteps to become a minister. But I have never known "rebellious" and "Stoltzfus" to be antithetical.

Back then wigs were made of horse hair, yak hair, or human hair (the most expensive): "A man could outfit himself with a hat, coat, breeches, shirt, hose and shoes for about what a wig would cost him. A wig also required constant care from a hairdresser for cleaning, curling and powdering." [4]

As wigs became more popular, it wasn't uncommon for many wig-makers to eek out a living in the same town. Some set up shop the way we think of storefronts today – others traveled from area to area, offering their services on the road.

Our family wig-maker, Christoph Jr., eventually married Catharina Bergmann – the name Catherine would become a popular name for Stoltzfus girls in the family for the next 150 years. My great-great grandmother was named Catherine, but at some point during her life

---

[3] When two men from successive generations share the same first and last name, I refer to them as Jr. and Sr. – this is not their official name, but just an easy way to differentiate between them.

[4] http://www.costumes.org/history/100pages/18thhair.htm

and for reasons I don't know, started going by Katie, and after that Katie seems to be used more often in my family.

In fact, there is an interesting pattern in the names of the wives chosen by those early generations of Steltzfuss/Stoltzfus men:

Paul Steltzefuss married a Margarethe.
John Steltzfuss married a Catherine.
Christoph Sr. married an Anna Margarette.
Christoph Jr. married a Catherina.
Nicholas married an Anna
Christian Sr. married a Catherine.
Christian Jr. (Nicholas's grandson) married an Anna.

Christoph Jr. and Catharina eventually moved back to East Germany in the early 1700s.

In 1717, or thereabouts, Catharina gave birth to a son. But this boy would not be just another male born within this family in the 1700s. He wouldn't follow in the steps of his parents, remain in Germany, father his own children, and then die. Something of the adventurer's spirit was born in him. Eventually he would change the course of his family's history, the course of my history.

The son's name was Nicholas Stoltzfus.[5]

---

[5] I am deeply indebted to those at The Nicholas Stoltzfus Homestead, particularly Paul Kurtz and Zach Stoltzfus, for providing me with direction and historical information regarding the Stoltzfus family before their immigration into the United States. Zach gave a presentation some time ago regarding these topics, and it was his expertise on the matter that revealed much to me about my ancestors leading up to Nicholas Stoltzfus's arrival in the New World. He was also kind enough to review these initial chapters for historical accuracy. For more information on how the Nicholas Stoltzfus Homestead is being preserved, or to arrange for a tour, please visit http://www.nicholasstoltzfus.com

Chapter Four
The Evolution of a Name

The weather was beautiful the day my great-grandmother was buried. The sun shone as if it was the first day it had ever seen. The May sky was blue. Spring was running its course. Summer was on its way. The life of that year reached its next transition.

The funeral was held in a small barn, and attendance was strictly by invitation only.   They had to cut the line at the great-grandchildren because there just wasn't space for more. It's always such an honor to be invited to someone's funeral in the Amish community, but most of the time it's more about how much space is available – the services are held in the area of the church, because the church people take care of the food and hospitality for the day.

The endless row of buggies seemed to take forever to arrive, and once they did, the young men helping to organize the event wrote a number in chalk on the side of each buggy to help match the proper horse with the proper buggy. The family received the first numbers based on birth order. It's a sort of Amish valet parking.

At the gravesite the casket was opened for one last viewing. It was moving for the family, saying good-bye. Then, the pallbearers lowered her casket into the ground. There was a final graveside sermon, and then, the digging began. The preacher read scriptures in Pennsylvania Dutch while the men took turns with four shovels, using the mound of dirt that had been removed to now fill the hole. The clods made plodding sounds on the casket, competing with the preacher's voice. Then, the sound became earth falling on earth.

All of the removed dirt was put back in place, forming a small hill, Mummi's own little patch of earth. And it was over.

My aunt says it was so different than a normal funeral, where you watch the casket go down and then you walk away. It was a completely different feel, just watching the grave get covered by people that love her, their last act of care and love for a woman who meant so much to them. So much silence. So many tears. All along the sun shone down from the bluest of May skies.

It was so honoring. And so final.

Steltzefuss.
Steltzfuss.
Stoltzfuess.
Stoltzfus.

The evolution of a name. Who knows why each subtle change was made? Ironically, the only time the name remained the same in my early ancestors was when John and Christoph Gottlieb shared the same occupation. But with Nicholas, the name had arrived at its final version, or at least the version that we recognize:

Stoltzfus.

Nicholas was born around 1717 in eastern Germany. It's a long way from eastern Germany to eastern Pennsylvania where Nicholas ended up, especially in the early 1700s. But as you consider the facts of Nicholas's life, the reasons for his trek become increasingly understandable.

Nicholas's father Christoph Jr., the wig-maker, died at the age of 29, meaning both Nicholas's father and grandfather died young. His mother remarried, to a man named Daniel Bellair, a pond maker in the Duchy of Zweibrucken – since this was Nicholas's only living relative that we know of, it is likely that Daniel may have taken Nicholas under his wing and perhaps helped him learn a farming trade.

But there was another, well-known group of people who were also farmers in that area. That's right – the Anabaptists. The Amish.

In the preceding decades, many Anabaptists, stripped of their rights as citizens, could only obtain farmland in the hills where it was assumed they would be unable to make a living – the soil was unworkable, and the conditions for farming were poor. Yet, using new techniques, they were able to provide for their families, and became renowned as successful farmers. Some of them farmed around Zweibrucken, close to where Nicholas lived.

There were two separate sects of Anabaptists living in Zweibrucken at the time: the Hook Mennonites wore hooks on their clothes and followed Jacob Ammon; the button Mennonites were followers of John Reist. [6]

Enter Nicholas.

Having taken on a farmer's trade, he set out, probably in his early 20s, working on his own. Many of the men in those days were self-employed farmers, contractors of sorts, hiring themselves out to whomever would pay them the most. Then Nicholas, son of a wig-maker, grandson of a Lutheran pastor, somehow gets hired on at a farm in Zweibrucken. This seemingly minute detail changed the course of our history.

He saw a girl and fell in love, but there was a problem: she was an Amish girl, and Nicholas was, by birth, a Lutheran. Marriage between a Lutheran and an Anabaptist was illegal – being a Lutheran was mandated by the State. Yet, the romance inched forward.

What was it about this girl that so drew Nicholas? Was it her beauty? Did they befriend each other while working side-by-side in the fields? Or could Nicholas, alone and without a family of his own, identify with the marginalized state of an Anabaptist woman? Whatever the case, Nicholas and the girl decided to marry, but before they could proceed they needed permission from the local magistrate.

Nicholas made the request, and it is noted in the town documents. It would appear the local magistrate, or someone with similar responsibilities, then wrote to a superior asking for input on such a rare request:

---

[6] Ernest Drumm, *The Revealed Life of Nicholas Stoltzfus; Out of the Archives of Zweibrucken.* Researched and com-piled by Levi Stoltzfus. Masthof Press, 2009.

Nicholas Stoltzfus, who went over from the Evangelical Luther religion to the Anabaptist sect [wishing] to marry an Anabaptist's daughter will want to establish himself in the land; instructions are requested.

The local authorities considered Nicholas's case, and he was met with this reply:

Most humbly we inform with reference to Nicholas Stoltzfus as on the 14th instant. On account of the recorded circumstance of the applicant, and because this person who benefited by the religion of his parents, the Evangelical (Lutheran) religion, for eight or nine years according to what his parents say, and then went over to the Anabaptists sect, for this reason the requested marriage certificate was denied, as recorded February 13

So because Nicholas was already Lutheran and benefited from a society founded on Lutheran ideals, his request was denied. When the couple received the note, I'm sure they were devastated. Imagine living in a time when permission to marry could be dictated by the local government. But they refused to give up. Nicholas decided to write an appeal.

Nicholas's appeal to this decision is "dialectal, poorly written and mixed with Latin terms." His communication is not another application for marriage, but recognition of the laws then in place and an appeal that the law be overlooked in his case:

> To the most high Duke, most gracious Prince and Lord concerning my proposed marriage, highly honored high official, that has been protested; the marriage with Rinkweyler landlord's daughter, an Anabaptist, the reason for submitting a request for permission is as follows. Because the parents of this party have left nothing to give, but are from Saxony where I was born, the deceased father Christopher Stoltzfus, and my mother, born of Friessen Bellens, true wife, Evangelical Lutheran religion, and I was living with mother in that land, but after my mothers death I very soon needed to go to strangers for employment, for this reason from that first time on, having given up my first

employment, I settled in and around Cron Wyssemburg, steadily, and had the opportunity to be among that kind of people and no other than Anabaptists, and got used to them and was among them and was instructed in their religion, and convinced to remain among them and had further opportunity to work for such people around Rinkweyler, yes, and even to marry among them was my decision, and since I am now 25 years old, and have nothing to expect from my parents, and by such a marriage I can assure my subsistence, so then if one would consider my circumstances in this time of need of support, and the worthy, princely Lord would most graciously permit me to marry.

Zweibrucken, January 14, 1744

Your most submissive and obedient

Nicholas Stoltzfus [7]

Twenty-five years old and completely alone. His mother dead. His stepfather may have still been living, but there was no legal requirement, no bond of love or responsibility between them.

Nicholas appeals to the Lord's reason (he is alone and this marriage will "assure his subsistence"), to his sympathy ("after my mother's death"), and to his pride ("the worthy, princely Lord"). The couple waited, for who knows how long. Then, finally, they received word.

Permission was granted, but only with the stipulation that they leave the country for a time, so in 1744 they married, and he converted from Lutheran to Anabaptist. I'm tempted to gloss over that sentence; after all, conversions today are commonplace. People convert from one denomination to another, from one way of doing things to another. Many who attend church will leave for another congregation or even another religion. Conversion is a mathematical term, as much as it is a theological one.

But conversion for Nicholas was anything but a matter of figures or a quick change of mind during which he decided to stop attending one church and start attending another. No, to convert to Anabaptism in the

---

[7] Ernest Drumm, *The Revealed Life of Nicholas Stoltzfus; Out of the Archives of Zweibrucken.* Researched and com-piled by Levi Stoltzfus. Masthof Press, 2009.

17th century was a monumental decision in which he laid down almost all of his rights as a member of that community – no longer could he live wherever he wanted or own land or work just any job. He took upon himself the stereotypes of what it meant to be Anabaptist. He became an outsider, all for love.

In other words, he was a hopeless romantic.

Nicholas and his first wife, whose name we do not know, resurfaced in the community records seven years later, in 1751, in paperwork filed over a horse dispute. How were they permitted to return? How long were they gone? Where did they go? So many questions for which we may never have answers.

Some records would indicate he was then a pond digger, a trade he may have learned, or at least become familiar with, thanks to his stepfather – ponds were commonly used as a habitat to grow fish. But whatever his way of earning a living, something life-changing happened to Nicholas in 1766, something that would have a profound affect on many Stoltzfuses alive today: Nicholas decided to leave the area where he lived, the country where he had grown up, for good. He decided to lead his family on a huge endeavor.

They would move to the New World.

Chapter Five
The Death of Nicholas

Had the Nicholas Stoltzfus family always considered a move to America? What we do know is that Nicholas Stoltzfus and his family left for America on the Ship Polly, captained by Robert Porter. In most cases, the tickets cost the voyagers all the money they had, meaning they arrived in the New World with only their possessions and the clothes on their back; if they didn't die on the journey, there was a good chance one of their family members had died or wouldn't survive long after they landed. For most of them, when they arrived, there would be no one to greet them.

The conditions in the boats were such that in 1765 a supplement to an existing German law was implemented in order to standardize these conditions, to make them safer and to protect the interests of the passengers from unscrupulous shipping companies:

> 1765 – Supplement to the German Shipping Bill. In the same Law Book mentioned in the above item there is set forth an act that was passed May 18, this year, to better protect the Germans, that came over in crowded ships. This act sets forth that to

protect these people and at the same time to enable the ship owners to recover their fares, that certain regulations must be made. Among these regulations it is set out that there must be room for each passenger, and that these rooms must be three feet nine inches high in the forepart and two feet nine inches high in the cabin and steerage, and that no more than two passengers shall be put together in one bedstead except if the Father and Mother want their children in the same bedstead with them they may do so. These berths were 18 inches wide and six feet long.

Can you imagine crossing the Atlantic in a room that was 3 feet 9 inches high? Or sleeping in a bed with your spouse that is 18 inches wide and 6 feet long? Or, if you were single, sleeping in one of these births with a stranger?

The act further provides that these ships carrying German passengers must have a well recommended surgeon and a complete chest of medicine – that the medicine must be given to the passengers free – that twice a week the vessel must be smoked with burning tar between the decks and that it should be well washed with vinegar twice a week.

Imagine the smell as you boarded the ship and descended into its dark belly with your family and everything you owned – the acrid smell of burned tar mixing with the pungent odor of wood soaked in vinegar. Twice a week the crew would clear all the cabins and fill the ship with a thick, acrid smoke, then wash down all the wood surfaces with vinegar to kill lice and get rid of any rats that survived the smoke.

It is also said that neither the purser nor other persons shall sell to passengers at a greater price than 50% profit on first cost, any wine, brandy, rum, beer, cider or other liquor or any spices or necessaries for sick persons – that no person shall carry any liquor or other things more than 30 shillings worth. The act also provides that the officer in Philadelphia appointed to carry out this law shall take with him a reputable German inhabitant of

Philadelphia to interpret into English the statements of the German passengers. It is also provided that the interpreter in a loud voice shall declare in German that the duties required by this act will be read to them in German and that they may inquire about any matter they may wish to know.

When Nicholas Stoltzfus, or any immigrant, boarded a ship to cross the Atlantic, not only were the sights and smells discouraging, but it was also highly likely that they couldn't communicate with the captain or the sailors, so the following provision was added:

> It is also provided that the master of the ship must give each person a bill of lading mentioning the trunks, crates, chests, bales or packages belonging to every passenger except of such goods they may want to keep in their own possession. It is also provided that the ship owner must declare when starting out what goods the Germans will not be allowed to bring from their home to America, and that if they have such goods he shall declare what taxes or duties they must pay on the same, so that they will not lose them. The act provided that the fares must be fixed and certain and that if the German passengers offer that sum the shipmaster must take it and dare not hold their goods to compel them to pay higher prices. Many other provisions were made in the act: but all with the same end in view, to prevent these ignorant people from being robbed.

The fact that these regulations needed to be outlined illustrates the corrupt culture of these crossings.

But Nicholas Stoltzfus and his family boarded one of these ships in 1766. He left no living relatives behind (that we know of) and none greeted him on the other side of the Atlantic. He traveled with a large trunk in which fit all of his earthly belongings. The family probably shared two or three bunks, holding each other close while the waves crashed against the sides of the boat. Perhaps he walked them to the deck, their legs shaking and unsteady, so that they could be seasick over the side. The days blurred into one. The sun's reflection off the endless ocean was blinding. At night it seemed they were the only people left in the entire world.

Then, one day, land. It was Philadelphia.

In the book, *Historic Background and Annals of the Swiss and German Pioneers* by Henry Frank Eshleman it reads

> 1766 – Ship Records of This Year. Five vessels carrying Palatines arrived in Philadelphia harbor this year: The Ship "Chance" under Capt. Charles Smith from Rotterdam September 23, 1766 with 106 passengers. The Ship "Betsy" under Capt. John Osman from Rotterdam October 13, with 84 passengers. The Ship "Cullodian" under Master Richard Hunter from Lisbon October 15, with 12 passengers. **The ship "Polly" under Master Robert Porter from Rotterdam October 18, with 53 passengers.** The ship "Sally" under Master John Davidson from Rotterdam November 4, with 7 passengers. The total number of passengers was 263. Among the familiar Southeastern Pennsylvania names in the list are: Muller, Weitzel, Arnold, Locher, Schaffer, Weber, Kehl, Meister, Lantz, Hasler, Becker, Weingartner, Lipp, Gross, Conrad, Locher, Weber, Flick, Frey, Martin, Sand, Zimmerma-Ott, Shffer, Singer, Hoffman, Wolff, Mosser, Keller, Volmer, Benner, Kauffman, Wagner, Miller, Frantz, Zlegler, Eckert, Oberlander, Fisher, Meyer, **Stoltzfus**, Muller, Walter, Herman, Donner, Schmidt, Jacob, Schreiner, Henninger and Amecker" [8] (emphasis mine)

So Nicholas Stoltzfus arrived, in 1766. A rather inauspicious entrance to the New World – just one family name out of 49; one small unit arriving in a group of five ships carrying 263 passengers. His journey on earth was in its last decade, but the journey of the Stoltzfus's in the New World, well, that was just beginning.

---

[8] Henry Eshleman. *Historic Background and Annals of the Swiss and German Pioneers.* Nabu Press, 2010.

I'm sure the joy they felt at arriving was soon put in check by the bustling chaos of the city. Where did they spend their first night? Did they wander the streets, looking for work, for a place to stay?

Most likely they connected with the Anabaptist community very quickly. Most Amish or Mennonites arriving in America carried letters of endorsement from bishops or other leaders from the Old World, and upon arrival, they were quickly integrated into a community that shared their common faith and language. A common heritage.

How was Nicholas welcomed into the American Anabaptist community? Was it easier back then than it is today to "become Amish"? Perhaps it was – in the 1700s there was less of a noticeable separation between Anabaptists and non-Anabaptists. Cars were not an issue, clothing was similar, most people wore hats or bonnets, and the use of electricity as a source of power for technological devices was in its infancy. Nicholas may well have made a seamless transition into the colonial Anabaptist community.

But what kind of America did they arrive to? In only 10 years the American Revolution would begin in full force, and the birth of a new nation would be upon them. The colonists were tiring of the empire's rule. It would seem the rumor of war, or at least unrest, followed Nicholas and his family from the battlefields of Germany to the other side of the ocean. During August of 1766:

> Violence breaks out in New York between British soldiers and armed colonists, including Sons of Liberty members. The violence erupts as a result of the continuing refusal of New York colonists to comply with the Quartering Act. In December, the New York legislature is suspended by the English Crown after once again voting to refuse to comply with the Act. [9]

The colonies grew more and more impatient with the taxation and imposing nature of the British rule. Meanwhile, the governmental structures of the colonies were becoming more advanced, as were the political and philosophical thoughts of the early-American thinkers, men like Benjamin Franklin, Thomas Paine and Thomas Jefferson, who

---

[9] http://www.historyplace.com/unitedstates/revolution/rev-prel.htm

molded the foundational thoughts on how our country would be formed.

Nicholas and his family were dropped into this boiling pot of political philosophies, economic changes and civil unrest. After their arrival, there are no tax lists or documents that shed light on the Stoltzfus family for four years. But we do know that, at some point, Nicholas's first wife died and he married his second wife, a woman named Anna. Then, in 1770, Nicholas is found again, this time in a Berks County Court House of Pennsylvania Deed Book. It says:

> This indenture made the thirty first day of January in the year of our Lord one thousand seven hundred and seventy, between Thomas Youngman of Cumru Township in the County of Berks and Province of Pennsylvania, a tanner and Catherine his wife of one part, and Nicholas Stoltzfus and Christian Stoltzfus both of Leacock Township of the County of Lancaster for the price of two hundred thirty one pounds of money for seventy acres and thirty one perches of land... [10]

They had survived their voyage and initiation into the new land. They settled. They spent at least some time in Leacock Township in Lancaster County – with friends? Perhaps the relatives of friends from the tightly knit community of Anabaptists from the Old World? Whatever the case, they had now achieved what had seemed a far-fetched dream while still living in Germany: they owned land. Seventy acres. They would have their own farm. They were servants to no other man.

In John A Parmer's presentation *The Nicholas Stoltzfus House: 10 Years of Progress,* he makes some interesting observations about that particular property purchase:

> On April 4, 1769, the Morris family sold approximately 249 acres, in two parcels, to Thomas Youngman...9 months later, on December 19, 1769, Youngman sold a 78 acre parcel of that land

---

[10] Ernest Drumm, *The Revealed Life of Nicholas Stoltzfus; Out of the Archives of Zweibrucken.* Researched and compiled by Levi Stoltzfus. Masthof Press, 2009.

to John Gerber...He too was an Amish family pioneer, having arrived in 1750 or before...further deed evidence would indicate that they never lived there, having purchased a 140 acre farm to the south just a year before. Now events get interesting! Just five weeks after the Gerber purchase, Nicholas Stoltzfus and son Christian, on January 31, 1770, purchase the adjoining 70-acre parcel from Youngman! Could this be coincidence, or were the Gerbers and the Stoltzfuses already acquainted? Just five years hence, young Christian Stoltzfus would marry Catherine Gerber, John's oldest daughter.

Nicholas would have found the Tulpehocken Creek a wonderful source of food – as a pond-digger in Germany he would have understood fish, how to catch them, farm them and certainly how to eat them. His training with the Anabaptists as a farmer in the difficult hills of Zweibrucken would have made Pennsylvania's fertile ground a welcome change (although I imagine they had a lot of trees and stumps to clear).

The house they built is preserved to this day, restored by The Nicholas Stoltzfus House Preservation Committee. The two-story, stone house sits quietly among the trees, although you can hear cars and 18-wheelers thundering past on a nearby highway. The Tulpehocken Creek still flows persistently, only a hundred yards away.

Nicholas's journey from Germany to American was not in vain. His decision to brave the Atlantic crossing with his family led to a completely new existence – instead of spending their lives as migrant farmers, constantly under the oppressive yoke of an intolerant government, they were now land owners, making a way for themselves in the world.

But Nicholas didn't have long to enjoy their farm – he died November 10th, 1774, at the age of 57, only four short years after purchasing the land. A few months after his death, with the American Revolution nearly at its peak, Patrick Henry delivered his famous "Give Me Liberty or Give Me Death" speech. [11]

---

[11] http://www.ushistory.org/declaration/revwartimeline.htm

It is in vain, sir, to extenuate the matter. Gentlemen may cry, Peace, Peace--but there is no peace. The war is actually begun! The next gale that sweeps from the north will bring to our ears the clash of resounding arms! Our brethren are already in the field! Why stand we here idle? What is it that gentlemen wish? What would they have? Is life so dear, or peace so sweet, as to be purchased at the price of chains and slavery? Forbid it, Almighty God! I know not what course others may take; but as for me, give me liberty or give me death! [12]

Painted on the background of Nicholas's life, in which he gave up everything for one chance at liberty, it is easy to see why Henry's sentiment was so commonly shared among the colonies.

I can only imagine the emotions of Nicholas's children in the days following his death, as they laid their father to rest. He seemed such a brave, extraordinary man, one who would not be stopped by the loss of his father at an early age. He disregarded the intolerant views of his old society. He approached life as an adventure and a challenge, living where he wished, doing what he wished, marrying whomever he wished.

The following is an inscription from the Stoltzfus Family Bible:

Dec. 23, 1736 is Christiana (Jane) Stoltzfusin born in this world, she died

Aug. 24 in the year 1745 was born to me a daughter in this world by the name Catharina (Catharine) Stoltzfusin

In August 1747 was born to me a daughter in this world by the name Elizabet (Elizabeth) Stoltzfusin

Aug. 10, 1749 was born to me a son in this world by the name Christian Stoltzfusz in the morning at 6 o'clock by sign.

June 29, 1751 was born to me a daughter in this world by the name Barbara Stoltzfusen was between 10 and 11 o'clock.

July 28, 1753 around 11 o'clock has God left a son be born unto me into this world by the name Daniel Stoltzfusz.

September 9, 1755 has God left a son be born unto me into this world by the name Nicholaus Stoltzfusz. The sign was Balances. The birth was 6 o'clock.

---

[12] http://www.law.ou.edu/ushistory/henry.shtml

Oct.10, 1757 has God unto me a daughter born into this world in the afternoon at 4 o'clock. The sign was virgin by the name Magttalena (Magdalena) Stoltzfusen

Nov. 1, 1774 has the old Nicholaus Stoltzfusz died and has left a wife and four children. June 11, 1781 the wife also has died, my mother and left the children above mentioned.

Written by me, Christian Stoltzfus. [13]

The authors of *Descendants of Christian Fisher* write:

> Tradition handed down from a granddaughter Catherine, who was married to Jacob Steinman, says that on the day of her grandfather's funeral, they carried him on a bier to a quiet resting place on his farm. They all proceeded on foot a distance of about two miles along the south bank of the Schuylkill River. They forded the river at a shallow point known as Cross Keys. [14]

So passed Nicholas Stoltzfus. But the Stoltzfus story, well, that was still in its infancy.

---

[13] Ernest Drumm, *The Revealed Life of Nicholas Stoltzfus; Out of the Archives of Zweibrucken.* Researched and com-piled by Levi Stoltzfus. Masthof Press, 2009.

[14] *Descendants of Christian Fisher (1757 – 1838).* Edited by Katie Beiler. Pequea Bruderschaft Library, 2009.

PART 2:
FIVE SONS

1774 - 1905

Nicholas Stoltzfus
m. unknown (d. unknown)
m. Anna
|
Christian Stoltzfus
m. Catherine Garber (d.1783)
m. Elizabeth King
|
Christian Stoltzfus
m. Anna Blank
|
Samuel Stoltzfus
m. Susan Beiler
|
Benjamin Stoltzfus
m. Sarah Mast
|
Catherine Stoltzfus

Chapter Six
How Stories Die

I wonder how Nicholas's son Christian felt, walking away from his father's grave that day, going back to the stone house on the banks of the Tulpehocken. He was 17 years old when he and his father arrived in Philadelphia - I'm sure the monumental crossing of the Atlantic was etched into his mind: the smell of the ship, the rolling waves, the sudden arrival in the clamor of Philadelphia.

He married Catherine Gerber when he was 24, only 6 months before his father died. Could he have recognized the difference between his life and his father's life? Christian could marry whomever he wished; they could live wherever they wanted; they already owned their own farm. All because of the sacrifice his father made by uprooting and moving to the other side of the world.

Christian and Catherine had their first child, John Stoltzfus, in February of 1776. Such uncertain times in which to bring a child. The thirteen small colonies were at war with one of the most powerful empires in the world. Battles were all around them – Quebec, South Carolina, the Atlantic Ocean. In July of that year, the Declaration of Independence would be read and printed for distribution. By September of that year, the British occupied New York City, and a few short months after that George Washington crossed the Delaware River and captured Trenton from the Hessians. [15]

These were not easy times to be Amish. Tradition states that during the Revolutionary War, several members of the congregations in Christian Stoltzfus's area (where Christian would eventually serve as minister) were taken to Reading and put in prison for refusing to serve in the military. Tradition also says that they were sentenced to death, but Henry Hertzell, a Reformed Church minister, stepped in and made sure the sentence was never carried out. [16]

Christian and Catherine had a second son, Jacob Stoltzfus, born almost three years later in August of 1779. The Revolutionary War still had four years left to run – the majority of the fighting that year continued in the New England States, New York and New Jersey, as well as in the South.

Their third and final child together, another boy, was born in July of 1881. They named him Christian. It would seem that Christian Sr.'s life was falling into order: land owner, married, and now the father of three healthy boys. But a piece of his father Nicholas's history seemed determined to show up in his own life: Christian's wife Catherine died May 18, 1783, after they had been married for only nine years. She was 34 years old.

I wonder what those years were like for Christian and his three boys, ages seven, three and not quite two. Knowing the Old Order Amish, the community would have pitched in to help with the raising of the younger boys. John, the firstborn, would have been old enough to help with chores around the house. So life went on at the Stoltzfus homestead, but the four bachelors would not have to forge ahead on their own for long.

Two years after Catherine's death, Christian Sr. married again, this time to Elizabeth (King) Lantz. Elizabeth was the daughter of Samuel

---

[15] http://www.ushistory.org/declaration/revwartimeline.htm

[16] Grant Stoltzfus. *History of the First Amish Mennonite Communities in America.* Masthof Press, 2002.

King, "the pioneer immigrant of the King family"[17]). Christian Sr. and Elizabeth were two second-generation Americans, both widowed in a young country. Elizabeth brought two young children into the family from her previous marriage, and together they went on to have additional children.

The Descendants of Christian Fisher notes that "after the second marriage of Christian Stoltzfus, he moved with his family to Lancaster Co., on the farm south of Bareville, where John L. Stoltzfus now lives. There he served as Bishop of the Amish churches of that locality." [18]

Christian Sr.'s third son with Elizabeth, Christian, Jr., is my direct ancestor. I am sure he did not remember Catherine's passing – he was only two – and likely did not recall his father's second marriage, to Elizabeth – he was only four when that took place. But I'm sure that he loved the memory of his biological mother (he would eventually name his first daughter Catharine), and I'm sure he considered Elizabeth nothing but his real mother (his second daughter was named Elizabeth).

Yet all of that was many years into the future for that child. In the mean time, his boyhood was filled with family. After all, he had two older brothers, plus two older stepbrothers (from Elizabeth's first marriage), and then his father and Elizabeth went on to have: Anna, Barbara, Abraham, David, Fanny, Catherine, Elizabeth and two children who died young: Solomon and Magdalena.

Then, a new century. The 1800s arrived, and the world bustled as trans-Atlantic travel became more and more common. The United States, in its infancy, welcomed immigrants from all around the world. Communication and transcontinental transportation methods improved. Progress seemed unstoppable.

It was with the dawning of a new century, in 1803 to be specific, that Christoph's Nicholas's Christian's Christian married Anna Blank. They went on to have nine children together: Catharine, Elizabeth, Barbara, John, Samuel, Rebecca, Annie, Christian and Susan. You can see the

---

[17] *Descendants of Christian Fisher (1757 – 1838).* Edited by Katie Beiler. Pequea Bruderschaft Library, 2009.

[18] *Descendants of Christian Fisher (1757 – 1838).* Edited by Katie Beiler. Pequea Bruderschaft Library, 2009.

continued emphasis on the heritage of names: the eldest daughter, Catharine, named after her grandmother who died young; Elizabeth, named after her great-aunt and grandmother; Barbara, named after a great-aunt as well as Christian Jr.'s half-sister; John named after an uncle, Christian Jr.'s oldest brother; Samuel shared a name with the King family's primary immigrant, his great-grandfather; Annie, named after her mother and great-grandmother; Christian III, named after his father and grandfather.

There was clearly a tight relationship between the generations, something that remains in the Anabaptist communities to this day.

Many historically significant things were taking place in 1812: Napoleon was directing his armies through Europe, taking city after city, country after country; Eastern Louisiana was admitted as the 18th State in the Union; James Madison was re-elected president of the United States. And Samuel Stoltzfus, my great-great-great-great-grandfather and the fifth child of Christian and Anna Stoltzfus, was born.

All of these events would have affected Samuel's family, but in the year of his birth, it was the War of 1812 that would have weighed heavily on their minds. The US declared war on Britain on June 18, 1812, which led to the British imposing a stranglehold on US trade overseas and causing serious economic hardship. The fighting came relatively close to Lancaster, with the eastern front being the Atlantic Ocean and, more specifically, the Chesapeake Bay region. The northern front of the war came as close as the Canadian line with battles in Niagara. The western and southern fronts were further removed: the Detroit area and the Gulf of Mexico.

Imagine living in a time without television, radio or the Internet, hearing the rumor of war but never knowing exactly what was going on. Newspaper headlines were quickly scanned daily to see just how close the war had come during the previous day or week. Enemy soldiers camped only a few hundred miles away, but they didn't have up-to-the-minute reports on how the battles progressed or how much longer until the enemy marched over their own fields.

But the United States prevailed.

The war provided for the rise of Andrew Jackson, whose victory outside of New Orleans (albeit after a peace treaty had already been signed) saved the city from destruction. The Treaty of Ghent ended the War of 1812 three years after it began. [19] The treaty also led to the resurgence in Anabaptist immigration into the United States, as the war had all but sealed off the waterways.

The Anabaptist role in the war was consistent with their pacifist beliefs. For example, Christian Troyer Sr. was brought to court for refusing to provide his wagon and team of horses to the war effort:

> On March 19th, 1814 in York, Christian Troyer was taken to court and it is listed in the minutes of the General Quarter Sessions of the Peace, Home District with Thomas Ridout Esq., Chairman, assisted by William Allan and Duncan Cameron as follows: "The following persons had been summoned to attend Court this day and shew cause why they have not sent forward their Teams with Sleighs as regularly impressed and directed so to do, for Government Service," The names of the persons in court were: Christian Troyer; John Oister (Oster); Michael Kiffer (Keffer); John Shank (Shunk); John Snider: and Joseph Michler. The Constable, Samuel Arnold, who impressed the sleighs with teams belonging to the above named persons did not attend, so they consequently were dismissed by the Court. [20]

This case would serve as only the beginning of a tension between the war-machine of the United States of America and the pacifist convictions of the Anabaptists.

Meanwhile, Samuel grew up. He carried on the farming tradition of his ancestors and stayed in Lancaster County. Time passed.

Samuel's grandfather Christian Sr., Nicholas Stoltzfus's son, died in 1832, two years before Samuel got married. What an important funeral the elder Christian would have had, the last Stoltzfus man remaining who had lived in Germany. I can imagine the Amish coming from miles around in remembrance of this Amish bishop, the son of the first Stoltzfus to step foot in The New World.

---

[19] http://www.gatewayno.com/history/War1812.html

[20] http://sheffield.typepad.com/dansheffield/2010/07/anabaptist-family-heritage-alternative-vision.html

I wonder how many memories died with Christian: how many stories of his father Nicholas and his grandfather Christoph? What tales did those generations laugh about or reflect on? Did any facts about Christian's great-great-great-grandfather Paul Steltzefuss vanish with the burial of Christian? Stories are not like genetic traits – they are not automatically passed down in the blood.

They must be told.

Then, in 1835, Samuel and Susan married, and in July of that year Susan Stoltzfus went into labor. She gave birth to their first child, a boy, and they named him Benjamin. Benjamin was born in Morgantown, PA.

With his family, we start to see just how difficult a proposition it was to bring children into the world in the 19th century. Whether it was by disease, or accident, or some genetic weakness, Benjamin's brother David, born fifteen months after Benjamin, died young. The 8th child in the family, Elizabeth, also died when she was only 7 years old, in 1856.

Close to the time of Benjamin's birth, a woman by the name of Hannah Mast gave birth to twin girls: twins who did much to shape the Stoltzfus family tree for the next 60 years.

I do have some selfish interest in the birth of these Mast twins: without them, I would not be in existence.

Chapter Seven
Conniving Twins

I don't know exactly how this next story came about – I only know the barest of facts. But this is how I like to imagine the lead up to the one of the most important swaps in my ancestry.

Rachel and Sarah Mast, twin teenage girls, lay quietly in their shared bed. The room was dark, and they could hear their parents ease toward their own bedroom. Minutes ticked by, and both thought the other was sleeping. Then one of them sighed and changed position. The other whispered, in a voice barely audible.

"Are you awake?" Rachel asked.

"Yes," sighed Sarah. Her voice didn't sound like she was up for a conversation.

Rachel rolled over so that she faced Sarah. The two teenagers had been inseparable since birth.

"What do you think about John?"

She was referring to John U. Stoltzfus, the Amish boy Sarah was dating.

"He's nice," Sarah said, rolling over to face Rachel. "Now go to sleep."

Rachel could tell that Sarah was smiling, even though it was too dark to see her face.

"Just nice? C'mon. What do you really think?"

Sarah groaned.

"I don't know. He's nice," she whispered again, then asked a little louder, "What do you think about Ben?"

Rachel was dating John's first cousin, Benjamin Stoltzfus, my great-great-great-grandfather.

Sarah could feel Rachel shrug, and she could just picture the frown of indifference on her face.

"Now who's gone quiet?" Sarah asked. "Just go to sleep."

But neither of the girls felt sleepy anymore. They stayed awake for a long time, talking about the boys, their other friends, their brothers and sisters. They thought they heard one of their parents come into the hall, so they stopped talking, held their breath, peeked through squinted eyes. The footsteps receded, but at first neither said anything.

"Are you still awake?" Rachel whispered.

Sarah groaned.

"Would you please go to sleep?"

"I can't sleep now; I've got an idea," Rachel practically hissed, then went quiet.

The two girls lay there. Sarah knew that voice – it was the voice that always led to trouble, but she waited to hear Rachel's idea. Still, no one said anything. Finally, Sarah's curiosity got the better of her.

"Okay, so what's the idea?" she whispered.

"We switch."

"What are you talking about? Switch what?"

"We switch."

Sarah's mouth dropped open.

"You must be kidding!" she said out loud.

"Shhh!"

"You must be kidding!" she said again, this time whispering.

Rachel giggled.

"You must admit, it would be kind of fun."

"But what if they get upset?"

"Oh, they won't get upset. They'll probably know right from the beginning."

"But what if they don't? What if they don't know we've switched?"
Rachel shrugged.
Sarah found a laugh rising up in her.
"Just this once!" she said, laughing.
"Shhh!" Rachel said, but her own laugh was louder than Sarah's.

The next weekend, when Benjamin and John came to pick up Rachel and Sarah, they actually (unbeknownst to the boys) picked up Sarah and Rachel. Legend has it that the girls looked so much alike that the two Stoltzfus boys had no idea that the girls had switched places! I guess the date went so well, and everyone was so happy with the new arrangement, that even after the young men became aware of what had happened, the two couples never switched back.

Fast-forward to January 1st, 1857, and somewhere in central Pennsylvania there was a double wedding. Benjamin Stoltzfus married Sarah Mast, and John Stoltzfus, his cousin, married Sarah's twin sister Rachel. I can only imagine the celebration, or how many times someone in one of the families leaned over to someone else and said:

"Well, it's a good thing they switched because you can tell they're each happy with the one they married."

The year 1866, when Benjamin was 31, marked the 100-year anniversary of the arrival of the Stoltzfuses in America. It was also one year after the Civil War ended – the bodies of over two thousand unidentified Civil War casualties were buried at Arlington National Cemetery that year (1/3rd of the 620,000 people who lost their lives in that war as a result of battle and disease would remain unidentified). In that same year Congress overturned President Johnson's veto, giving all former slaves the rights of citizenship as guaranteed by the 14th Amendment. [21]

John Stoltzfus (Nicholas's Christian's Jacob's John), also known as Tennessee John, wrote the following in the latter half of the 1800s while reflecting on a bygone century. It is a piece that gives us some insight into how people of those days were viewing the world:

---

[21] http://www.historyorb.com/events/date/1866

The manner of life of our ancestors was simple in food and drink and clothing. Coffee was little used; the diet consisted of water, milk, tea, soup, bread and milk, etc. They sowed flax and spun it, which was good work for the girls. They did well if they finished spinning by February. They also spun wool on small as well as larger spinning wheels. Industry and honesty made them happy, as did also frugality, good conduct, and virtue.

The men plowed and sowed by hand. Wheat was cut with a sickle. One could often see twenty or more reapers cutting in rows, of both sexes. Later the cradle was used to cut the grain. They threshed with horses and flails and did well to finish by March. Flour was hauled in wagons to Philadelphia, and the wheat to mills about twelve miles away and sometimes further.

About the year 1800 or near this time, the turnpike from Philadelphia to Pittsburgh was opened. This was considered a great achievement. Great numbers of teams used this road, hauling wheat, meat, etc. to Philadelphia and other places, as well as store goods to Pittsburgh and other points in the West. Good horses were sold at that time for from 70 to 80 [dollars]. A government mail coach used this road once a day from east to west, with which ten to twelve, more or less, passengers a day traveled each way.

Invention and discoveries began to appear in the world, to the astonishment of human beings, as though the world were just now awakening out of its sleep after five or six thousand years. There were sowing machines, mowing machines, threshing machines, and sewing machines. Instead of being able to thresh only twenty or thirty bushels per day with horses if all went well, one can now, with a machine, thresh and clean as high as five hundred bushels or more in a day. The railroad also came in this century. Where one could formerly haul in a wagon with six horses, four tons more or less, twenty or thirty miles a day, they can now move a hundred and fifty to two hundred tons, one hundred and fifty to two hundred miles in twenty-four hours. Where formerly eight to ten passengers a day traveled on the turnpike each way, there are now eight to ten trains a day each way, each perhaps carrying three to four hundred passengers at a speed of four hundred to five hundred miles a day or in 24 hours. A letter from Ohio to Lancaster, PA, formerly cost the receiver 25 cents and was on the way perhaps four or five days; now it goes in twelve hours and costs the receiver nothing. A message can be sent a thousand miles and the answer received by telegraph in twelve hours or less. Writing changed to printing. The Gospel, a little book, was first written over a period of many years, but now over a ton of paper is consumed in a single printery in one week and broadcasted over the world so that printing has very likely reached its high point, by means of which the fashions of the world and other vanities are pictured to the eye.

Although I have now mentioned in part what concerns the farmer and transportation, there are still many other arts and sciences in manufacture, etc. I remember that nails were once cut by foot on a machine and the heads struck afterwards, that material for shirts was spun and woven by hand and sold at fifty cents a yard, and now one can get manufactured shirt muslin at seven cents a yard. In many other things which are of less value to humanity, there have been wonderful inventions.

If our fathers who left this world a hundred or only seventy years ago could suddenly return to this life, would they not observe the change in the world with great surprise? The children who are born now cannot conceive the toil and industry, simplicity and humility, and the life of their pious forefathers. If the father or mother of a household died and one had to go some distance to the burial place, four horses were hitched to a covered wagon, the corpse was placed upon the wagon. The household which accompanied usually went on the wagon and often had bundles of straw for seats. The mourners rode behind, both men and women. There were no Dearborn wagons then yet.

Many of the forefathers who came from Germany, or went to the west, moved into the "bush", first built cabins, and began with good spirits to clear and fence in their land, without much murmuring or complaining and looked courageously into the future. They did not have as many rocking chairs with cushions as now, also no lounges and no carpets. They built their houses for the protection of the body and did not think that they would need a second or third for one household.

The brethren and sisters received each other with joy always. And if they came from Germany with a letter (of membership) they were gladly received with hand and kiss, and all worked together with glad and charitable spirit. The food, when there was a "meeting" was soup, pie, bread, etc., and water to drink. Those who sat near together drank from one vessel and ate from a common dish with spoons, each one cut bread for himself, since it came onto the table in quarter-loaves. There were at that time no cook stoves, but great open hearths into which one put pieces of wood four feet or less in length, for cooking.

Those who are now living and have arrived at an old age, can see for themselves the change in the church, which is one body in Christ, as it is going on, as well as the change in the world, according to human wisdom and the permission of a kind Creator, which will not be according to the imaginations of men, but in the strength of God with the glorious appearing of Jesus Christ without sin, to allow those who trust in him for redemption. [22]

This piece does a great job in illustrating the world in which Benjamin Stoltzfus lived, the life to which he was accustomed. But time doesn't stop. It keeps moving forward. Even Benjamin Stoltzfus, once the baby boy of Samuel Stoltzfus, grew old.

Benjamin's daughter Catherine is my primary concern. It is with Catherine that the stories are no longer just things we find in books, dates and names that have to be deciphered. We can wonder about less, fill in fewer gaps with our imagination, because, unlike any of the generations we've discussed so far, there are people on this earth who remember her, who knew her.

---

[22] *Descendants of Christian Fisher (1757 – 1838)*. Edited by Katie Beiler. Pequea Bruderschaft Library, 2009.

Chapter Eight
A Death That Led to My Life

Catherine Stoltzfus entered the world November 17, 1873. It was 99 years and a couple of weeks after Nicholas Stoltzfus (her great-great-great-grandfather) had died, the first of her ancestors to enter America. It was also 103 years and 33 days before I would be born. Her birth makes a strange dividing line for me between the people that exist only on paper and those who are still remembered in person by the living.

Her parents, Benjamin Stoltzfus and Sarah Mast, had been married for 16 years, and they already had five children: Rachel (named after Sarah's twin, with whom she so notoriously switched boyfriends), Samuel (named after Benjamin's father), Hannah (named after Sara's mother), Elizabeth (after Benjamin's younger sister who died shortly before their wedding) and Stephen (named after Sarah's father). After Stephen's birth, and before Catherine was born, they lost two children in a row: Rebecca at 22 months old and then Sarah at 23 months old.

In the year 1900, approximately 20% of all children died before the age of 10.[23] That's one out of five, and in Catherine's family, this statistic

---

[23] http://www.ipa.udel.edu/education/courses/econ490/Production_of_Health.pdf

proved itself true. The leading cause of child mortality in the early 1900s was congenital malformations, diarrheal conditions, pneumonia and influenza. Benjamin and Sarah's first five children survived; then two died under the age of two – imagine the joy and determination (and perhaps a little nervousness) with which they welcomed Catherine into the world.

She had one younger sister, Lafena, born four years after her. In "Life and Changes of Grandpa's Days," John Lapp writes that Lafena "as a child had a disease and her mind was somewhat shattered after that. She stayed single, and after her brothers and sisters were no longer capable of taking care of her, she then went to the nieces and nephews. She sang a lot, and we have many memories of her." Lafena was Mummi's aunt.

Catherine's father Benjamin became a minister when she was only 6 and a bishop when she was fifteen.

Then, at the age of 20, she married Samuel Lapp, becoming Catharine Lapp. But it was a last name she would only have for a short time.

I wonder if the doctor arrived in Lancaster by way of the Gordonville train station. In 1898, there were four tracks slicing their way through that small town (population 413), and nearly 200 trains passed through every day. Today you are lucky if you see one train all day. I can imagine the relatives of my great-great-grandmother (Catharine Lapp at the time) waiting by the tracks, perhaps still sitting in their buggy. This doctor was their last hope.

The intriguing part about history is that we know what will happen. We know who will live and who will die, and in his own strange way this doctor saved my life that day.

I can only imagine what the doctor was feeling as his train click-clacked from Philadelphia to Lancaster. Had he done many appendix operations before? Had he done any? Doctors had only recently begun treating appendicitis by removing the appendix, as opposed to draining it as they had for centuries. Opening a body up, removing organs, cleaning the infection, sterilizing and suturing the internal areas, knitting the flesh back together, stopping the bleeding – the skills, equipment and knowledge that allowed these crucial things to happen were still in their infancy.

In the late 1800s, appendectomies were rarely successful.

Apparently our kind doctor was nervous – he arrived intoxicated, wreaking of the alcohol he had been drinking all the way from Philadelphia. In those days the patient needed alcohol to dull the pain. The doctor sometimes used it to dull his own senses from the violent, bloody scene an operation like that could become. But legend says our doctor overdid it.

He was driven to my great-great grandmother's house on a cold December day in 1898, the air clearing his head. He got down from the buggy and carried his bag into the house. The horses' mouths threw steam up into the air, their hides smoking with heat, like the steeds of the four horsemen.

They ushered the doctor inside – it was two weeks before Christmas. The children's minds were full of the holidays, wondering what gifts they would get that year, salivating over the thought of the family meals. A frosty glaze coated the windows, but that didn't stop the neighbor kids from huddling around outside, wiping away the frost with their cold fingers, watching as the doctor asked the family to lay Samuel Lapp on the large kitchen table.

The kitchen table – these were the hubs to the wheel of life. Breakfast together around the table, then out for chores or school or work, then back to the table for lunch, then out again, then back to the table for supper, tired eating at the end of a long day. Kitchen lanterns hissed late into the night over those tables. Dreams and nightmares, joys and sadness: the kitchen table played host to them all.

Samuel lay there on the kitchen table, only 26 years old. He would have been feverish by then, perhaps clutching his gut in pain. He needed help to walk to the table, assistance to rise up on it and then lie down. The doctor fumbled nervously through his bag as Samuel was given something to drink, something to numb the pain, and something to bite down on.

I had my appendix removed when I was 24 years old. The night before, I went to bed with a stomachache, wondering why the spaghetti dinner affected me so strangely. In the morning, it was worse: pain radiated out from the lower, right side of my abdomen. If I sat still it felt dull, like a toothache, but when I moved a sharp pain shot outwards. Maile drove me to the hospital. We waited in the emergency room for 8 hours. That afternoon the doctor did an ultrasound and confirmed that my appendix was swollen. The surgery that night lasted an hour? 30 minutes? I don't know because I was under anesthesia, and when I regained consciousness my stomach muscles were sore and the doctor had given me three button-sized scars in exchange for my appendix.

But in 1898, no such bartering was available.

The eyes of the children peeking through the windows would have widened as Samuel Lapp's shirt was pulled back.

"Come away!" their parents yelled from across the yard. "Get away from there!"

They scattered, relieved to be torn from that sight.

The doctor that no longer has a name pulled the small scalpel from his bag, hands shaking. Perhaps Samuel felt the cold steel slide into his skin, or perhaps the pain he had been in for days was already clouding his mind.

His blood ran out on to the sheets covering the family table as the intoxicated doctor cut him apart and removed the offending organ. But Samuel did not survive the operation. The exchange required for his appendix was his life – it fluttered around the room for a moment, then vanished into the cold December air.

My great-great grandmother Catherine, only 25 years old, sat in the back room with her three children: Anna, Benjamin and John. A widow. Her family surrounded her, hugged her, and wiped her tears. The children sat there wondering what kind of a doctor brought this into the house.

John Lapp (Samuel Lapp's son, only 3 months old at the time of his father's death), later wrote down his memories and the stories told to him throughout his life. The following is included in the booklet entitled "Life and Changes of Grandpa's Days":

> My father died when I was three months old. He died during an appendix operation performed at home on the kitchen table. In those days there was not much heard of going to the hospital, nor of appendix operations. Even a rush matter or emergency would have had to be with a horse and wagon. His age was twenty-six. Mother was left a widow with three children. My sister Annie was four and brother Benjamin was two. I was three

months old. Father was buried at Gordonville Cemetery, Lancaster Co.

On the day of Samuel Lapp's funeral (my dad), his good friend Sammie Stoltzfus was sick and couldn't come to the funeral. So on the way to the cemetery the funeral wagon stopped in front of Sammie Stoltzfus house. They put the coffin with Samuel Lapp outside the window so Sammie could view him. They were about the same age. He was also married.

I wonder how that doctor felt on the train back to Philadelphia. Relieved perhaps, that it was over? Stone drunk? Would he remember the surgery in the morning? Would his life be racked with guilt because of the Amish man with appendicitis that he killed on that December day? As his train click-clacked back into the city, the sights and sounds of a Christmas not far off surrounded him.

If I were a ghost, I would hover over him in that train and shout. I would tell him not to feel bad – his slight of hand, his willingness to try, may not have saved Samuel Lapp. But on that day, December 10, 1898, that doctor saved my life. And the life of my mother's family. The lives of my children. Would we be here if it were not for him?

One death leads to so many lives.

Catherine and her three children moved back in with her parents: Benjamin Stoltzfus, now a bishop, and his wife Sarah (the twin who pulled off the boyfriend exchange). John, the youngest, remembered his grandfather fondly:

> This was my grandfather that became very close to me because I had no father. I well remember him. I often walked with him around the mill. He died in 1902. I was four years old then.

Benjamin Stoltzfus was gone. Great-great grandson of Nicholas Stoltzfus, son of Samuel Stoltzfus, husband to a Mast twin, father of nine children. A preacher and a bishop. A caring grandfather to his daughter Catherine's orphaned children. He survived the turn of the century, dying on December 21st, 1902, at the age of 67 (74 years, minus one day, before I was born).

His grandson John, after losing his father and his grandfather in the time span of a few short years, also remembers taking his chocolate Easter bunny out of the packaging to find that the local store owner, knowing the families hardships, had taped a penny to the bottom of the treat.

Life went on for my great-great-grandmother Catherine. Did she have hopes of remarrying? Did she envision the rest of her life lived as a widow? Whatever the state of her emotions, she carried on. She sewed for other people to earn money, and she kept a garden.

Her son John attended school in Morgantown with his sister Annie, while his 10-year-old brother Benjamin was hired out to his uncle Sammie J. Stoltzfus and attended Weavertown School. It was not uncommon in those days for families with many children, or families experiencing hardship, to send their children to live with relatives. The relatives took on the financial responsibility of raising and schooling the child, and it eased the burden on the child's family of having that extra mouth to feed.

It wouldn't have been easy for Catherine to send out her oldest son, but in those days, it seems everyone was faced with hard choices.

Before I tell you more about Catherine's life, I need to tell you about someone with whom her life would intersect: Amos King

Amos was one of eleven children: Christian, Aaron, Amos and Rebecca were the oldest four. Then Amos's parents had Menno, who died before his second birthday. Then came Moses. Amos's sister Katie, number 7, died when she was 8 years old. Priscilla, the next daughter, died before she was five. John was the Kings' 9th child. Two more girls were born, Elizabeth and Levina, but neither survived to see their second birthday.

Amos lost those siblings when he was 6 years old, 11 years old and 13 years old. Two more of his sisters, Levina (1 ½ years old) and Katie (8 ½ years old), died when he was 15. They passed one day apart, one week before Christmas of 1889. I wonder how the fact that he lost five siblings affected the psyche of this little boy.

While we do not know for certain the cause of Levina and Katie's death, it seems rather suspicious that the winter of 1889 was also the very time the Russian flu spread literally around the world. According to a "Wired Science" Internet article:

> The data on the disease were assembled for the first time from local records in 172 European and American cities. The Russian flu is particularly interesting because it was the first major epidemic to strike Europe after the laying down of dense railroad connections. In 1889, there were already more than 125,000 miles of rail lines connecting European cities. (That's more mileage than exists today, the authors note).
>
> The outbreak began in the spring of 1889. It peaked first in St. Petersburg, Russia, in December of that year. By then, it had spread all across Europe and North America and was front-page news in many places across the country. In papers like *The Evening Bulletin* in Maysville, Kentucky, the flu hit the front page in the days after Christmas. The paper printed dispatches from cities across the world. "It is safe to say that over one-tenth of the population is affected by it," a Boston reporter wrote. Meanwhile, doctors in Pittsburgh "expected[ed] 'la grippe' to reach here in all its violence before another month has passed."[24]

This particular strain of flu carried with it the normal flu symptoms: fever, sore throat, body aches. Its incubation period was 1 to 3 days and generally took anywhere from 2 to 10 days to run its course. [25] Approximately 1 million people died from the Russian, or "Asiatic," flu.

But Amos survived.

A year and a half before the Christmas when his two sisters died, something swept through the northeastern United States that had a more positive affect on 13 year old Amos: the Blizzard of 1888.

> The Nor'easter that strikes the U.S. Northeast in March comes on the heels of a warm spell that has opened buds on trees in New York's Central Park. New York's temperature drops to 10.7° F on March 12, then plunges to a March 13 record of 8°

---

[24] http://www.wired.com/wiredscience/2010/04/1889-russian-flu-pandemic/
[25] http://www.ehow.com/about_6062435_russian-influenza.html

the next day . . . winds off the Atlantic build up to 48 miles per hour, bringing unpredicted snow that continues off and on into the early morning of Wednesday, March 14. The 3-day accumulation totals 20.9 inches in [New York City], but snowdrifts 15 to 20 feet high bring traffic to a standstill. Parts of New England get up to 50 inches, and drifts as high as 40 feet bury houses and trains. Washington is isolated from the world for more than a day . . . [26]

Saratoga, New York, got 58 inches of snow. This blizzard, one of the most intense in recorded history, came when Amos was a teenager. He would tell stories about the deep, deep snow to his wide-eyed grandchildren. They asked for those stories over and over again, dreaming that some day they would see snow that drifted up to the roofs of the houses.

---

[26] http://www.answers.com/topic/1888

Chapter Nine
The 115-Year-Old Journal

This story will circle back around to my great-great grandmother Catharine, but for now we will leave her where she is, a widow with three children whose father has just passed away. Necessity demands that we continue following the rabbit trail of Amos King. It amazes me, these winding and twisting roads that history must follow to reach the present moment.

I heard rumors about this Amos King, stories of what he was like as a man. You see, Mummi was his daughter.

Many of my great-aunts and great-uncles are still living: Mummi's sons and daughters. One of these is Amos Stoltzfus, and when I started combing the countryside for stories, his name kept coming up again and again.

"If you're serious about writing a book about the Stoltzfus side of your family, you have to talk to Amos," they'd say. I also heard rumors not only of the stories that Amos remembered but also of an old journal that might still be in existence, a journal from the 1800s documenting the days of my ancestors.

My grandmother gave me Amos's number, so I called him. He lives in Maryland with his wife Hannah. We agreed on a time to meet, and I drove down to visit with him, to see what stories we could exhume together.

Hannah greeted me at the door as if I were her son. Amos came slowly down the stairs, fresh off a hip-replacement surgery. We shook hands. He spoke softly, at an even pace. His words come in thoughtful measures. I asked him for stories about our ancestors, and he did not disappoint.

At lunchtime, we went into the kitchen, and Hannah served us some of the best chicken salad sandwiches I've ever had. I'm not usually a fan of chicken salad sandwiches, but that day I ate two.

"I have to go look for something," Amos said, rising slowly and walking back upstairs. It wasn't long before he reentered the kitchen and placed something on the table in front of me.

It was a little notebook: it's spine was broken, and some of the pages, now unattached, have the tendency to float out. The cover was brown with a black stripe along the left hand side. Nothing was written on the outside of it, so that it appeared like any other journal you might find, old and deteriorating, in a landfill or trash can somewhere. Yet, if you would open it, you would be surprised.

In the center of the front cover was the following inscription:

May 29 1893,
Amos C. King's Book,
West Earl Lanc. Co Pa.
Second Book. May 29, 1893

This is the journal of my great-great-grandfather, Amos King. There must have been at least one other at some point, but somehow the years managed to discard it. We have no idea if it is the last – he seemed a prolific writer, from all accounts, so it seems hard to believe he would have stopped journaling after 1896. Yet the front and back of the book contain so many notes from later dates that I wondered if perhaps this was the last notebook he kept, adding only one or two things over the years.

The inside covers, both in the front and back of the journal, have very little leftover space – writing which began in the middle of those blank spaces expanded over the years as additional notes were added. Things like: *In God We Trust, 1934. Feb. The cold month. For nearly 4 weeks from zero to 26 below zero. At some places colder than for 100 years.*

Then, on the first page, the journal begins. The daily existence of Amos King comes into being with a beautiful script, a sharp cursive unlike any handwriting from the 21st century. The topics can seem repetitive, unless you allow yourself to picture this young boy, already having lost so many people in his life, taking a few minutes at the end of each busy day to record the passing of time. I imagine him in his room, or at the kitchen table, an oil lamp or candle flickering out at the darkness around him

The journal begins on May 29, 1893, and each ensuing day is marked with only a number until the new month comes into being.

I read most of the journal into my recorder during a few more visits with Uncle Amos – he would sit there with me while I read. He explained some of the farming techniques that my great-great-grandfather Amos talked about in his journal. He knew some of the people mentioned. He knew all of the places. What an amazing experience – reading a 117-year-old journal about my great-great-grandfather Amos King, all the while getting commentary from my great-uncle Amos Stoltzfus.

This is how it went (I include only the first seven months here – the journal is written out in its entirety at the back of the book):

May 29 Today Father and Mother went down to Uncle Christian Stoltzfus and Aaron and I worked on the woodpile. And its cloudy and damp weather.

My great-great-grandfather Amos's father and mother were Benjamin King and Catharine Stoltzfus (she is not any of the multiple Catharine Stoltzfus's we have discussed).

Aaron was Amos's older brother by two years. Of all his siblings, they seemed to spend the most time together, working, going to Sunday meetings and singings held by the Amish youth.

30. Today we made some tobacco land ready. And this evening we planted a lot of tobacco. 1893.

31. Today Father and Aaron were making fence. And I shoveled the potatoes. And planted some tobacco.

June 1. Today we started shoveling corn. And I and Moses planted some corn over. And this afternoon Father and Johns were in Farmersville with thirty dozens of eggs at fourteen cts a dozen. And this evening we planted some tobacco.

2. Today we were shoveling corn. And this evening it commenced to rain. But we need some rain too.

3. This forenoon we went to Conestoga. And it was Aaron and I and Beckie. Aaron and Fannie Glick and David and Susie Zook. We had two horses and a market wagon. We were at Uncle Aaron Stoltzfus for dinner. And at Christ ... for supper. And at Isaac Stoltzfus's over night. And it's warm weather.

Amos King's uncle Aaron Stoltzfus was his mother's youngest brother. So even he had Stoltzfus blood in him.

4. Today we were at the meeting at Abram Kurtz. And at Jonas Stoltzfus for supper. And this evening we were at the singing at Isaac Stoltzfus. And tonight we went home full of sleep.

In May of 1893, young Amos King was 18 years old – in about five years he would marry Katie Stoltzfus (not my great-grandmother), daughter of Jonas Stoltzfus. If this is the same Jonas Stoltzfus at which he spent the night on June 4th, 1893, I wonder if there were any sideways glances with the young Katie, 15 years old at the time. I wonder if the next day, while shoveling corn and planting tobacco, Amos thought about her.

Another note – Jonas Stoltzfus's wife Catherine was an older sister to the Mast twins, Sarah and Rachel, the ones who switched dates and had the double wedding on New Year's Day in 1857, 36 years before! The years pass so quickly! The generations just keep on blending, one into the next.

5. Today Aaron was shoveling corn. And I and Moses were putting ... greens on the tobacco plants. And this evening we planted some tobacco.

Moses was Amos's younger brother – he would have been 12 at the time. Uncle Amos said the greens were probably some sort of powder that protected the tobacco from pests.

6. Today Aaron was shoveling corn. And this evening it rained powerful. Amos C King born Sept 6, 1874

There are times throughout Amos's journal where he refers to himself in the third person, affirming his identity. Perhaps he was just practicing his signature, as many do. Or perhaps, after watching four of his siblings die, this was some sort of subconscious attempt at verifying his continued existence.

Whatever the case, as he grew older his random inscriptions transformed from the simple writing of his name and birth date to brief statements about God and faith.

7. Today we were planting tobacco the whole day. And we planted about a thousand plants. It's cloudy weather.

8. Today Aaron was shoveling corn. And I was shoveling potatoes. This evening we planted tobacco.

9. Today Aaron and I were shoveling corn. And this evening we made done planting tobacco. It's wet weather.

10. This forenoon Aaron and I were shoveling corn. And Father was in Farmersville. And this afternoon he went to up to Isaac Stoltzfus. And Aaron went to Pinetown to fetch a load of boards. And it's very warm.

19. Today we started scraping corn and we sold our two young steers to Mr. Stridemore for 4 ¾ cents a pound. They weighed 1590 pounds, both of them.

20. Today we started haymaking. This forenoon Father went in Lancaster on the train. In 1893 May sometime the World's Fair, Chicago commenced. Aaron was scraping corn.

21. Today Aaron was scraping corn and this evening we put some hay in. And it's warm weather.

22. Today we were making hay. This evening we had a nice shower. Adam Kauffman helped us.

23. This forenoon we were hoeing tobacco and this evening we cleared one field of hay. It's good hay weather.

24. Today we were busy making hay. And the hay is coarse and pretty near all clover.

25. This forenoon Father and Mother went down to Grandmother's. Aunt Lizzie is still sick. And we were all at house. This afternoon it is raining. This evening Father and Mother came home.

Aunt Lizzie is Amos's aunt, his Father's youngest sister Elizabeth. I do not have any information on what her sickness was or how long before this journal entry she had been ill. Born in 1849, and 44 at the time of this entry, she never married.

26. This forenoon Father went in Farmersville with 49 dozen of eggs. And Aaron and I planted tobacco

27. This forenoon it rained. And I and Moses fetched a barrel full of buttermilk at the West Earl Creamery. And this afternoon John Neuhaus's and Grandmother were here. And Aaron and I were hoeing tobacco. And it's damp and cloudy weather.

28. This forenoon Father made the rest of the grass of. And Aaron and I were hoeing tobacco. Still cloudy weather.

29. *Today Aaron was patching the barn roof. And I was shoveling tobacco. And this evening we made done haymaking. We had a pretty descent hay crop again. And it's still damp and cloudy weather.*

30. *Today we were hoeing tobacco. And I shoveled tobacco.*

July 1. Today Aaron and I were shoveling corn. And Father went to Ephrata. He bought a new ... binder from Mr. Stricher for one hundred and five dollars and the old binder in trade. And this evening Aaron went away.

2. *Today I and Beckie were at the meeting at Noah Fisher's. And this afternoon we had a lot of visitors. It was Christ King, Enos Stoltzfus, Jacob King, Jacob Zook and John Ebersole. And this evening we were at the singing at ... Beiler's place.*

3. *This forenoon we were ... corn. And Mrs. Sprechers was here to set the binder up. And it's raining.*

4. *This forenoon we were picking blackberries*

5. *This forenoon we were picking cherries and this afternoon we started harvesting. The corn crop is looking good.*

6. *Today we were harvesting. The binder is doing well.*

7. *Today I and Moses were picking cherries. This afternoon we were binding. This evening it rained.*

8. *This forenoon Aaron and I were shocking wheat and it's damp weather and this afternoon we made done binding wheat. This evening it rained. A nice shower. This evening Christ came home and we had ice cream.*

9. *This forenoon Aaron and Fannie Glick were here. And Simon Zooks Christ and Barbara Zook. And this afternoon Aaron and Beckie went down to John Stoltzfus's and this evening we were at home.*

10. *Today we were busy hauling wheat into the barn.*

11. Today we were handling wheat on stacks. We have a German fellow to help us. It's dry weather right now.

12. Today we were busy handling wheat and we had very good harvesting weather and it's very dry weather.

13. Today we made done harvesting and this evening we had a little storm. And tonight we had a nice rain. Wages for harvesting was $1.25.

14. Today we were suckering corn. And Father went into Farmersville. Look where you walk in this world.

They used to "sucker" corn – the little shoots that grow out the side of the stalk would get twisted off.

"Look where you walk in this world" is one of the first little spiritual tidbits that we find in his writing, and these expressions become more apparent as the journal progresses.

15. Today we shoveled tobacco and the rest were hoeing tobacco. Christ came in this world to save the sinners from sin.

16. Today we were all at the meeting at Henry Zook's. And this afternoon Jacob King and Katie Yoder and Fannie Fisher were here. And this evening we were at the singing at Jacob Stoltzfus, a large singing.

17. This morning Father and Mother and Grandmother and John were down to Uncle David Stoltzfus in Chester County and we were hoeing tobacco. This evening Aaron and Aaron Glick went in Lancaster.

18. Today Father and Mother were visiting in Chester County until this evening when they came home. And Aaron and I were hauling dung. Wonderful warm weather.

19. This forenoon we were hauling dung and this afternoon we were spreading dung.

20. Today we started plowing. And I was hauling ... fence away. And we have dry weather just now. And Father and John were with Grandmother.

21. Today I was plowing but it's too dry to plow, and Aaron was cleaning the fence. Order is heaven's first law.

22. Today I was plowing and Christian Stoltzfus from Morgantown was here. And Beckie was at John Glick's quilting, and this evening I was at the auction at Bareville. And this evening Aaron and Aaron Glick went away. And we have a dry summer.

23. Today I was at home and Christ Riehl's and Grandmother were here and this evening I was at the singing at Christ Stoltzfus. And Aaron's was at the Isaac Stoltzfus singing.

24. Today I was plowing and Father and Aaron were making stake fence. Love your neighbor as yourself.

25. Today Aaron helped thresh at Abram ... and I was plowing. Father was reaping oats.

26. Today we were shoveling and hoeing tobacco and this evening we had a little shower. Thou shalt not steal.

27. This afternoon we hauled some oats in and this evening we threshed some oats. And Aaron and I were at the camp meeting at Brownstown.

"What?" exclaimed my great-uncle Amos from the other side of the kitchen table. "Read that again!"

"And Aaron and I were at the camp meeting at Brownstown," I read.

"A camp meeting?" he exclaimed. "A camp meeting! Well, I never!"

Uncle Amos just couldn't get over the fact that his grandfather Amos had gone to a camp meeting with his brother Aaron. We couldn't imagine this would have been looked on kindly by the Amish church they attended.

I did some searching around on the Internet and discovered this church in Akron, PA, an area that Amos King very well could have been referring to as Brownstown back in the late 1800s. The history section of their website provides the following information:

The year 1992 marks the one hundredth anniversary of Grace Church in Akron. However, our church was originally a part of the Evangelical Association, a denomination founded by Jacob Albright about 1800.

At the General Conference of that denomination held in 1885, there arose differences of opinion concerning the powers of the General Conference and the Bishops. This resulted in a division and two groups known as the Majority and Minority were formed.

The Minority group reorganized as the United Evangelical Church. Since the court awarded all the church property to the Majority group the people in Akron who favored the Minority group met for worship in the East Akron school house (at the intersection of Main and Diamond Streets) and in the homes of some of the members. It was with great anticipation and joy that a new church was built in 1892. The cornerstone laying service took place on Sunday, August 23, 1892. Services were held Saturday night and three services on Sunday in the tabernacle in the rear of the church building with seating for about 600 people. Rev. G.W. Hangen was the minister at that time.

Rev. A.A. Delong preached a sermon in the English language on Saturday night. On Sunday morning Rev. J.H. Shirey preached in the German language. He preached an English sermon in the afternoon and after the sermon an opportunity was given to have names placed in the cornerstone, a dollar was to be contributed by each adult and fifty cents by each child under ten. There were 147 names placed in the stone. Rev. Shirey preached again Sunday night. The grand total of all the offerings taken was more than $450.

The church was dedicated on Sunday, November 20, 1892. Bishop C.S. Haman preached on Saturday night and again on Sunday morning, this time in the German language. Presiding Elder S.S. Chubb preached in the afternoon to a large audience. All available sitting and standing room was used and many were unable to enter the church. Rev. Chubb preached again on Sunday evening and again there were not enough seats to accommodate all the people. According to the records the church building cost $3300 and the members had a building fund of $800. On dedication day all but $16 was raised.

The first Sunday School session was held on Sunday, November 27, 1892 at 1:30 P.M. with 130 persons in attendance.

But wait! Here's the interesting part:

> From the beginning our denomination has stressed evangelism. The charge conducted an annual camp meeting at Rothsville from 1892 to 1895. Later a camp meeting was held annually at Millway from 1903 to 1916. People came from far and near to hear the preaching and many were converted and added to the church.

Are these the camp meetings that my great-great-grandfather Amos attended? Was he drawn to leave the Amish at any point? He doesn't discuss it in his journal anywhere, but the fact that he mentions these camp meetings, when he mentions so few other out of the ordinary events, seems to suggest they were a highlight to him.

We were both surprised to read that. And as Uncle Amos put it, "Well, I never!"

Chapter Ten
A Life in One-Sentence Days

Reading a journal is slow work, especially when it's written in a cursive script straight out of the 1800s. Some of the words were difficult to decipher. But Amos and I continued on.

28. This forenoon we turned the oats. This afternoon we threshed the rest of our oats. We got 235 bushels and we threshed 25 bushels of wheat.

29. This forenoon we were hauling dung and it rained a little shower and Father and Beckie went in.

In those days hauling manure was no easy task. They usually had a one horse wooden sled with steel runners, and they'd load it down with manure, pull it out into the field, and spread it with a pitchfork.

30. Today Father and Mother were at the meeting at Jacob Beiler's, and we were at home all day. Til this evening we were at the singing at Noah Smoker's.

31. This forenoon we were spreading dung, and this afternoon we hauled dung. Avoid evil companions.

"Avoid evil companions," Uncle Amos said quietly, as if to himself.

"He likes to drop those gems in among his writing, doesn't he?" I asked.

Amos nodded.

"He was a godly man. 'Avoid evil companions.' He didn't just write these proverbs in his journal. He lived by them."

August 1. Today we made done hauling dung. And this afternoon we were spreading dung. And we have very dry weather. Wheat is worth 58 cents.

Every time I read the phrase "made done," Amos would chuckle to himself.

"Made done," he'd say, shaking his head back and forth. "Did he really write that? Made done."

2. This forenoon we made done spreading dung. And Father was plowing. And it's dry weather.

3. Today I was plowing and Father and Aaron were making fences. And it's now three weeks that it didn't rain on any account.

4. Today we were plowing and making fences. And the corn and tobacco is going to die for want of rain.

5. Today I was plowing and Aaron and Moses were topping tobacco. And we have still dry weather.

6. This forenoon Father and Mother went down to Grandmother's. Aunt Lizzie is still sick. And Aaron and Beckie went to Henry Zook's. And this afternoon at John Glick's. This evening they were at the singing at Ezra Stoltzfus's. And we had a hail and thunderstorm and our corn and tobacco is pretty badly cut.

7. Today I was plowing and Aaron worked in the tobacco patch. This evening Aaron and I and Beckie were over at Aunt Lizzie's, who is still sick.

8. Today Aaron helped thresh Abram's ... and I was following and we sold chicken's to Isaac Meyer's. We had 103 pounds of young chickens at 11 cents a pound. Amount is $11.33. And 85 pounds of old chickens at 9 cents a pound amount to $7.65. The whole amount was $19.21 and so on.

9. This forenoon I helped to thresh at Abram Riehl's and Aaron's helped threshing at Elias ... wages are $1.00 and $1.25. Father went to Grandmother's.

10. This forenoon Aaron helped to thresh out Monroe ...

11. Today Aaron and I went for elderberries. We were as far as Bowmansville. It is a very warm day.

12. Today we sawed down our hickory tree out in the meadow. We have very dry and warm weather. And this afternoon Father and Mother went to Uncle Abram Stoltzfus's and Uncle John King's overnight.

13. Today we were at the funeral at Joel Zook's. Their baby died. It was 3 months and 9 days old. And this afternoon we went with Christ to David Smoker's. And this evening we were at the singing at John P Fisher's.

My great-great-grandfather Amos spoke with a particular precision when discussing death. "3 months and 9 days old," Amos wrote. It is as if they want to remember not just the years, but each of the days as well.

14. This forenoon I was plowing and this afternoon we were cutting wood. I think this is a wonderful world.

15. Today I was plowing and Aaron was quarrying stone for Abram Stoltzfus. And it's terrible dry and warm weather. Evil habits are gathered by unseen degrees, as brooks make rivers and rivers turn to seas.

16. Today Aaron's helped to thresh at Joe Hoover's and Father went to Grandmother's. And Lizzie is poorly. And Christian Stoltzfus and Nancy Stoltzfus and Grandmother...Hard times on farmer's just now.

82

17. Today Aaron's and I helped to thresh at Levi Hoover's, and this evening we had a little shower but no account. And it's now 6 weeks that it didn't rain on any account.

18. Today Aaron helped to thresh at Simon Zook's, and Moses and I were suckering tobacco. The crop is poor.

19. Today they made done threshing at Isaac Zook's. And Moses and I started cutting tobacco. And Father and Mother were at John Neuhauser's.

20. Last night Aunt Lizzie died and this afternoon Father and Mother and Aunt Barbara went down to Grandmother. And Aaron and John were at Jacob Zook's for dinner and I was at home.

21. This forenoon Aaron was quarrying stones. And Moses and I were putting away tobacco. It's dry weather.

22. Today was the funeral of Aunt Lizzie King. And we were all at the funeral. It was a very large funeral. She was 44 years and 3 months old.

23. Today Aaron was plowing. And I and Moses and John were putting away tobacco. Cloudy weather.

24. Last night it rained and stormed, the whole night. And this afternoon Aaron and I were plowing but the ground isn't soaked. We have stormy weather.

25. This forenoon Aaron and I were plowing, and this afternoon Aaron went up to David Beiler's to help thresh. Father went over to Grandmother's.

26. Today Aaron helped to thresh at David Beiler's. I was plowing and we had very warm weather. The thermometer reached over 100 degrees.

27. Today we were at the meeting at Isaac Stoltzfus's. And this afternoon Aaron and I were with Isaac Glick. This evening we were at Jacob Glick's awhile.

28. Today I helped to thresh at Jacob ... and Aaron helped at John Glick's. And Father fetched a load of sulphur coal at M. Stauffer's Coal and Timber Yard. *Love your neighbor as yourself.*

29. Last night was the stormiest night that we've had for a long time. And we had heavy rains too. And the corn is badly tangled down.

31. Today we started making out potatoes. And Grandmother was here.

September 1. This forenoon we were making out potatoes. And last night Jonas Zook's barn burned down.

2. Today we made done making out potatoes. We have a fair crop again. This evening Aaron went away.

3. Today Christ was at home. And Uncle Christ Stoltzfus's girls and Lethenia Kauffman were here. This afternoons we were at Joe Hoover's. And this evening we were at the singing at John Beiler's.

4. Today I was plowing . And Aaron's and Moses were putting away tobacco. Our tobacco crop is poor.

5. Today we started threshing. We had John and Simon Zook's engines. Tonight it rained a little.

6. This forenoon we made done threshing. We got 389 bushels of wheat. And we sold $5.00 worth of chickens. And this afternoon we helped thresh at John Zook's.

7. Today we were busy putting away tobacco. And it's dry and cloudy weather. *Avoid evil companions.*

8. This forenoon I fetched 3,173 pounds of phosphate at Leacock Station from G. Baird at $27.00 a ton.

9. Today we started cutting corn. It's terrible bad to cut.

10. Today Aaron and Beckie and I and Aaron and Fannie Glick were at David Blank's. And this afternoon we were at Jonas Lantz. And this evening we were at the singing at ... Beiler's.

11. Today Aaron and I were cutting corn and Father and Mother went over to Grandmother's and they brought Grandmother and Aunt Susie ... along

12. Today Aaron helped to thresh at Jacob Stoltzfus's. And I was cutting corn. Moses was harrowing.

13. Today Aaron and I were cutting corn. And Moses was harrowing. It's dry and warm weather.

14. This forenoon it rained a little. And Aaron and I were hauling stone. This afternoon we were cutting corn. And we cooked some apple butter. This evening Father took 10 bushels of potatoes at ... cents a bushel at Brownstown.

15. Today Father and Mother were at the funeral of John Petersheim. He was 70 years, 2 months and 18 days old. And Aaron and I were cutting corn. This evening we had a thunderstorm.

16. Today we made done cutting tobacco. And this evening Aaron and Beckie went to Elias Stoltzfus.

17. Today Aaron and Beckie were at the Lower Pequea meeting at Samuel Umble. The young folks were baptized. They were Enos Stoltzfus, ... Umble, Amos Algyer, Molly ... , Rachel Stoltzfus, Sara Petersheim and Annie Umble. And this afternoon I was at John King's. And this evening I was at home. And Aaron and Beckie were at the singing at Joshua Lapp's. And it's fresh and clear weather. Thou shalt not steal.

18. Today Aaron and I were cutting corn and Father was plowing the tobacco patch.

19. Today Aaron and I were cutting corn and Moses was harrowing.

20. Today Aaron and I were cutting corn and Moses was harrowing. This evening Father and Mother went to John Zook's. And Aaron and Beckie went to John King's.

21. Today Aaron and I were cutting corn and Moses was harrowing. And it's cloudy weather.

22. Today Aaron and I were cutting corn.

23. Today we made done cutting corn. And it's damp and rainy weather. And Father and Beckie went in Farmersville. September 23, 1893.

24. Today we were at the meeting at ... Beiler's place. And Aaron and Aaron Glick's were at the meeting at Christian Esh's. This afternoon Father and Mother were with Grandmother. This evening we were at the singing at ... Beiler's. It was a large singing. Mind your steps.

25. Today we started sowing wheat. And Aaron worked at John Zook's. This afternoon it rained and John Zook's fetched 20 bushels of wheat.

26. Today we were sowing. And Aaron worked at John Zook's. Moses was harrowing. And we had a mason to fix the chimneys. Nice weather.

27. Today I was sowing. And Father and Mother were at the sale at Nancy Stoltzfus.

28. Today I was plowing corn stubbles. And we sold Christ's horse for $70 to Clayton Rook. He bought 8 steers at $3.20 per hundred. They average 840 pounds, And a bull for $2.75 per hundred. He weighed 750 pounds.

29. Today we made done plowing corn stubble. And we have dry and warm weather again.

30. Today we made done sowing. And Aaron worked at Simon Zook's.

October 1. Today we were at ... And Christ was at home. And Uncle Christ Stoltzfus was here. And Aaron was at the singing at Levi Smoker's.

2. Today I and Moses were picking apples. And Aaron was hauling lumber with our teams at Millway Station.

3. Today we were picking apples and quarrying stones. And Father went in Farmersville, from there to Ephrata. And it's dry and warm weather.

4. This forenoon Aaron's worked on this road. And Moses and I started husking corn. This afternoon it rained. It's necessary.

5. Today we were husking corn. And we paid our school tax. It was $22.00.

6. This evening Father and Mother went over to Grandmother's. And we were husking corn.

7. This morning Father and Mother went on the train down to Daniel Stoltzfus. And we were husking corn. And it cleared off again. And this evening they came home.

8. Today they were at the meeting at Jacob Zook's. And I was at home the whole day. And this evening we were at home too.

9. Today we were finished husking corn. And our corn crop is about 3/4ths of a crop.

10. Today we were husking corn.

11. Today Aaron and Moses and I were husking corn. And it's splendid husking weather.

12. Today we were husking corn. And it's cloudy weather. And I guess it will rain.

13. Today we sold $21.00 worth of chickens to Isaac Meyers. And Father and Mother and Aunt Becca went down to old John Stoltzfus. And this afternoon it rained and stormed wonderful. This evening they came home.

14. *Today we were husking corn and Father took Aunt Beckie over to Uncle Christ Stoltzfus.*

15. *This forenoon Christ and Daniel Fisher were here. And this afternoon we were at Jacob Stoltzfus. And it's cold and stormy weather.*

16. *Today we were busy husking corn.*

17. *We have nice corn this year. But it isn't so plenty as last year. Good husking weather.*

18. *Today we were busy husking corn.*

19. *Today we were husking corn and this evening we were at the husking at Daniel Esh's.*

20. *Today we were husking corn. And it's damp.*

21. *Today we made done husking corn. This afternoon Beckie went over to Grandmother's.*

22. *Today Father and Mother and Aaron were at the meeting at Christ Petersheim's and it was a large meeting. Beckie and I over at John Glick's. This evening we were at home. And it's cloudy weather.*

23. *Today it rained the whole day. And Isaac Stoltzfus and Barbara Zook were here. And Aaron and I worked the potatoes in the cellar.*

24. *Today we were hauling corn fodder. And Aaron fetched a load of coal at Leacock Station.*

25. *This forenoon Aaron and I were hauling corn fodder. This afternoon I was making fence.*

26. *Today Father and I were in Lancaster. We bought a stove at G M Steinman's Store for $16.00. We sold some potatoes. And Aaron was hauling coal to burn lime.*

27. Today Father and Beckie were at the meeting at Jonas Lantz. Some strange preachers were there. It was Christian Troyer and Mr. Peachy. And we made done hauling corn fodder.

28. Today I fetched a load of coal at Leacock's and Aaron was filling in.

29. Today Aaron was away. It's cold and stormy weather. This evening I was at the singing.

30. This morning Aaron and I started quarrying stones. But we stopped after a while. We bored air holes and Aaron lighted it and the powder can caught fire which he had in his hand and the can exploded. And it burned him pretty badly. Then I worked around the barns. Father worked in the summerhouse.

31. Today I worked where I wanted and Father went in Farmersville. We had a heavy frost.

November 1. Today I helped thresh with Jacob Stoltzfus. And Aaron is pretty sick today. We have nice weather.

2. Today we made done threshing at Jacob Stoltzfus's. And Isaac Hoover and I were quarrying stones and it's warm and pleasant weather.

3. Today Isaac and I were quarrying stones.

4. Today it rained the whole day. And I cleaned and dunged the stables and so forth.

5. Today we were at the meeting at John Miller's. This afternoon we had some visitors. They were Aaron and Fannie Glick, Samuel Stoltzfus, John Beiler and Uncle Elias Stoltzfus. And this evening we were at the singing at John Miller's. And it was a large singing.

6. This forenoon Isaac Hoover and I were quarrying stones and in the afternoon we were filling limekiln.

7. Today Father and Mother and Grandmother and Nancy Stoltzfus were in ... with two horses. Isaac and I were filling limekiln.

8. Isaac and I were filling lime kiln. And Father and Mother were visiting in Conestoga.

9. Today we made done filling limekiln and Father and Mother came home. And this evening Christ King's came and stayed overnight.

10. This forenoon Father and Mother were with Christ's over to John Zook's. And I fetched a load of coal at Stauffer's Coal and Lumberyard.

11. Today I dunged the stables and cleaned the cistern out. And Father and Moses and John went in Farmersville. This evening Daniel Lapp was here.

12. Today Beckie and I and Christ were at Christ Stoltzfus's for dinner and for supper at Sarah Stoltzfus. This evening we were at the singing at John Fisher's. It was a good singing.

13. This forenoon we sold two cows to S Sensinig. One for 15 dollars and the other for 30 dollars. And Moses and I were ... stones in the ground. Father went out to Stauffer's to pay his coal bill.

14. Today we made done picking stones. And Father and Aaron went to Farmersville.

15. Last night it rained and snowed and its rough and cold weather.

16. This morning Eli Stoltzfus started hauling lime. And it's rough and stormy weather. This afternoon Father took a hog to Sensenig that weighed 299 pounds at 8 cents a pound.

17. This forenoon they made done hauling lime. We got 1012 bushels at 8 cents a bushel. Amount $80.96. This afternoon we were hauling coal. And Beckie helped to bake pies at John Zook's.

18. Today I dunged the stables and Father went in Farmersville. This evening I was at the auction in Mechanicsburg. Aaron went away too.

19. Today we were at the meeting at John Zook's. This afternoon Aaron went to Aaron Glick's. I was at home and Father and Mother went with Simon Zook's. And in the evening we were at the singing at John Glick's. And it's cold and stormy weather.

20. Today Aaron and I were quarrying stones. And this afternoon Father took a load of chickens to Jay Stoltzfus. Had $15.30 worth of chickens. From there he went to Grandmother.

21. Last night Christ came home. And today Christ and Aaron were quarrying stones. And I worked around the barn. And this afternoon it commenced to snow. And it's rough and stormy weather. We have dull times but plenty to eat.

22. Today Christ and Aaron were quarrying stones.

23. Today I helped to thresh at John Zook's and Father took a hog to S Sensinig for 8 cents a pound. It weighted 294 pounds. Christ and Aaron were quarrying stones.

24. Today Christ and I were quarrying stones and Aaron was filling limekilns.

25. This forenoon I dunged the stables and Christ and Aaron were filling limekilns and this evening Aaron and I were in Farmersville.

26. Today Aaron went away. And I was at home. This evening we had a singing at Stephen Stoltzfus's.

27. This forenoon Father went in Lancaster on the train, and I fetched two loads of coal and so on.

28. Today we worked at the stone. And this evening we worked at the auctions at Mechanicsburg.

29. Today we were filling limekiln.

30. Today was Thanksgiving Day. And Christ and Aaron were at Jacob Glick's. And Father and Mother were at Grandmother's. And this evening we were at the singing at John P Fisher's. Always speak the truth.

December 1. This forenoon Christ and Isaac Hoover were quarrying stones. And this afternoon it rained.

2. This forenoon they were quarrying stones. And Father and Mother went in Farmersville. Christ and Aaron went in Lancaster and I worked.

3. Today we were at the meeting at Daniel Stoltzfus, and it rained the whole day. And it rained this whole day. In the evening we had a good singing.

4. Today Christ went to Grandmothers, and we worked around the barn. And this afternoon Father took a load of turkeys to JP Stoltzfus. He had $20.34 worth of turkeys.

5. Today John Allgyer and Becky Glick married.

6. Today they were hauling lime. And we have a pretty decent snow. And this afternoon I took a sleigh ride, and we have cold weather.

7. Today Samuel Esh and Annie Stoltzfus married. And Christian Lapp and Leah Zook married. And we were at the wedding, and it was an excellent wedding. But it's cold weather just now.

8. This morning we came home from the wedding. And we didn't work much on any account.

9. This forenoon I dunged the stables and this afternoon Christ and Aaron were at the auction at Meyer's Store in Mechanicsburg. I was at home.

10. Today I was at the meeting at Black Jacob Stoltzfus. And this afternoon we had some visitors. They were Gideon Beiler, Isaac Glick, Aaron Glick, Joshua Lapp, Mollie Blank, Annie Beiler. It was a pleasant day. And tonight we were at the singing of Jacob Stoltzfus.

11. This morning Christ went down to Jacob Smoker's. And I was at Wenger's Mill. And in the afternoon I fetched a load of cinder ash at this mill. This evening

Aaron and Beckie went in Farmersville. And our dam is all frozen over. And we have cold weather. Love one another.

12. Today John King and Beckie Lapp married. And David Blank and Beckie Beiler married. And Samuel Lapp and Katie Stoltzfus married. And Christ and Aaron were at John King's wedding. And Father visited old Johnny Stoltzfus.

"And Samuel Lapp and Katie Stoltzfus married." This is the Samuel Lapp who will die on his kitchen table in 1898, almost five years to the day later. This is the Catherine Stoltzfus who will be left a widow with three small children. And it is also the Catherine Stoltzfus who will eventually become Amos's second wife.

Our timelines are such tangled threads.

13. Today Father went over to Grandmother. And Aaron and I were hauling dung. And it's rough weather.

15. Today is cold and stormy weather

16. Today we worked around the barns and so on.

17. Today we were at the meeting at Benuel Stoltzfus. This evening we were at home.

18. This forenoon I was at Wenger's Mill. And this afternoon Christ and ... and I went in Conestoga.

19. Today Isaac Glick and Annie Yoder married, and we were at the wedding. And it was an excellent wedding. And tonight we were at Isaac Stoltzfus's. And it's very warm and pleasant weather.

20. This forenoon we came home. And this afternoon I fetched a load of chopping. And this afternoon Christ went into Mechanicsburg.

21. Today Christian Beiler and Fannie King married. And we were at the wedding and it's very warm and pleasant weather. Father made ready to thresh.

22. Today we made done threshing. We got 340 bushels from the four stacks. And we sold $4.60 worth of turkeys to Meyers.

23. Today we started stripping tobacco. And Aaron went in Brownstown. This evening we were at the auctions at ... This afternoon it rained a little.

24. Today Simon Zook's were here. And we were at home. This evening we were at the singing at John Smoker's. This morning David Glick died. We leave muddy rags.

25. This forenoon I was with Samuel Stoltzfus. Afternoon I was at Black Jacob Stoltzfus. Christ and Aaron's were at Joel Fisher's. And it's warm Christmas weather but bad and muddy roads.

26. This forenoon Christ and Aaron came home. And David Glick was buried. He was 53 years, 4 months and 20 days old. And Father went in Farmersville. It's rough weather.

27. Today Christ and Aaron's were filling limekiln. And Father and I butchered a bull. And it's warm and pleasant weather. Wheat is worth 60 cents. Chickens are worth 6 cents a pound.

28. This forenoon Isaac Hoover helped to fill the limekilns. And this afternoon it rained. And we butchered a hog. And it's warm weather. This evening Christ went down to David Smoker's.

29. Today we were stripping tobacco and I fetched a load of chopping at Wenger's Mill. And Beckie helped to bake at Simon Zook's.

30. Today it snowed the whole day, but the ground ain't frozen. And we were stripping tobacco.

31. Today we were at the meeting at Simon Zook's. And we had some visitors. They were Daniel and Molly Lapp, Aaron and Fannie Glick, Benuel and Katie Stoltzfus, Amos, Elam and Katie Stoltzfus, Daniel and Susan Zook, Benjamin and Annie Umble, Jacob, Katie and Susan Yoder, Daniel Fisher, Danny Beiler,

Barbara Glick, Lydia and Annie Beiler, and Joseph and Jonathan Yoder from Mifflin County. This evening we were at the singing at Simon Zook's.

Notice the reference to "Amos, Elam and Katie Stoltzfus." Katie is the same girl whose Father showed up once before in his journal. Amos would marry her in 1898.

Amos's journal goes on for two more years, in a similar singsong way, reducing each day to its most basic elements: the tasks at hand, the people who crossed his path, and a few extraordinary occurrences. It ends in 1896 when he is 22 years old.

Two years later, after this journal ends, he married Katie Stoltzfus. And with each passing year, the intersection of his life with that of Catherine Lapp, widow of Samuel Lapp, grew ever nearer.

PART THREE:
FOUR DAUGHTERS

1905 – 2010

Catherine Stoltzfus
m. Amos King

|

Katie King
m. Samuel Stoltzfus

|

Priscilla Stoltzfus
m. Emanuel Beiler

|

Verna Beiler
m. Merrill Smucker

|

Me

Chapter Eleven
The Twists and Turns of a Storyline

Twists and turns of a storyline that determined my existence reached a hectic pace at the end of 1898. First, on November 17th, my great-great-grandfather Amos married Katie Stoltzfus, daughter of Jonas Stoltzfus and Catherine Mast. Two months later Samuel Lapp died on a kitchen table, the victim of appendicitis.

The strange thing is that Amos and his new bride Katie probably would have been at Samuel's funeral – it's entirely possible that Katie would have dashed to Catherine's house when she received word of his illness and impending surgery. You see, Katie and Catherine were first cousins: Katie's mother was an older sister to the Mast twins, Rachel and Sarah, who had switched boyfriends.

If these two female cousins were nearly as close as their mothers had been, they would have spoken often before, during and after Samuel's passing. Catherine and Samuel were probably at Amos and Katie's wedding. Who knows? Maybe the four were close friends.

I imagine Amos and Katie standing by Samuel Lapp's graveside, watching the casket lowering slowly into the grave, occasionally looking over at Catherine and her three young children. If they were anything like my wife and I, they would have gone home from that funeral and held each other a little tighter, spoken of how they could not go one without each other. We often say things like that: "I couldn't do it without you."

But every day people force themselves to go on without the one they thought they couldn't go on without.

Catherine went on.

Katie, Amos King's first wife, was the 9th of 10 children in her family. In her first four years of marriage to Amos she had two children: Lizzie and Jonas. Then, in 1902, she got sick.

I wonder how her sickness began. Perhaps she woke one morning to a feeling of achiness and fatigue. She could have had a sore throat and a low-grade fever. By all accounts, Amos was a gentle, kind man, slight of stature with thick, bushy black eyebrows and dark, wiry hair. Maybe he sent her back to bed those first few days. I can imagine her arguing with him; after all, Christmas was approaching, and preparations were needed to make the holiday special for their two young children.

But after a few days of not eating, she felt weak and ended up bed-ridden. Logically they would have called for the doctor who, upon further examination (and if the family stories are correct), would have noticed the greenish-grey membrane covering her tonsils. Or, if bleeding had already begun to occur, the back of her throat would have appeared black. As diphtheria settled in, she developed a barking cough, and her neck could have swelled up as wide as her head.

In the early 1900s, no cure or successful treatment for diphtheria existed: there were 100,000 to 200,000 cases each year, resulting in 13,000 to 15,000 deaths.[27] Diphtheria was not a pleasant way to die: an obstructed airway made breathing difficult and coughing painful. She probably spent Christmas Day in a coma. I can imagine Amos splitting his time between his two children (Lizzie and Jonas) and the rest of the family, then going in to sit beside Katie's bed, praying. But the toxin spread throughout her body, and she died on December 26, 1902. The day after Christmas.

Amos was 28 years old, a widower, with two young children.

---

[27] http://www.cdc.gov/vaccines/pubs/pinkbook/downloads/dip.pdf

Who knows how Amos King, whose wife Katie died in 1902, and Catherine Stoltzfus Lapp, whose husband died in 1898 of a failed appendectomy, ended up together? What set of circumstances brought this widower and widow, along with their five children, together? While we do not know the details, one thing can be said: they had a lot of things in common.

Both were part of a long line of Old Order Amish. Both lost multiple siblings to sickness or accidents. Both lost spouses when they were still in their mid-20s. As mentioned previously, Catherine and Katie were first cousins, so Amos and Catherine would have known of each other's plight. In fact, Amos and Catherine themselves were third cousins, sharing a great-great-grandfather in Christian Stoltzfus (Sr.), although their family trees were created separately by Christian's first and second wives: Amos through Christian's first wife Barbara, and Catherine through his second wife Susanna.

So who knows how they came together? I have a hunch though, and it has to do with a set of Mast twins audacious enough to switch beaus, pretending to be one another. If those two women were as mischievous and "involved" as they were when they were two little girls plotting the great exchange, then I'd guess they had something to do with it. In fact, I'd be surprised if they weren't somehow responsible.

So, a shared set of life-experiences? A more romantic situation? A pair of conniving aunts? We may never know what brought Amos King and Catherine (Stoltzfus) Mast together. But what we do know is that they married each other in 1905, and suddenly, as if out of the ashes of a nearly destroyed world, my ancestors begin coming into view. Their newly combined family had five children from their previous marriages: Catherine brought Anna (11), Benjamin (9) and John (7); Amos contributed Lizzie (5) and Jonas (3), born only four months before his mother's death.

Jonas, after the death of his mother, had been taken in by Levi Fisher's family at the age of 4 months. They kept him until Amos and Catherine married, at which point he returned with his father and new stepmother. I try to imagine what that would have been like for Amos, picking up his three-year-old son and taking him home, now that he had a wife, and the boy had a mother to care for him.

Yet, I descended from none of those original five, which is why the combined deaths of Samuel Lapp and Katie (Stoltzfus) King led to my existence. If Samuel never would have come down with appendicitis, or if Katie would have survived her fight with diphtheria, would I even be here?

Amos and Catherine went on to have six children together: Sarah, Katie, Priscilla, Amos, Samuel and Rebecca. Amos died in 1914 when he was only 4 days old, and Samuel died the day after Christmas in 1917. He was only 2 ½ years old and passed away fifteen years to the day after Amos's first wife, and 19 years and a few weeks after Catherine's first husband, his namesake.

I find it hard to fathom, these lives filled with so much loss. If, like my great-great-grandfather Amos King, I lost four siblings before I got married, then lost my wife after only four years of marriage, then lost two of my own children, I wonder how I would cope with that. But there was a strength in my ancestors, a strength I do not recognize in myself. Perhaps it's there. Perhaps, should trials come my way, I would find it rising from unknown depths within me. I can only hope it is never tested.

There is something special to me about the second child that Amos and Catherine had together: Katie King. She would be my great-grandmother, my Mummi, the gracious old lady I remember seeing from time to time at my grandmother's house. Before I went digging for stories, I never knew she shared the name of her grandmother as well as that of her father's first and second wives: Katie.

No matter whom you speak with, it's clear that Amos King was a man of stories. His granddaughter (my grandmother) Priscilla remembers how all the children would crowd at his feet around the bench in their house as he told tales about the old days that kept them wide-eyed. Catherine, walking in and out of the room, often corrected him, a voice harping in the background calling him to task on exaggerations or simple, missed facts. He would argue back – she never conceded ground. But the stories always continued.

During one of my trips to my great-uncle Amos's, he told me how his grandfather Amos King used to sit on the steps beside the barn. Little

Amos would wander up next to his Grandpa King and sit on the step beside him. His Grandpa King would always tell him a story.

"The snow was so deep we couldn't used the sleigh. We couldn't even go to church," Grandpa King whispered intently to a wide-eyed Amos.

"What about the horses?" little Amos would ask, already knowing the story.

"The snow was up to the horses flanks," Grandpa King said, as if he were still amazed, his thick black eyebrows now filled with gray. "They floundered, and bucked, and nearly fell in the snow. We had to turn back. There were fifty-foot drifts in New York. Fifty feet of snow! When it finally started to melt we'd hitch up the sleigh and ride over the top of the snow, bundled up in buffalo robes. Sometimes the sleigh would tip, and we'd all fly out. Then we would empty the sleigh of all the snow, right it again, and set off."

Grandpa King shook his head slowly back and forth, as if he was amazed at his own story. Little Amos Stoltzfus wished he could see snow that deep. But he didn't want the horses to get lost.

After Amos King passed away, they found writing on the walls of his old barn. Dug right into the boards, his curving script went on, probably much as it did on paper, perhaps a little larger, talking about who was married in what year and how the farming was that year and what their tasks were for the day. I'm sure he scattered proverbs throughout the straight lines of writing. But when the barn was torn down the boards were burned.

My great-uncle Amos Stoltzfus (now over 70 years old), the same one who used to sit on the step listening to his grandfather tell stories, the same one who walked me through his grandfather's journals, still can't quite believe someone didn't keep those old boards.

"It's a shame," he said sadly, shaking his head. "It's a real shame."

Chapter Twelve
Surviving the Great Depression

My Mummi, daughter of Amos and Catherine, was born on December 5th, 1908. She grew up with five older half-brothers and sisters as well as three full-siblings, but most of us never knew which were of common parents – they loved each other with a love forged by perseverance through hardship and death. They seemed extraordinarily close.

When Mummi, in her old age, started going around to live with her children, her four living siblings occasionally visited her – they were all in their late 80s or 90s. Some were hard of hearing, and many were losing their sight, so they would sit in a tight circle, close together, holding hands, leaning in toward one another, talking quietly in Pennsylvania Dutch: over 400 years of life in that small group.

Mummi did not have an easy childhood. When she was five years old her younger brother Amos died – he was only four days old. Then, in 1917, when she was nine years old, her younger brother Samuel died the day after Christmas. He was only 2 ½.

Yet her recollections of her early days were filled with wonder and excitement, not with sadness or melancholy. She told me stories about being a young adult during the Great Depression, when farmers struggled, and a penny to a child was like $10 today. She told me how crowds of people gathered to wait for the first car to drive through town, the main road still unpaved. They waited and waited, and when it finally came, one of the neighborhood dogs chased it for miles – they didn't think the dog would ever come back. She told me about the first airplane to fly over Lancaster County and how people were scared of it, thought the end of the world must be right around the corner.

She worked hard in those days, helping around the house, washing clothes, tending the garden, canning food. In the winter, there was less work and more time for fun – snow forts and snowball battles, sledding and ice-skating. They sold their eggs to the grocery story and used the money to buy a few groceries or articles of clothing that they couldn't make, like boots.

Everyone needed work in those days, and it wasn't unusual for a stranger to knock at the door enquiring about a day's wages. If it was during a busy season, wages were $1.00 a day, and sometimes the older "tramps" would come looking for a handout or a meal. In the words of Mummi's older brother John, their mother Catherine "never shut the door to a hungry man."

Harvest was a busy time for everyone. The threshing rigs were each manned by four or five hands, usually young boys. They'd often show up in the evening and set up for the following day, sleeping in the barn overnight. In the morning, they'd wash in the trough and come inside for breakfast, prepared by Mummi and her mother and sisters. Everyone was up early. Sometimes, during harvest, there would be 15 – 20 men and little boys coming in to the table. The neighbors came by to help if they were needed.

Mummi also helped bake pies and cakes, feathered chickens and gathered vegetables from the garden. She'd help carry cold water out to the stubble fields (which her brother John admitted "was a little rough on bare feet"). Those days were busy times, and a lot of work had to be done to make sure they could get through the winter.

On Tuesday the 20th of November, 1928, Amos and Catherine King's daughter Katie married Samuel Stoltzfus. It was 9 days before Thanksgiving that year.

To give you an idea of what our country was like in 1928, the first United States office building with air conditioning opened in San Antonio. The first transatlantic television image was received. Mussolini was modifying the Italian electoral system, paving the way for his continued rule and participation in World War II. Velveeta Cheese and Mickey Mouse made their first appearance. Herbert Hoover was elected president in November, and Babe Ruth was hitting home runs.

And somewhere in Lancaster County, PA, Samuel and Katie married.

But eleven months after their wedding, the world turned on its head.

The United States economy was expanding exponentially in the 20s. But by August of 1929, that expansion had peaked. A prevailing sense of uneasiness began whispering its way across the country. On September 3rd, 1929, stock market prices reached their highest level ever. Then, October 24th: Black Thursday. 12,895,000 shares sold. October 29th, Black Tuesday: 16,410,000 shares sold, and the New York Times index of industrial stocks dropped nearly 10% in one day. By November, stock prices halved from their September highs.[28]

Communities were thrown into chaos in the 30s, with farmers losing their land, migrant workers drifting around the countryside looking for work, and small camps, Hoovervilles, were set up to take in those who were starving and couldn't find work. Entire families wandered from state to state with no goal in mind other than a day's work or something resembling a meal.[29]

The colonial spirit that had welcomed the great-great-great-grandfathers of that generation was challenged like never before. What had once been a country founded on hope and democracy and rugged individualism was now floundering in despair and starvation. The average family income in 1929 was $2300 – by 1933 that had dropped 40%, to somewhere around $1500. Imagine today, going from an annual income of $30,000 to $18,000. More and more banks went out of business each year: in 1930, 1350 banks failed; in 1931, 2293 banks

---

[28] http://www.amatecon.com/gd/gdtimeline.html
[29] http://kclibrary.lonestar.edu/decade30.html

suspended operation; in 1932, 2293 banks failed; and in 1933 over 4000 banks closed their doors.[30]

Yet the Amish, including my great-grandmother's family, were uniquely positioned to survive just such a time. Their farms, some held in the family for over a hundred years, were mostly paid off. They kept minimal, if any, debt. Multiple generations lived in one farmhouse. They were mostly self-sustaining, as far as food went. They had large families and worked hard, enabling them to work their own farms without bringing on hired hands. And their sense of community meant that, if hard times or bad luck did strike, there was a larger crowd of people looking out for them.

In the midst of these years, my great-grandparents tried to make their way.

---

[30] http://www.amatecon.com/gd/gdtimeline.html

Chapter Thirteen
An Unexpected Guest

Their first house was much closer to Samuel's family than Katie's, and she missed her brothers and sisters. Sometimes, when Samuel would be out in the fields shouting and carrying on with his brothers, working and having fun, Katie would sit in the kitchen and cry, missing her own family. Sometimes Samuel and Katie would spend the night at one of his brothers' houses – they'd stay up half the night playing games or just talking and laughing, then eat breakfast before going home and going to bed.

The climate of worry that gripped the country in those days did not prevent my great-grandparents from starting a family soon after they were married – on June 7th, 1930, their first child was born: Annie K. Stoltzfus. Their second child Priscilla, my grandmother, was born in January of 1933. Then came Naomi in '36, Amos in '39 (the one with whom I read through great-great-grandfather Amos's journal), Samuel in '42, and Katie in '45. They were a veritable every-3-year, baby-making machine until Sadie was born in '47. But then they returned to the 3-year plan, and Lloyd, the baby, and the one in whose house Mummi would die, was born in '50.

Mummi was a feisty mother – her children remember her as strict but loving. In the words of her son, Amos, "When she said something, you knew she meant it and you'd better dance. If you talked back to Mom you got those looks that said, 'You'd better never do that again.'"

But I only remember her as a white-haired elven lady, bent over double when she walked. Her kind eyes and gentle smile have found a permanent place in my memory. She listened well and enjoyed a good conversation more than most, speaking in short bursts like a morning songbird.

Her husband Samuel, my great-grandfather and the one we called Daughty, was more laid back, sometimes using his voice to scold, but he rarely paddled the children. With him order was more important – everything had its place. But it didn't always stay that way, especially when the kids decided to play cops and robbers in the haymow. Their tunnels and caves sent the hay flying, and this challenged their father's naturally laid-back demeanor and brought out a dormant temper.

As Daughty got older, some of the grandkids were a bit scared of him because he'd stare at them when they'd go outside to play, his eyes squinting with suspicion – he didn't want them dirtying up his barn! The grandchildren also remember driving out the lane late at night in their buggies – if the horse left a mess on the drive, Daughty would be out there cleaning it up with his shovel before they even got out to the road.

Daughty's obsession with tidiness also affected his ability to farm and was probably something that kept him from being very successful at it. He'd often go over all his cornfields three times, hoeing it by hand – a farmer just doesn't have time to do that, but Daughty was always more about quality than quantity.

But mostly Daughty was remembered as a quiet, good man with a hearty laugh and heartier appetite, someone who enjoyed life, treated his family well and loved his wife. I remember an old man with a large, Santa Claus beard. I don't remember ever hearing him speak, but he died when I was very young.

I called my grandma to see if she could tell me more stories about the past. She thought about it for a moment, thinking through which days she would be available. She has a very busy schedule for a 78 year old.

We agreed on a day and I drove over to where she lives with my parents. Well, not with my parents exactly, but in a small house attached to my parent's house. Some people call this kind of addition a Mummi-end, and lots of Amish build them on to their houses when their parents reach a certain age, one of the endearing ways that they take care of the older generation.

I called her on the way over to make sure she was home.

"We should go to my sister Annie's house and ask her what she remembers," Grandma said.

"Oh, okay," I said, although I wasn't too sure about just going by someone's house without calling first. But Grandma seemed to think it was a good idea, so I picked her up and we drove about five miles to my great-aunt Annie's house. She is still Amish.

Her husband is Lloyd, referred to as Lloyd D. They lived on a beautiful little farmette, also in an addition built on to one of their children's houses. They were both in their 80s.

We pulled in the driveway, and Grandma led the way to the door.

"Hello? Anyone home?" she called out when no one responded to her loud, impatient knocking. Then she opened the storm door. I felt more and more uncomfortable – showing up without calling first was already something of a stretch, but then just walking in when someone didn't answer their door?

"Maybe no one's home," I suggested.

"Oh, no," Grandma insisted, "she's home."

She said the words as if she just knew. As if she could sense it. You cannot argue with that kind of reasoning.

Then she walked inside and continued calling out, "Hello? Anyone home?"

I followed her inside, reluctantly.

Finally a voice called out from the nether-regions of the house. A tired-sounding voice.

"Who is it?"

My grandma answered in Pennsylvania Dutch, including some words that sounded like a warning that she wasn't alone. I've always wished my parents had taught me that language, but they preferred to use it when we were younger to talk about Christmas gifts and other things that little ears shouldn't hear.

112

"Did we wake you up?" Grandma asked Annie as she came into the room. Grandma didn't sound all that concerned or sorry if she did. I guess that sometimes I forget they are siblings, and I would talk or do the same things to my own sisters, even if they were 80 years old.

Only two of my grandma's siblings are still Old-Order Amish – Annie is one of them. She came out to the room adjusting her covering and straightening her glasses. She looks a lot like my grandma: small facial features, piercing but kind eyes, and a quick smile.

"No, no. I just have a backache. It hurts terrible bad, so I was resting. That's all."

"Hello, Annie," I said.

"Well, hello there," she said. I shook her hand.

"This is Shawn," Grandma said. "He's the one writing the book."

"Well, I guess I know who he is," Annie said, smiling and pretending to be offended.

"He wants to know if we remember anything about Mummi and Daughty."

"Oh, well," she said. "I'll have to think."

Along with some stories my great-uncle Amos had shared with me during my visits with him, these are the memories we were able to salvage about their growing up years.

The first house my Mummi and Daughty Stoltzfus (Samuel and Katie) lived in sat north of the town of Intercourse, back a long lane. It was the first farm on the right on Hollander Road. There's a house about halfway down that lane, and that's where Mummi and Daughty lived when they first got married, on the farm owned by his parents.

Mummi didn't go away much in the evening when the children were young, but a few times they were alone when thunderstorms came – they were all deathly afraid of thunderstorms, retreating to the safest places in the house when the lightning started to strike.

On another of the rare occasions that Mummi and Daughty went out without them, the children decided to surprise their parents and milk the cows themselves. In those days they milked by hand, and they were so proud when Mummi and Daughty got home and the milking was already finished.

They lived in that farmhouse until Annie was twelve years old, and my grandma was nine, but then their Uncle Steph wanted to start farming, and that farm was for him, so they had to move. They moved to the house at the end of the lane because they couldn't find a farm of their own to rent or buy, and they stayed in that house for a year.

Eventually, they found a farm to rent on Queen Road. They called it the Rosenberry Farm. They were happy, those days at Rosenberry: the wash house had a bell that the children all liked to ring; there was an orchard, and they'd climb up in the trees looking for bird's nests; there was a dairy, and they milked the cows by hand. Best of all, their landlord forbade the use of kerosene or gas lanterns, so they had to use the electricity. And there was an inside bathroom – unbelievable luxuries for an Amish family.

Mummi and Daughty took their young son Amos to a doctor for treatment of his asthma, and since they were Amish, they hired a driver to take them. On one particular trip, it was Mummi and Daughty and three of the children: Naomi, Amos and Sam. As they were being driven home, they came to a bend in the road close to the covered bridge. Young Sam, only a year or two old, pulled on the door handle, opened the door, and flew out.

The Eby's lived right there at the corner, so Mummi and Daughty carried Sam inside. His head was gashed open. Mummi and Daughty rushed with him to the hospital, and sent Naomi and Amos walking home to tell the rest of the family, since they hadn't been that far away from their home when the accident took place. Naomi was three years older than Amos, and when they were nearly at their house, she stopped him.

"Now I'm going to tell them what happened," she said in a warning voice, referring to Annie and Priscilla, their older sisters. "Don't you tell them!"

They argued about it the entire way home – who would get to pass on this exciting, terrifying news to their sisters about the accident.

In the end, it was Naomi. Amos couldn't persuade her otherwise.

Then there were the butchering days. Early in the morning on a winter day, all the men began to arrive, shuffling their feet in the cold and greeting each other with comments on the weather. The crops were in the barn, the tobacco hanging and drying, nearly ready for sizer boxes.

Grandma remembers it as a day of great confusion and activity. The men filled huge copper kettles with boiling water, killed the pigs, and used the boiling water to scrape off the hair. Then the butchering took place, and they divided the pig into sections. The intestines were scraped out and cleaned vigorously – they would be used for sausage casings.

The slaughtering could be done in a day, but the canning and "womenfolk" work went on for a few days. They made the puddings and mince for mince pies. The puddings went in a crockpot and were covered with a layer of fat, then stored in a cool place in the cellar.

The men went from place to place, the families helping each other to finish the butchering before winter.

My grandma and her sister Annie remember one thing: if they were sent away to their Uncle John's overnight, they could expect a new brother or sister when they got back. The pending arrivals were never spoken about, at least not with the children. In one instance, they were sent up to the spare room to fetch a crib, and suddenly, they heard a baby crying downstairs. Their younger brother Samuel had just arrived, and they hadn't even known Mummi was expecting.

They lived at the Rosenberry Farm for five years, and then Daughty got the urge to buy his own farm, so he borrowed the money and moved into a farm just east of the town of Intercourse, on Newport Road. It was a wake up call for the Amish children – the new place had no electricity and an outside toilet.

But the main things that they remember about that house have nothing to do with outhouses, because during the time that they lived there, three huge events took place: Daughty ended up in prison, they received a visit from a notorious couple, and Mummi and Daughty nearly left the Amish.

Chapter Fourteen
When Daughty Went to Prison

In 1931, an Amish man took the rare step of submitting four articles to a county newspaper. In Donald B. Kraybill's book *The Riddle of Amish Culture*, he quotes the Amish man's writing:

> Among all the Amish people in Lancaster County, you couldn't find one who ever took any high school, college or vocational school education. Yet I don't believe there's a class of people in the entire world that lead a happier life than do our people on the average. For pity's sake, don't raise the school age for farm children...for if they don't do farm work while they're young, they seldom care for it when they're older . . . [he then speaks of an educated female acquaintance who could not boil an egg] even though she was a bright scholar, a good dancer, busy attending parties, in fact very busy equipping herself to be modern flapper with lots of pep. [He then argued that experience is a better teacher than higher education and concluded that] Brother, if you want an educated modern wife, I

wish you lots of wealth and patience and hope the Lord will have mercy upon your soul.[31]

Schooling was clearly in the forefront of the Amish discussion in the 30s. But why?

One room schools were being closed by the State of Pennsylvania, replaced with larger, consolidated schools. Rumors abounded of pending legislation that would raise the minimum age requirement for schooling from 14 to 15 or even 16, rendering the one-room schoolhouses (which everyone attended in those days) insufficient when it came to completing a student's education. Amish children would have to begin attending public high schools for at least one year.

Then it started happening. In Lancaster County, the township of East Lampeter began building a new consolidated elementary school with plans to close ten one-room schools in the area (where many of the local Amish school children were educated). A group of citizens, mostly Amish, got the help of some lawyers from Philadelphia and obtained a court order to halt construction. This was soon overturned, and construction continued. The new school opened in 1937 – "some children attended a one-room school that was still open, but others hid at home."[32]

By 1937, Daughty and Mummi were 33 and 29 years old, respectively, and had three children: Annie, born in 1930, my grandmother Priscilla, born in 1933, and Naomi, born in 1936. Would they have started to worry about the schooling situation as their young family grew, or with only one school-age child, would it have been at the back of their minds? No matter what they thought about the schooling ordeal in 1937, in a few short years this matter of education would provide my family with one of its most legendary stories.

Just as the school was built in East Lampeter, legislators discussed changes that would have a huge impact on the Amish culture. In those days, the school codes required children to attend school at least until they were 16, but allowed farmhands and domestic workers to drop out

---

[31] Donald B Kraybill. *The Riddle of Amish Culture.* Johns Hopkins University Press, 2001.
[32] *The Riddle of Amish Culture.*

117

when they turned 14. The changes under discussion would raise the age to fifteen for domestic workers and farmhands as well as extend the school year from eight to nine months.

These rumors stirred eight Amish bishops, from all sixteen districts, to action. They petitioned their legislator. The Amish were mobilized in a way that far superseded their action against the East Lampeter School. It was the beginning of a 2-year battle. Kraybill describes how the end of 1937 was a somber one for the Amish:

> In December 1937 three events shrouded the traditional gaiety of the Amish wedding season. First, the consolidated East Lampeter School had opened its doors despite Amish protests. Second, their Thanksgiving offering, formal petitions, personal meetings with state officials, and pleading letters had not exempted Amish fourteen-year-olds from school. Many, in fact, were hiding at home. Third, the Amish learned that Moderns cherished education and would not cater to rural peasants. Amishman Aaron King, living on the settlement's eastern fringe, was jailed for refusing to send his fourteen-year-old daughter to high school. King was convicted after a federal district court turned down his appeal in December 1937 . . . they faced a frightening question: Would they be willing to sit in prison for the sake of their children?[33]

The struggle continued. The Amish began petitioning for the right to build their own private schools. They also argued the case for work permits, and 54 such permits were given to Amish 14-year-olds in 1939. The onset of World War II gave them some time, as the nation turned its thoughts and energies to war and away from petty, local school board skirmishes.

But when the war ended, the break was over, and the government began clamping down on the Amish resistance toward public schools. They started arresting Amish fathers in large numbers – at least two dozen were imprisoned in the fall of 1949. The Amish lobbied and

---

[33] Donald B Kraybill. *The Riddle of Amish Culture.* Johns Hopkins University Press, 2001.

petitioned, but by the fall of 1950, "98% of the work applications from Lancaster County were rejected by the Department of Public Instruction," resulting in the incarceration of 36 Amish fathers.[34]

My great-grandfather Samuel was one of these Amish men, most likely arrested in the fall of 1949.

Samuel's son Amos remembers that it happened in the winter – he was 10 years old at the time and putting tobacco in sizer boxes in the tobacco shed at their Newport Road farm. The brittle brown leaves had hung in the barn through the fall and were finally ready for packing. The local constable, known well by the family, pulled into their lane and got out of his car.

How did he say it?

"Samuel Stoltzfus, you're under arrest."

"Samuel Stoltzfus, I'm going to have to arrest you."

"Sorry, Samuel, you'll have to come with me."

However he said it, the news was not received well. Daughty stooped down and got into the man's car, and the door slammed behind him. It was an emotional night for the family with lots of tears and unspoken worries. Mummi felt helpless. There was nothing she could do but keep the house going until they heard news from someone.

I wish I had asked my great-grandfather what that night was like. What was it like being processed into a prison? Where did he spend the night, and with whom did he share a cell? How long did he think he would have to stay? What was it like when the prison employee walked in and told him he was free to go?

There's a newspaper picture of three Amish men emerging from prison. Above them, the sign stretches in an arc: Lancaster County Prison. The front entrance is meshed in heavy, black, iron bars. The first released Amish man stands on the sidewalk, his hands in his pockets, looking around, as if waiting for a ride. Two more Amishmen come out of the darkness behind him.

When Daughty returned home, there was a lot of rejoicing.

The arrests continued over the next 4-5 years until an agreement could be reached on the instillation of Amish-run vocational schools that

---

[34] Donald B Kraybill. *The Riddle of Amish Culture*. Johns Hopkins University Press, 2001.

would fulfill the year of education currently under dispute.[35] But for the Amish this didn't solve the dilemma of school consolidation, and eventually they would go on to start the Amish one-room schoolhouse system still in place today.

In the weeks following Daughty's arrest, after he had returned home, the family received two peculiar visitors: Julius and Ethel Rosenberg. The couple knocked at the door and asked if they could come inside. They said they had some pressing information regarding the recent arrests that they wanted to pass on to the Amish families involved.

The couple sat in one of the rooms with Daughty and Mummi. The children listened from the other room – the Rosenbergs' city-slicker clothing and manner of speech intrigued 11-year-old Amos. The visiting couple pulled out a copy of the Bill of Rights and presented it to the parents, explaining their rights under the Constitution. Apparently they were trying to make friends with the Amish community, perhaps in order to influence them into the Communist movement of which they were part.

Daughty and Mummi listened to what they had to say, wanting to ask these people to leave their house but feeling awkward about it. If they had known more about the Rosenbergs at the time, they would have been even more hesitant about giving them their time. Less than one year after their meeting, Julius and Ethel were arrested by the federal government for treason.

The Rosenbergs had married in 1939 and had become full members of the American Communist Party in 1942, but dropped out one year later so that Julius could start espionage activities. When his previous membership with the Communist Party was exposed, he lost his job with the Signal Corps. Ethel Rosenberg's younger brother Sgt. David Greenglass eventually informed the authorities that Julius Rosenberg had been passing state secrets to the USSR, leading to Julius's arrest. Ethel was arrested less than two months later.

The trial, beginning in March of 1951, drew the attention of the nation – young Amos Stoltzfus, son of Daughty and Mummi, remembers

---

[35] Donald B Kraybill. *The Riddle of Amish Culture.* Johns Hopkins University Press, 2001.

seeing a picture of the Rosenbergs in the newspaper not long after they had been in his house. The trial lasted just over three weeks and the Rosenbergs maintained their innocence. But in the end they were convicted and sentenced to death under the Espionage Act – they would be the only two civilians executed for these types of activities during the Cold War.

They died in the electric chair in 1953, less than four years after sitting with my great-grandparents in their living room.[36]

Back in the 1940s and 1950s, Amish interaction with the English, or non-Amish, was judged much more strictly than it is today, and it was this more stringent outlook that nearly led to Mummi and Daughty leaving the Amish.

Around 1951, probably just after the schooling incident and the chance meeting with the Rosenbergs, Samuel began working at Smoker Elevator, a local business owned by an Amish man, Ike Smoker. The Amish church, as they have the authority to do, deemed the business too modern – there was electricity in the shop and a few other things along those lines. Because of this decision, ten or so of the Amish who worked there were excommunicated, and it was made plain to them that the only way to return to the Amish church was to find other work at a place that wasn't so "worldly."

Daughty was one of their employees.

Mummi took their excommunication very hard – their children would have been around the ages of 21, 18, 15, 12, 9, 6, 4, and 1. One day she took Amos up into the bedroom to pray, and she cried and cried – she didn't want to leave the Amish. It was a serious time, and Daughty considered the option even more once his brother Abe left, but Mummi was so desperately against it.

In the middle of all this, their church had special meetings, trying to decipher what was going on and what should be done. Some of the leaders stood around outside the church, their voices raised as they held intense discussions over what they thought the approach should be. At other times, some of Daughty's friends who had been excommunicated from the Amish church (and weren't coming back) would visit the

---

[36] http://www.atomicarchive.com/Bios/Rosenberg.shtml

house. The children overheard them talking in hushed tones: the wives worried and tearful, the men determined, yet uncertain.

Eventually, though, Daughty gave in to Mummi, and they returned to the Amish church. He paid his penance, found other work, and life went on.

Daughty was relatively quiet, and it was natural for an Amish man to keep his stress and worries to himself. But several of his children were under the impression that the stress of owing money on the farm on Newport Road is what led to him selling it.

In any case, three years after they moved to that farm, they sold it. Part of this involved selling off the twenty or so steers that Daughty had raised, but the morning of the sale a small disaster occurred: the steers got out. The kids chased them up and down Newport Road and through the surrounding fields.

Daughty ran around, even more stressed than usual, worried that the steers, in all of their running and evading and dodging, would lose weight and bring less at market. But they were all recovered, and Daughty made a pretty penny on his investment.

In 1955 Daughty took his son Amos out to buy him his first horse and buggy for his 16th birthday. They went out to try a new horse fresh off the track – Vicky Rivera was its name. The horse had been retired from the track because it would lose its head when it got in among other horses. It was pretty wild, but Amos decided that it was the horse for him.

Daughty wasn't too sure.

Amos convinced his dad that they should take the horse out and test it, so they hitched her up to their buggy and drove away. They were heading north and a car was coming toward them. Just then a dog ran out to chase the car and spooked the horse, which ran right on over in front of the car!

The driver lost control, flew behind Daughty and 16 year-old Amos, and launched over a bank. The driver was okay, and after some effort they retrieved the car from the field and he drove away.

Then Daughty started shouting at Amos, emotional and upset.

"I told you we didn't want this horse!"

Amos thought that was it – he'd never get to keep it. But Daughty started to calm down and eventually Amos convinced him. They purchased Vicky Rivera.

That horse continued getting Amos into trouble – it just fought and fought to run, and sometimes Amos had to stand up in his seat just to hold her back. One time he was driving through the small town of Intercourse like that, standing up in his seat and holding the horse back. Vicky Rivera was covered in a white lather and pulling hard at the bit, trying to run away.

When Amos arrived in front of the schoolhouse, a New York tourist saw how worn out the horse looked and came running into the middle of the road trying to stop Amos.

"You're running that horse to death!" the lady shouted, grabbing for the reigns.

"Lady," Amos shouted as the horse flew past her, "can't you see I'm not even sitting in my seat trying to hold this horse back!"

After my great-grandfather left Smoker Elevator, he went to work for a boat manufacturer in town. The company took him and his family on vacations down to Maryland, something my grandmother remembers well. Vacations in those days were uncommon, but because of great-grandfather's work, they got to go to a bay and even had access to a boat.

An Amish family with access to a boat!

There are some enduring memories of Daughty water-skiing, his beard shooting backward in the breeze. I'm sure his skin was pale as a ghost's. I'm sure his smile was bigger than the bay. What I wouldn't give for a photo of the original Squirrel, water-skiing.

Chapter Fifteen
Death in the Spring

Maile and I somehow got it in our heads that we were going to have chickens. So we went to the local feed supply store and put in an order for four layers, five boilers, and two guinea fowl (to eat the ticks in the woods that border our house). They lived in our kitchen for four weeks, in a large plastic bin under a heat lamp. The nights are cold in May.

The layers were black and tiny. The guinea's were even smaller – one was gray, the other white. They reminded me of puppies with oversized eyes and fuzzy bodies. But the white ones, the boilers: their feet were huge, preparing to carry their perpetually heavy bodies, and they gobbled up food like Pacman.

Eventually, we moved them out into the chicken coop that Dad and I created out of two old Frederick Fair tables my grandfather had originally made, perhaps twenty years before that. The coop took longer to build than I thought, and nothing was ever quite square – I'm sure my Daughty Stoltzfus would have been disappointed, but it was very much done in the "throw-it-together" tradition of both of my grandfathers. You cannot please all of your dead ancestors all of the time.

After about ten weeks, the white boilers waddled around on feet barely able to support their incredible girth. They were most certainly ready for the chopping block. Now what? I called an Amish man in the area and left him a message. He called me back and left a message.

"We're not butchering right now – it will be about six weeks before we are ready."

By then these chickens would be too heavy to walk. I looked on the Internet, trying to see how difficult it would be for me to do it myself. I wasn't so sure.

Then my dad spoke with an Amish lady at the farmer's market my parents go to. She had fond memories of butchering chickens with her own mother, years ago.

"Bring the chickens to my house," she said. "If you cut the heads off, I'll get them ready for you."

So on a rainy Tuesday morning my dad and I drove over to Rebecca's house. She is my mom's second cousin, married to a Stoltzfus. In the back seat the five chickens protested valiantly at every turn, jumping on top of each other and flapping up a whirlwind of dust and feathers that filled the van. I opened my window.

We pulled into Rebecca's house – she doesn't live far from the Rosenberry Farm where my grandma grew up. She opened her door and watched me take out the chickens. She smiled. Her husband came out and told us we could chop their heads off in the pasture. But the chickens scared their horse, so they had to lead him into the barn before the decapitations could commence.

Rebecca's husband put two nails in the railroad tie, and I took out the first chicken. My dad stretched the chicken's head through the nails, and I pulled on the feet. I'm going to be honest with you – it wasn't a pretty sight. The first four took multiple swings of the axe. I'm not proud of it. It is what it is.

After the head came off of each chicken, I tossed the body to the side where they mostly rolled over on their backs and kicked their legs at the sky, trying to run away from something that already happened. Before the final chicken, Rebecca's husband (who had come out with us, probably for entertainment purposes, watching the English butcher their chickens) said in a monotone voice:

"You know, when I was a boy, and one of the guys was getting married, he was the one who had to cut off the heads. And if he didn't get it in one shot, he wasn't fit to be married."

I looked up at him, and he had a twinkle in his eye. My dad made sure that the last bird's head flew off in one stroke.

"That was close," my dad said. "I thought I wasn't going to be fit to be married."

Rebecca met us in the barn with buckets of boiling water. We dipped the chickens in and pulled their feathers out. Then we carried them inside and Rebecca showed me how to go about the rest of the process: cut off the feet, clean up the neck area, remove the wings at the joint, then the thighs. Cut away the breasts and pull back the rib cage without breaking the intestines or gall bladder. Everything else pulls out.

I didn't learn this in high school.

My grandma told me a story about chickens. When her parents took her and her brothers and sisters to her Grandma Stoltzfus's house for Sunday lunch, the first thing she would ask is what they wanted for lunch.

"Chicken or ham?"

If they wanted chicken, she walked out to barn and grabbed one of them, cut its head off, and started plucking. They didn't have a refrigerator or a freezer, so the only way to keep chicken fresh was to keep it alive.

If they said ham, that was a little easier. She climbed up into the attic and grabbed one of the heavily smoked hams that hung in the heat. They were packed in saltpeter. The wood floorboards in the attic were grease-stained by the hams, dripping their fat.

And that was Sunday lunch.

Soon after my grandparents married, chicken became available in the grocery store, prepacked and separated. White meat or dark meat. Drumsticks or thighs. This was a welcome miracle.

My grandmother, Priscilla, first met my grandfather, Emanuel, when he came along with one of his older brothers to work for Daughty. She was 13 or 14 at the time, having reached the age when girls started to glance outside of their own homes, wondering what the future might have in store for them. Since she was in that mindset of exploration, you would think that the moment a strapping young man showed up at her father's place, her first giddy thoughts would be of love and marriage.

In reality, when my grandfather showed up at my grandmother's house for the first time, she didn't give him a second thought. But a few years later, when she was 16, they went on their first date. Grandpa was 19. Knowing him, I can't imagine he was going to let any grass grow under Grandma's feet.

It started after a youth gathering or a singing. Night descended on the surrounding fields, and the Amish youth started up their hoedowns. One of the guys would ask a girl to go with them on a walk, and then, if the walk went well, they'd ask to take the girl home. This is how it all began for Grandma and Grandpa. Their courtship went along as usual, like any Amish courtship in the 1940s. And after two years of courting, when Grandma was 18 and Grandpa was 21, they got married.

Of course Mummi had her opinions at first.

"I wasn't so sure," she once said of my grandpa, with a mischievous gleam in her eye. But Mummi (or Daughty) didn't have any serious concerns. They knew Grandpa's family, and he treated their daughter with respect.

Their courtship was uneventful (or at least that's how my Grandma remembers it, 60 years later), and in 1951 they got married at Uncle John's house (Daughty's brother). In the morning, the betrothed couple went into where the wedding was going to be held, accompanied by two couples, unmarried attendants. As everyone else filed in, they walked past the couple and shook their hands before taking their seats.

Then, while the crowd waited in their seats, my grandparents went upstairs, and the preachers talked to them. Sixty years have passed since that day – Grandma says she can't remember what they asked or told her: words of advice? Words of warning? Encouragement? Whatever the meeting's purpose, eventually she and Grandpa made their way back downstairs and walked to the front again with their attendants. The preacher came and stood at the front as well.

The congregation sang a few songs, and then Grandpa and Grandma stood up at the front and said their vows. Just like that, they were married. After that, they went back and sat down again, and the congregation sang a few more songs. Then it was time to eat lunch.

During lunch, the married couple always sat in the corner, and after they were seated, the single boys went upstairs and picked out a single girl; those couples went into where the wedding meal was taking place. What happened to the single girls who weren't chosen? What if there were too many girls? I don't know. But once everyone was in the hall, they sang hymns and other songs, and the singing went on for most of the afternoon until it was time to set up for supper.

After supper, there was a hoedown in the barn with square dancing. The festivities went long into the night. I like to imagine walking past the barn where Grandma and Grandpa danced that first night as a married couple, surrounded by friends and hope for the future. I try to picture my grandfather, so young, whisking my grandmother across the wooden floorboards, both of them moving with a youthfulness I never had the chance to witness in real life. I imagine that the lantern light sneaks out through the boards forming the barn walls, interrupted in Morse code flashes as dancers swing by inside. It's a true celebration, the way weddings should be.

That night my grandparents, newly wed, went home. There was no honeymoon to Vegas or Canada or even the Pennsylvania "mountains" a few hundred miles away – it was right back to regular life and work and family, almost as if nothing out of the ordinary had happened. The only difference was that now they lived together. They had a room for that first year in Mummi and Daughty's house.

That is, until the winter came. When the harvest work was completed, and all of the weddings were finished, Grandma and Grandpa went visiting. They went to aunts and uncles and cousins every weekend that winter, usually spending the night Friday and having Saturday dinner and supper, staying through Saturday night and then going with them to church before heading home on Sunday. It was a fun time, the start of a new life. This is also when the relatives gave their gifts to the newlyweds. Every weekend that winter they traveled, and they didn't move into their own home until spring.

20 years before I was born, July 12th, 1956, was a day that ended up being a very important one in my own history. It was the day my mother, Verna Beiler, was born.

Grandma and Grandpa were at Mummi and Daughty's when my grandmother's water broke – they rushed to the doctor's office, and he sent them straight into the hospital.

Mom came only after a long, slow delivery. In those days the mother and her baby stayed in the hospital for an entire week (not something Grandma complained about), but when their week was up, they left and the new baby was greeted at home by her older sister Kate, nearly three, and an older brother Omar, about eighteen months old. For six weeks, my grandma struggled to take care of these three young children, but it was a lot of work and her body was still recovering. A cough that started out innocently turned into double pneumonia.

They were still Amish in those days. One of Grandma's family members came to the house to watch over Kate and Omar, but my mom was too young so Mummi took her home, where she cared for her for one week. When Grandma finally brought my mom home, Mummi wanted to tell her how to take care of my mother – it was hard for Mummi to give her back.

The grandchildren and great-grandchildren of Amos King, the story-teller, and Catherine King (whose first husband died from appendicitis) remember them in the late 1950s and into the 1960s, traveling from house to house to live with their children in their older days. When they came to my grandmother's house, even when she was a teenager, the younger generation knew in no uncertain terms that they were "supposed to behave themselves."

In spite of these feelings, the children wanted to take something out to them when they drove in the lane, maybe some flowers they picked from the yard or a little trinket. In return the King grandparents brought with them small treats and the sound of stories. They sat on old rockers and weaved their way front and back, front and back, their deep eyes remembering all that had changed since their childhood in the late 1800s. So much had changed.

Then came the spring, 43 years before I got that phone call in Wendover, England late on an almost summer's night. It was 1962. It was my great-great-grandfather Amos's 88th spring: the 88th time he watched the snow melt and the earth thaw, the 88th time he saw the farmer's plow their fields and spread the manure, the 88th time he saw the daffodils spread their yellow heads towards the sun.

On April 1st, 1962, he died.

I wonder what his last thoughts were like – was he relieved to be evacuating a life during which he had lost so much? Was he remembering those early days of his boyhood, the times in his journal when he worked hard for his father and spent the weekends with friends and at church? Surely, after all those years, his faith was unwavering.

Avoid evil companions, he had written.

Watch where you walk in this world.

I wonder how well he remembered his first wife Katie and the four short years they had together, those early days when it was just them and two little ones and such hope for a long and happy future.

His second wife Catherine was there when he died, by his side. This would be the second husband she buried. The grandchildren remember how Amos's naked body was placed on a hard board, under a thin sheet – this was the old tradition. They remember how his body, slight and bony in his old age, protruded up against the sheet, unyielding and scary. An 88-year-old man's body, covered by only a thin sheet, seemed like almost nothing, as if everything had been spent.

Catherine survived her husband by exactly 369 days. She, too, would die in the spring, at the end of a long, cold winter, following so many of her family members into eternity. Epidemics, World War I, World War II, the inventions of television and radio and the automobile: so many changes took place from the late 1800s, when she was born, to the 1960s, when she passed away.

There is something right about dying in the spring, I think. There is something about facing the death that winter brings, staring it in the face, and refusing to let it take everything. Then the warm breezes arrive from the south, and the tips of the trees come alive, and the grass begins to green.

I can understand the willingness to die then, knowing that spring has in fact come again and life will continue, with or without you.

Just about every Friday night, Grandma and Grandpa went to her parent's house, Mummi and Daughty's place. Even as their families grew, nearly every week they'd go there. The cousins would run around outside playing while the adults sat inside talking, telling stories or simply sharing local news.

In the early days of my grandparent's marriage they lived on a farm, and my grandpa helped out. He worked there for three years before taking a job at a local factory, Singing Needles: he worked in the packing area. But the Amish church didn't like that he worked there – it was too worldly – so they moved down to a farm close to the town of White Horse and Grandpa started farming again.

There are many difficult things that happen when an individual or family decides to leave the Amish. There are probably as many reasons to leave as there are individuals who have left. But eventually my grandpa made the decision: they were going to leave the Amish.

Because my grandparents left the Amish church with a group that included an Amish pastor, they were not shunned by the Amish community – but this doesn't mean it was an easy decision or a painless process. I would imagine that Daughty's own wrestling with whether or not to remain Amish made their decision easier to understand. And other siblings had already left. But for Mummi it was difficult.

In her final years, she seemed to care much less about the dividing line between the Amish and the "English." In fact, it is sometimes difficult for me to reconcile the Mummi I remember (quiet, gentle and accepting) with some of the stories of her younger self. But I suppose these are the changes that will come over all of us, should we live nearly 100 years.

Still, watching your children walk away from your own tradition is never easy. It was even more difficult for her when my grandmother stopped wearing her covering. These are the moments that I'm talking about: subtle, perhaps, to outsiders. Yet within a community, within a family, all become stark reminders of decisions that have been made. Changes to the familiar. Deviations from the ways of those who came before.

Chapter Sixteen
My Birth and My Daughty's Death

She woke up in the morning with a stomachache and thought back to her dinner from the night before: orange juice and pizza, the likely culprit. She wondered if she'd be able to go to work that night – she was a waitress at a local restaurant, and she'd been getting better tips than usual since she'd taken to propping the serving tray on her pregnant stomach. But as the morning went on, she realized this was no regular indigestion. Her baby was on the way.

Her husband helped her into the car and they drove to the hospital through Monday morning traffic. He used the impending arrival as an excuse to speed down the center lane. This would be her first child, and she took some comfort in the fact that her mother would be at the hospital that day – her mother volunteered on Mondays, sorting mail and delivering it to the patients and employees of the hospital.

Once in the delivery room, the baby made good progress, but he got stuck on his way out, so the doctor's reached for the forceps. This was more than the father could handle: he turned white as a ghost, and in his mind the room began to spin.

"My stomach's feeling kind of funny," he said.

"Mr. Smucker," said one of the nurses. "You need to sit down. Over there, in the corner. Put your head between your knees and breathe."

He barely made it to the chair. Soon one of the nurses was at his side, helping him catch his breath.

Why is that nurse helping him? His wife wondered frantically as the pain increased. *I'm the one having the baby!*

Just as the father came out of it, the baby arrived.

And that baby was me.

By the time 1983 rolled around, my great-grandparents Daughty and Mummi had been married for 55 years. Their daughter Priscilla (my grandmother) tells the story:

> Daughty died in 1983 when he was 78 years old. I was 50 when dad died. I didn't feel like I was ready to lose my dad. Right before he died, he had gout in his feet, and I took him somewhere to be treated, and he said he wasn't feeling well. I don't think he worked much after that.
>
> I was in the hospital with my mom when he died. My brother Sam was there, and we were in with him – it was a Sunday morning, so everyone else must have been at church. Dad had only been in over night – we didn't feel like his family doctor was paying much attention to him, so we took him to the hospital on a Saturday afternoon, and he was in overnight, and the next day he died.
>
> We were shocked – we knew he wasn't supposed to eat salt (of course to that he said if he couldn't eat salt he'd rather not eat – he couldn't stand eating food without salt). He wasn't very careful. And we knew he had heart problems. Anyway, they were going to do a heart catheterization on Sunday, but he didn't make it. We saw the line go flat. The nurse was in there with him. They worked on him a bit, but Mummi told them that he wouldn't want to be put on any machines.
>
> It was hard for Mummi. What a shock. She was 75.

Chapter Seventeen
A Journal Entry From the Fair

54 years ago my grandparents, young and Amish and looking to start a new business, took ham and cheese sandwiches to the annual fair in Frederick, Maryland. They set up a little tent with two of their friends outside the grandstand, holding little in the way of expectations. But in those days they occupied one of three food stands on the fairgrounds, and suddenly they were making sandwiches as fast as they could. They'd go behind the tent, laughing so hard they couldn't help customers, doubled over in disbelief at how busy they were, overwhelmed. That week they were forced to buy ham in Frederick to meet the demand. They bought out every grocery store in town.

My mom grew up attending the Great Frederick Fair every year, and, after she married my dad, the two of them would attend every year, taking us with them when we were old enough to stay out of the way.

29 years ago the colors and sounds of the fair represented all that was right about the world to this 5 year old boy. Grandpa slipped me $5 bills and I'd sneak across the midway, buy a pack of candy bars or a funnel cake. Then I'd sit under one of the back tables out of the way of the workers. Eventually I'd lay down, feeling the rough gravel through the thin blanket, hearing the guy in the next tent bark out "the greatest deal of the century." I'd fall asleep, dreaming of lollipops and stuffed animals the size of skyscrapers.

Three days ago my oldest two kids came down on Friday night, and spent all day Saturday helping at the fair. My son Cade ran pretzels from one side of the tent to the other, yelling out "special!" when someone sold a special order. My daughter Lucy fell asleep behind the trailer, just inside the tent. When I peeked back there and saw her sleeping, I was amazed and saddened at how fast 29 years can go.

Chapter Eighteen
One Easter Morning

My Grandpa Beiler, husband of Priscilla (daughter of Mummi and Daughty) was someone impossible to forget. I never witnessed his anger, though stories of it were legendary. What I remember of him is that he never let anyone stop him from doing what he wanted to do. He always, no matter what the topic of discussion, bore the premonition of a smile somewhere around the corners of his mouth. On Sunday afternoons he gave me a quarter to comb his hair, during which he nearly always fell asleep.

My mom remembers driving down one of these Lancaster County roads, early in the morning. Approaching in the distance, she saw a truck pulling a trailer loaded down with sheds. The truck drove down the middle of the road, well over the speed limit.

"I'm sure that guy is going to get over," she kept telling herself as she drew closer and closer to the oncoming truck and trailer. But it never strayed from where it straddled the yellow line, and she was forced into the ditch.

As she drove away, she looked into her rearview mirror with amazement.

"That was my Dad!" she exclaimed to herself.

That's how my Grandpa did things. Full steam ahead, up the middle, take no prisoners. When pulled over by a police officer for not having the correct licenses on the aforementioned truck and trailer, he conceded to the officers request that he park the thing along the highway overnight and come back the next day with the correct paperwork. Five minutes after the cop drove off, so did my Grandpa.

But in 1985, he contracted a serious kidney disease. I guess his son Omar had at least a little bit of his father in him, because when the doctors brought up the idea of a family member donating a kidney to Grandpa, Omar turned to his sister Kate and made a suggestion.

"Well, if anyone has to give a kidney to him, it should be her."

Everyone knew that Kate only had one kidney.

Initially the doctors let Grandpa do some kind of self-administered dialysis through a tube that went directly into his abdomen. He was only allowed to do this in extremely clean, disinfected, sterile areas. Being my Grandpa, and not wanting to waste any of his own time, he administered the bag of fluid to himself while driving down the highway on his way to market, hanging the bag from the little hook above his door.

During this time he opened and operated Burtonsville Market with a business partner. He loved it – the action, the people, the business. And he was finally making money.

Then numerous infections set in at the place the tube went into his abdomen, and he nearly died (I'm sure it had nothing to do with his method of self-administration), so his doctors moved him on to dialysis. After being on dialysis for some time, perhaps a year or so, he eventually received a kidney transplant.

The doctors later told us that what he had was Polycystic Kidney Disease, a kidney disorder in which multiple cysts form on the kidneys, enlarging them and impeding normal kidney operation. It is a genetic disorder – if your parents have it, you can get it.

The odds are 50%

50%.

There are so many things passed down from one generation to the next: our physical traits, our emotional strength, our mental health. Diseases. Tendencies. Ways of looking at the world.

We are not islands.

One night, during their annual stay in Florida, Grandma and Grandpa got ready for bed. During the previous week, my Grandpa had stopped joining Grandma on her walks around Pinecraft. During one of his last walks with her, he had been forced to take a break, stop along the road, and sit down.

"I just don't have it in me," he had said, trying to catch his breath.

Grandma turned off the kitchen light and looked at him for a brief moment. He lay on the sofa, eyes closing. He looked exhausted.

For some strange reason, he had spoken on the phone to just about everyone in the family that night. Either he had called them, or they had called him.

Maybe we should go to the doctor, she thought. But it was Saturday night, and the next morning was Easter Sunday. Soon they'd be driving back to Pennsylvania. She made a mental note to make sure he got to the doctor as soon as they returned home.

He went to bed.

"I guess I'll stay up and read a little bit," Grandma told him.

They had been sleeping in separate beds, because Grandpa was so restless in his sleep.

Not too much later, Grandma went to bed.

The next morning Grandma woke up with a bad feeling. Grandpa was being too quiet.

She walked over to his room and found him there, in his bed, completely still. He had died in his sleep. It was 1991.

In Pennsylvania, early that Easter morning, my aunt Kate woke up with a start. She looked quickly around the room.

I swear I just heard someone say my name, she thought to herself.

Then the phone rang. It was Grandma.

"Oh, Kate," she said, not knowing how to say it. "Dad died last night."

I was fourteen when Grandpa died. I remember the solemnity of watching his coffin go down into the grave, the permanence of the gravestone. I remember the meal afterwards, with so many Amish relatives.

Most of all I remember that, for some reason, my two cousins, one of my sisters and I walked the five miles from the cemetery to Grandma's house. It was a warm spring day, and halfway home I took off my new black shoes (they gave me blisters) and walked barefoot the rest of the way. The road felt cold and smooth under my feet.

Chapter Nineteen
Taking Care of Each Other

Mummi lived on her own for 16 years after my great-grandfather died. Daughty left her enough money to support herself, and she was so independent that, even in her later years, the kids had a hard time deciding how long she should continue living on her own. Age comes on all of us slowly, in such gradual stages. Her eyesight began to dim. Her hearing went slowly. Her children began to worry.

There was no major event that led to the end of her independent life. But there were small signs. She liked to put her towels inside her gas oven so that they would dry and get warm, but sometimes she forgot they were in there, and she'd start up the oven. Her daughter Priscilla once arrived at the house and found a scorched towel hidden under the bushes. Soon it became apparent that other accommodations would have to be made.

Mummi probably never would have chosen to start going around to live with her children, but she knew they had her best interests at heart, so when they asked her to move out of her house, she did it willingly. She started taking turns with each of the kids.

When she first moved in with Ben and Katie, Mummi's nightly walk from her bedroom to the bathroom could be a little disconcerting. But

Ben started to anticipate those late journeys. Her cane thump-thump-thumped along the floor, the bathroom door creaked open then latched shut, and he heard her slam her cane down on the counter at the edge of the sink. Then the door whined back open, and the cane thumped, and the door closed.

One morning Ben went into the bathroom and saw that Mummi's cane handle had thumped down on his eyeglasses. Mumbling to himself he picked them up off the floor and put them on, then got on with his day. He didn't feel right that morning: his balance seemed a little off, and one side of his field of vision was blurry. But he kept going: breakfast, then out the door.

Driving down the road another wave of blurriness and imbalance hit him.

Am I having a stroke? Ben wondered to himself, shaking his head, blinking his eyes.

He had lunch with some friends that day but didn't mention his uneasy feeling. Finally, later in the day, he was home again and decided to bring it up with his wife Katie.

"I'm just not feeling right," he said. "I think I might be having a stroke. This whole side of my vision is blurry."

Katie started laughing.

"What's so funny? There's nothing funny about a stroke."

"You're missing the glass in one side of your glasses," she said.

Ben put his finger up and pushed it through. Sure enough. He went to the bathroom and felt around on the floor, and his hand stirred up the piece of glass. He popped it back in. No stroke.

Mummi seemed to make the same treks in everyone's house.

Amos and Hannah have a 3-dimensional painting in their hallway of a boat at sea. During the day, it looks like the sun is blazing in the painting, but at night they have a black light shining on it, and what appeared to be the sun is suddenly the moon, glowing. The black light causes stars to appear, and the lights in the boat's cabins come on.

While Mummi was staying with Amos and Hannah, they also had another guest in the house. One night this guest witnessed Mummi thump-thumping on her cane down the hallway, past the painting. The black light set her white hair and nightgown to glowing.

"I was sure it was an angel," the visitor claimed.

By this time Mummi's eyesight was poor, and her hearing was not so good. But she loved audio books, and Hannah would often put one on for her to listen to, turn the volume up so Mummi could hear it, then go upstairs and clean – it was so loud for Hannah that she could hardly think!

One day while Mummi was listening to a story, Hannah, from all the way upstairs, heard Mummi slam her cane against the floor and yell.

"No!" she exclaimed in disbelief.

Hannah ran downstairs.

"Mummi, are you okay?"

"I just don't think I can take this anymore!" Mummi said, referring to the suspense in the story she was listening to.

"Well, then I'll just turn it off. Don't worry," Hannah said, turning off the sound. A quietness settled on the house.

A few minutes later Hannah could hear Mummi calling for her from the sitting room.

"Yes, Mummi?"

"Maybe you had better turn that back on. I should probably hear how it ends."

Mummi's 90th birthday was a festive affair although Mummi sometimes seemed amazed at the fuss everyone was making.

"What's that to celebrate?" she said, a mischievous look in her eye.

Surrounded by many of her children, great-grandchildren, and great-great-grandchildren, Mummi had a way of relating with everyone, even at that age. She carried on fluid conversations about life (although those talking with her had to lean in close and speak loudly). Whatever faculties were dimming, she always kept a strong memory and would often ask if so-and-so was still dating so-and-so and how that particular person's sickly child was and how some of her old friends were doing. She seemed to remember everything.

What she lacked in eyesight, she made up for with creativity. Mummi's great-granddaughters Naomi and Catherine looked so much alike that many people thought they were twins. She would always ask them to come up close so that she could see the color of their eyes – one had blue eyes, and the other brown, and that's how she could tell them apart.

It was the same way with Susan, another one of Mummi's great-grandchildren.

"I love when you wear that red nightgown," Mummi would always tell her. "That way I can tell who you are."

Then she smiled.

For all of those years that Mummi went around, she never got depressed or felt sorry for herself. She tried to stay busy all the time, not wanting to be a bother. She'd always ask for the minimum for herself, sometimes going a few days in between having her hair braided because she didn't want to add work for someone else.

Sometimes, when she was staying at her daughter Naomi's house, she would help hang the laundry or fold clothes. One day a neighbor, visiting the house, exclaimed,

"Who takes care of who around here?"

Mummi looked up with her patient eyes.

"We just take care of each other."

As she made her way from house to house, many of her children, grandchildren and great-grandchildren remember one thing specifically about Mummi: her praying.

She would often retreat to the room where she stayed, sitting on a chair or the edge of her bed, and pray for long stretches of time.

One night, while she stayed with her daughter and my grandmother Priscilla, her granddaughter Verna's husband, my father, (who lived in an adjoining house) heard a noise. He was alone in the house with Mummi, and he walked over quietly, not wanting to startle her. He didn't see Mummi, but a loud, sing-song voice greeted him. Still not knowing what was going on, he crept over to Mummi's bedroom door.

Then he heard it: Mummi was praying. Her voice rose and fell as she sang and spoke in Pennsylvania Dutch, naming each and every one of her children and grandchildren. She had a special request for each of them.

"It shows how valuable older people are," one of her grandchildren said later.

"If we could pattern our life after Mummi, why, we would do well."

142

Chapter Twenty
Our Names, Our Roots

My wife's stomach grew in 2009 as our fourth child prepared to join us. Another life beginning. Another piece of the puzzle. Who knows? Maybe this child will become a grandparent some day, a great-great-great-grandparent whose descendent will write a book about their ancestors, marvel at the lack of technology, take pause at lives that fit between two parentheses.

But as the due date grew closer, something about this pregnancy took a different route. For our other three children, we compiled lists of names beforehand with alternates and possible last-minute changes. We researched meanings and double-checked initials for any inadvertent spellings of unfortunate words. With number four, though, the whole name thing wasn't happening.

At night I'd ask my wife, Maile, the same question.

"So, have you thought of any names that you like?"

She'd groan, roll over in bed, and mumble something that sounded like "donwannatalkboutit." So I'd consent, turn out the light, and lay there thinking through our previous lists, wondering if any of those names would work.

Finally one night after I asked the same question once again, she sat straight up (not an easy feat for a woman who is 8-months pregnant).

"I know!"

"What?"

"You can name this baby!"

"What?"

"You heard me! You name the baby."

"You've got to be kidding."

"No, it'll be fun. You can name it whatever you want. I don't want to get involved. Plus it will give me something to look forward to, something to help me through the pain."

"But what if I name it – "

"I don't care. Sh! I don't want to hear."

"But what if I name it – "

"Seriously! Stop talking. I don't want to hear any names. You pick. I'll love it."

And so it happened that the sole responsibility of naming our fourth child fell to me. This gave me no small amount of anxiety – what if I chose something and Maile was horrified or only kind of liked it? We decided that I would let her know the child's name after he or she came out – we didn't know if we were having a boy or a girl, which doubled the amount of work I had to do beforehand.

Finally, I narrowed it down to two names. I was ready. The day arrived.

Maile gave birth on July 1st, 2009. A little boy came into the world, 243 years after Nicholas Stoltzfus arrived in this country.

No matter how much changes with the environment or location or methods, birth itself never changes: there is blood and water and pain; there is pushing and breathing and movement. There is anxiety and relief. And joy. And love.

The doctors moved that little boy up on to Maile's chest, and his watery eyes mirrored mine. I leaned over, my mouth close to Maile's ear, and through the lump in my throat I whispered:

"Samuel James."

James is Maile's father's name.

The name Samuel has many roots. It is the name of my uncle, a businessman in Texas: Sam Smucker. It is the name of another uncle, a businessman right here in Lancaster: Samuel Beiler. It is the name of my dad's cousin, a preacher: Sam Smucker. It is the name of my great-grandfather, Daughty, Samuel Stoltzfus. And many others.

The roots of that name go deep in my family tree. Who knows which version of Sam our Samuel will be: preacher? Businessman? Something else? The capabilities of all of them are in him. The weaknesses, the strengths.

It was a Sunday afternoon late in the summer of 2010. My three sisters and I were all at Mom and Dad's house. One of my sisters had four children at the time, and they love playing with our four kids. The eight of them laughed and ran and yelled at each other like small puppies just learning that the yard is not the edge of the universe.

Then Grandma came outside. Priscilla Stoltzfus Beiler, daughter of Mummi (Katie Stoltzfus), granddaughter of Amos King, great-granddaughter of Benjamin Stoltzfus, the one who married the Mast twin. And 8 of her great-grandchildren were there to greet her. My youngest daughter ran up and tugged on the hem of her dress, looking for sweets. Grandma kept Hershey Kisses in her kitchen and told them that they could run inside and have one.

My kids call her *Grandma*, even though she is their great-grandma. Someday, I suppose, they'll know the difference, but right now that is just her name; it's what I call her, and it seems fitting that they call her that, too. Names are always changing, it seems. What will I be called when I am 77 years old?

As I mentioned before, Grandma lives in a "Mummi-end" on my parent's house. She's only in her 70s and still completely independent, but I know the time will come when having her just down the hall will be convenient for everyone. One thing the Amish do well is take care of their older generations, and thankfully that tradition has been passed down, in spite of the fact that my family is no longer Amish.

Grandma sat down in one of the patio chairs. We all lounged out there and talked, told old stories about Grandpa. We talk about his affinity for ridiculously wild dogs and brown vans and how he wore his hat cockeyed on his head. We remember how crazy he was. I mention that when I went with him on those early mornings to market, he always smelled like black coffee.

The corn in the field behind my parent's house is six feet high, a dark green wall that hides the horizon. We all kind of prefer Autumn, when the farmer takes it down and you can see for miles: rolling hills dotted with farms, like ships rising on the crest of giant mid-Pacific waves. But there's something about the not-yet-harvested corn that is comforting — it keeps your gaze close, stops you from getting lost somewhere off in the distance.

As we sat there, a strange thought seeped into my mind: what will it be like when I am Grandma's age? What if that was me sitting there, my spouse gone, my kids grown, my kids' kids grown, my great-grandchildren scampering around the yard? What kind of a life would I be looking back on? What kind of a legacy will I have left?

In that instant I was more thankful than I have ever been. For my heritage. For my culture. For my family. There is something hidden in the middle of those cornfields that will always be inside of me, no matter where I live. I have to believe that even if my children would move away, even if my great-great grandchildren return to Lancaster someday as tourists, that their spirits will be inexplicably drawn to this place. That it will hold a curious feeling of melancholic nostalgia for them. That it will cause such a strange paradox of emotions to rise in them: emptiness and fulfillment, longing and satisfaction, sadness and joy.

These, after all, are the emotions that rose in me, as I sat there with my family on a warm Sunday night, late in the summer.

APPENDIX A
Amos C. King's Book
May 30 1893 - 1896

30. Today we made some tobacco land ready. And this evening we planted a lot of tobacco. 1893.

31. Today Father and Aaron were making fence. And I shoveled the potatoes. And planted some tobacco.

June 1. Today we started shoveling corn. And I and Moses planted some corn over. And this afternoon Father and Johns were in Farmersville with thirty dozens of eggs at fourteen cts a dozen. And this evening we planted some tobacco.

2. Today we were shoveling corn. And this evening it commenced to rain. But we need some rain too.

3. This forenoon we went to Conestoga. And it was Aaron and I and Beckie. Aaron and Fannie Glick and David and Susie Zook. We had two horses and a market wagon. We were at Uncle Aaron Stoltzfus for dinner. And at Christ ... for supper. And at Isaac Stoltzfus's over night. And it's warm weather.

4. Today we were at the meeting at Abram Kurtz. And at Jonas Stoltzfus for supper. And this evening we were at the singing at Isaac Stoltzfus. And tonight we went home full of sleep.

5. Today Aaron was shoveling corn. And I and Moses were putting ... greens on the tobacco plants. And this evening we planted some tobacco.

6. Today Aaron was shoveling corn. And this evening it rained powerful. Amos C King born Sept 6, 1874.

7. Today we were planting tobacco the whole day. And we planted about the thousand plants. It's cloudy weather.

8. Today Aaron was shoveling corn. And I was shoveling potatoes. This evening we planted tobacco.

9. Today Aaron and I were shoveling corn. And this evening we made done planting tobacco. It's wet weather.

10. This forenoon Aaron and I were shoveling corn. And Father was in Farmersville. And this afternoon he went to up to Isaac Stoltzfus. And Aaron went to Pinetown to fetch a load of boards. And it's very warm.

19. Today we started scraping corn and we sold our two young steers to Mr. Stridemore for 4 ¾ cents a pound. They weighted 1590 pounds, both of them.

20. Today we started haymaking. This forenoon Father went in Lancaster to the train. In 1893 May sometime the World's Fair, Chicago commenced. Aaron was scraping corn.

21. Today Aaron was scraping corn and this evening we put some hay in. And it's warm weather.

22. Today we were making hay. This evening we had a nice shower. Adam Kauffman helped us.

23. This forenoon we were hoeing tobacco and this evening we cleared one field of hay. It's good hay weather.

24. Today we were busy making hay. And the hay is coarse and pretty near all clover.

25. This forenoon Father and Mother went down to Grandmother's. Aunt Lizzie is still sick. And we were all at house. This afternoon it is raining. This evening Father and Mother came home.

26. This forenoon Father went in Farmersville with 49 dozen of eggs. And Aaron and I planted tobacco.

27. This forenoon it rained. And I and Moses fetched a barrel full of butter milk at the West Earl Creamery. And this afternoon John Neuhaus's and Grandmother were here. And Aaron and I were hoeing tobacco. And it's damp and cloudy weather.

28. This forenoon father made the rest of the grass of. And Aaron and I were hoeing tobacco. Still cloudy weather.

29. Today Aaron was patching the barn roof. And I was shoveling tobacco. And this evening we made done haymaking. We had a pretty descent hay crop again. And it's still damp and cloudy weather.

30. Today we were hoeing tobacco. And I shoveled tobacco.

July 1. Today Aaron and I were shoveling corn. And father went to Ephrata. He bought a new ... binder from Mr. Stricher for one hundred and five dollars and the old binder in trade. And this evening Aaron went away.

2. Today I and Beckie were at the meeting at Noah Fisher's. And this afternoon we had a lot of visitors. It was Christ King, Enos Stoltzfus, Jacob King, Jacob Zook and John Ebersole. And this evening we were at the singing at ... Beiler's place.

3. This forenoon we were ... corn. And Mrs. Sprechers was here to set the binder up. And it's raining.

4. This forenoon we were picking blackberries

5. This forenoon we were picking cherries and this afternoon we started harvesting. The corn crop is looking good.

6. Today we were harvesting. The binder is doing well.

7. Today I and Moses were picking cherries. This afternoon we were binding. This evening it rained.

8. This forenoon Aaron and I were shocking wheat and it's damp weather and this afternoon we made done binding wheat. This evening it rained. A nice shower. This evening Christ came home and we had ice cream.

9. This forenoon Aaron and Fannie Glick were here. And Simon Zooks Christ and Barbara Zook. And this afternoon Aaron and Beckie went down to John Stoltzfus's and this evening we were at home.

10. Today we were busy hauling wheat into the barn.

11. Today we were handling wheat on stacks. We have a German fellow to help us. It's dry weather right now.

12. Today we were busy handling wheat and we had very good harvesting weather and it's very dry weather.

13. Today we made done harvesting and this evening we had a little storm. And tonight we had a nice rain. Wages for harvesting was $1.25.

14. Today we were suckering corn. And father went into Farmersville. Look where you walk in this world.

15. Today we shoveled tobacco and the rest were hoeing tobacco. Christ came in this world to save the sinners from sin.

16. Today we were all at the meeting at Henry Zook's. And this afternoon Jacob King and Katie Yoder and Fannie Fisher were here. And this evening we were at the singing at Jacob Stoltzfus, a large singing.

17. This morning Father and Mother and Grandmother and John were down to Uncle David Stoltzfus in Chester County and we were hoeing tobacco. This evening Aaron and Aaron Glick went in Lancaster.

18. Today Father and Mother were visiting in Chester County until this evening when they came home. And Aaron and I were hauling dung. Wonderful warm weather.

19. This forenoon we were hauling dung and this afternoon we were spreading dung.

20. Today we started plowing. And I was hauling ... fence away. And we have dry weather just now. And Father and John were with Grandmother.

21. Today I was plowing but it's too dry to plow, and Aaron was cleaning the fence. Order is heaven's first law.

22. Today I was plowing and Christian Stoltzfus from Morgantown was here. And Beckie was at John Glick's quilting, and this evening I was at the auction at Bareville. And this evening Aaron and Aaron Glick went away. And we have a dry summer.

23. Today I was at home and Christ Riehl's and Grandmother were here and this evening I was at the singing at Christ Stoltzfus. And Aaron's was at the Isaac Stoltzfus singing.

24. Today I was plowing and father and Aaron were making stake fence. Love your neighbor as yourself.

25. Today Aaron helped thresh at Abram ... and I was plowing. Father was reaping oats.

26. Today we were shoveling and hoeing tobacco and this evening we had a little shower. Thou shalt not steal.

27. This afternoon we hauled some oats in and this evening we threshed some oats. And Aaron and I were at the camp meeting at Brownstown.

28. This forenoon we turned the oats. This afternoon we threshed the rest of our oats. We got 235 bushels and we threshed 25 bushels of wheat.

29. This forenoon we were hauling dung and it rained a little shower and father and Beckie went in.

30. Today Father and Mother were at the meeting at Jacob Beiler's, and we were at home all day. Til this evening we were at the singing at Noah Smoker's.

31. This forenoon we were spreading dung, and this afternoon we hauled dung. Avoid evil companions.

August 1. Today we made done hauling dung. And this afternoon we were spreading dung. And we have very dry weather. Wheat is worth 58 cents.

2. This forenoon we made done spreading dung. And father was plowing. And it's dry weather.

3. Today I was plowing and father and Aaron were making fences. And it's now three weeks that it didn't rain on any account.

4. Today we were plowing and making fences. And the corn and tobacco is going to die for want of rain.

5. Today I was plowing and Aaron and Moses were topping tobacco. And we have still dry weather.

6. This forenoon Father and Mother went down to grandmother's. Aunt Lizzie is still sick. And Aaron and Beckie went to Henry Zook's. And this afternoon at

John Glick's. This evening they were at the singing at Ezra Stoltzfus's. And we had a hail and thunderstorm and our corn and tobacco is pretty badly cut.

7. Today I was plowing and Aaron worked in the tobacco patch. This evening Aaron and I and Beckie were over at Aunt Lizzie's, who is still sick.

8. Today Aaron helped thresh Abram's ... and I was following and we sold chicken's to Isaac Meyer's. We had 103 pounds of young chickens at 11 cents a pound. Amount is $11.33. And 85 pounds of old chickens at 9 cents a pound amount to $7.65. The whole amount was $19.21 and so on.

9. This forenoon I helped to thresh at Abram Riehl's and Aaron's helped threshing at Elias ... wages are $1.00 and $1.25. Father went to grandmother's.

10. This forenoon Aaron helped to thresh out Monroe ...

11. Today Aaron and I went for elderberries. We were as far as Bowmansville. It is a very warm day.

12. Today we sawed down our hickory tree out in the meadow. We have very dry and warm weather. And this afternoon Father and Mother went to Uncle Abram Stoltzfus's and Uncle John King's overnight.

13. Today we were at the funeral at Joel Zook's. Their baby died. It was 3 months and 9 days old. And this afternoon we went with Christ to David Smoker's. And this evening we were at the singing at John P Fisher's.

14. This forenoon I was plowing and this afternoon we were cutting wood. I think this is a wonderful world.

15. Today I was plowing and Aaron was quarrying stone for Abram Stoltzfus. And it's terrible dry and warm weather. Evil habits are gathered by unseen degrees, as brooks make rivers and rivers turn to seas.

16. Today Aaron's helped to thresh at Joe Hoover's and father went to grandmother's. And Lizzie is poorly. And Christian Stoltzfus and Nancy Stoltzfus and grandmother...Hard times on farmer's just now.

17. Today Aaron's and I helped to thresh at Levi Hoover's, and this evening we had a little shower but no account. And it's now 6 weeks that it didn't rain on any account.

18. Today Aaron helped to thresh at Simon Zook's, and Moses and I were suckering tobacco. The crop is poor.

19. Today they made done threshing at Isaac Zook's. And Moses and I started cutting tobacco. And Father and Mother were at John Neuhauser's.

20. Last night Aunt Lizzie died and this afternoon Father and Mother and Aunt Barbara went down to grandmother. And Aaron and John were at Jacob Zook's for dinner and I was at home.

21. This forenoon Aaron was quarrying stones. And Moses and I were putting away tobacco. It's dry weather.

22. Today was the funeral of Aunt Lizzie King. And we were all at the funeral. It was a very large funeral. She was 44 years and 3 months old.

23. Today Aaron was plowing. And I and Moses and John were putting away tobacco. Cloudy weather.

24. Last night it rained and stormed, the whole night. And this afternoon Aaron and I were plowing but the ground isn't soaked. We have stormy weather.

25. This forenoon Aaron and I were plowing, and this afternoon Aaron went up to David Beiler's to help thresh. Father went over to grandmother's.

26. Today Aaron helped to thresh at David Beiler's. I was plowing and we had very warm weather. The thermometer reached over 100 degrees.

27. Today we were at the meeting at Isaac Stoltzfus's. And this afternoon Aaron and I were with Isaac Glick. This evening we were at Jacob Glick's awhile.

28. Today I helped to thresh at Jacob ... and Aaron helped at John Glick's. And father fetched a load of sulphur coal at M. Stauffer's Coal and Timber Yard. Love your neighbor as yourself.

29. Last night was the stormiest night that we've had for a long time. And we had heavy rains too. And the corn is badly tangled down.

31. Today we started making out potatoes. And Grandmother was here.

September 1. This forenoon we were making out potatoes. And last night Jonas Zook's barn burned down

2. Today we made done making out potatoes. We have a fair crop again. This evening Aaron went away.

3. Today Christ was at home. And Uncle Christ Stoltzfus's girls and Lethenia Kauffman were here. This afternoons we were at Joe Hoover's. And this evening we were at the singing at John Beiler's.

4. Today I was plowing . And Aaron's and Moses were putting away tobacco. Our tobacco crop is poor.

5. Today we started threshing. We had John and Simon Zook's engines. Tonight it rained a little.

6. This forenoon we made done threshing. We got 389 bushels of wheat. And we sold $5.00 worth of chickens. And this afternoon we helped thresh at John Zook's.

7. Today we were busy putting away tobacco. And it's dry and cloudy weather. Avoid evil companions.

8. This forenoon I fetched 3,173 pounds of phosphate at Leacock Station from G. Baird at $27,00 a ton.

9. Today we started cutting corn. It's terrible bad to cut.

10. Today Aaron and Beckie and I and Aaron and Fannie Glick were at David Blank's. And this afternoon we were at Jonas Lantz. And this evening we were at the singing at ... Beiler's.

11. Today Aaron and I were cutting corn and Father and Mother went over to grandmother's and they brought grandmother and Aunt Susie ... along.

12. Today Aaron helped to thresh at Jacob Stoltzfus's. And I was cutting corn. Moses was harrowing.

13. Today Aaron and I were cutting corn. And Moses was harrowing. It's dry and warm weather.

14. This forenoon it rained a little. And Aaron and I were hauling stone. This afternoon we were cutting corn. And we cooked some apple butter. This evening father took 10 bushels of potatoes at ... cents a bushel at Brownstown.

15. Today Father and Mother were at the funeral of John Petersheim. He was 70 years, 2 months and 18 days old. And Aaron and I were cutting corn. This evening we had a thunderstorm.

16. Today we made done cutting tobacco. And this evening Aaron and Beckie went to Elias Stoltzfus.

17. Today Aaron and Beckie were at the Lower Pequea meeting at Samuel Umble. The young folks were baptized. They were Enos Stoltzfus, ... Umble, Amos Algyer, Molly ... , Rachel Stoltzfus, Sara Petersheim and Annie Umble. And this afternoon I was at John King's. And this evening I was at home. And Aaron and Beckie were at the singing at Joshua Lapp's. And it's fresh and clear weather. Thou shalt not steal.

18. Today Aaron and I were cutting corn and father was plowing the tobacco patch.

19. Today Aaron and I were cutting corn and Moses was harrowing.

20. Today Aaron and I were cutting corn and Moses was harrowing. This evening Father and Mother went to John Zook's. And Aaron and Beckie went to John King's.

21. Today Aaron and I were cutting corn and Moses was harrowing. And it's cloudy weather.

22. Today Aaron and I were cutting corn.

23. Today we made done cutting corn. And it's damp and rainy weather. And father and Beckie went in Farmersville. September 23, 1893.

24. Today we were at the meeting at ... Beiler's place. And Aaron and Aaron Glick's were at the meeting at Christian Esh's. This afternoon Father and Mother were with grandmother. This evening we were at the singing at ... Beiler's. It was a large singing. Mind your steps.

25. Today we started sowing wheat. And Aaron worked at John Zook's. This afternoon it rained and John Zook's fetched 20 bushels of wheat.

26. Today we were sowing. And Aaron worked at John Zook's. Moses was harrowing. And we had a mason to fix the chimney's. Nice weather.

27. Today I was sowing. And Father and Mother were at the sale at Nancy Stoltzfus.

28. Today I was plowing corn stubbles. And we sold Christ's horse for $70 to Clayton Rook. He bought 8 steers at $3.20 per hundred. They average 840 pounds, And a bull for $2.75 per hundred. He weighed 750 pounds.

29. Today we made done plowing corn stubble. And we have dry and warm weather again.

30. Today we made done sowing. And Aaron worked at Simon Zook's.

October 1. Today we were at ... And Christ was at home. And Uncle Christ Stoltzfus was here. And Aaron was at the singing at Levi Smoker's.

2. Today I and Moses were picking apples. And Aaron was hauling lumber with our teams at Milway Station.

3. Today we were picking apples and quarrying stones. And father went in Farmersville, from there to Ephrata. And it's dry and warm weather.

4. This forenoon Aaron's worked on this road. And Moses and I started husking corn. This afternoon it rained. It's necessary.

5. Today we were husking corn. And we paid our school tax. It was $22.00.

6. This evening Father and Mother went over to grandmother's. And we were husking corn.

7. This morning Father and Mother went on the train down to Daniel Stoltzfus. And we were husking corn. And it cleared off again. And this evening they came home.

8. Today they were at the meeting at Jacob Zook's. And I was at home the whole day. And this evening we were at home too.

9. Today we were finished husking corn. And our corn crop is about 3/4ths of a crop.

10. Today we were husking corn.

11. Today Aaron and Moses and I were husking corn. And it's splendid husking weather.

12. Today we were husking corn. And it's cloudy weather. And I guess it will rain.

13. Today we sold $21.00 worth of chickens to Isaac Meyers. And Father and Mother and Aunt Becca went down to old John Stoltzfus. And this afternoon it rained and stormed wonderful. This evening they came home.

14. Today we were husking corn and father took Aunt Beckie over to Uncle Christ Stoltzfus.

15. This forenoon Christ and Daniel Fisher were here. And this afternoon we were at Jacob Stoltzfus. And it's cold and stormy weather.

16. Today we were busy husking corn.

17. We have nice corn this year. But it isn't so plenty as last year. Good husking weather.

18. Today we were busy husking corn.

19. Today we were husking corn and this evening we were at the husking at Daniel Esh's.

20. Today we were husking corn. And it's damp.

21. Today we made done husking corn. This afternoon Beckie went over to grandmother's.

22. Today Father and Mother and Aaron were at the meeting at Christ Petersheim's and it was a large meeting. Beckie and I over at John Glick's. This evening we were at home. And it's cloudy weather.

23. Today it rained the whole day. And Isaac Stoltzfus and Barbara Zook were here. And Aaron and I worked the potatoes in the cellar.

24. Today we were hauling corn fodder. And Aaron fetched a load of coal at Leacock Station.

25. This forenoon Aaron and I were hauling corn fodder. This afternoon I was making fence.

26. Today father and I were in Lancaster. We bought a stove at G M Steinman's Store for $16.00. We sold some potatoes. And Aaron was hauling coal to burn lime.

27. *Today father and Beckie were at the meeting at Jonas Lantz. Some strange preachers were there. It was Christian Troyer and Mr. Peachy. And we made done hauling corn fodder.*

28. *Today I fetched a load of coal at Leacock's and Aaron was filling in.*

29. *Today Aaron was away. It's cold and stormy weather. This evening I was at the singing.*

30. *This morning Aaron and I started quarrying stones. But we stopped after a while. We bored air holes and Aaron lighted it and the powder can caught fire which he had in his hand and the can exploded. And it burned him pretty badly. Then I worked around the barns. Father worked in the summer house.*

31. *Today I worked where I wanted and father went in Farmersville. We had a heavy frost.*

November 1. Today I helped thresh with Jacob Stoltzfus. And Aaron is pretty sick today. We have nice weather.

2. *Today we made done threshing at Jacob Stoltzfus's. And Isaac Hoover and I were quarrying stones and it's warm and pleasant weather.*

3. *Today Isaac and I were quarrying stones.*

4. *Today it rained the whole day. And I cleaned and dunged the stables and so forth.*

5. *Today we were at the meeting at John Miller's. This afternoon we had some visitors. They were Aaron and Fannie Glick, Samuel Stoltzfus, John Beiler and Uncle Elias Stoltzfus. And this evening we were at the singing at John Miller's. And it was a large singing.*

6. *This forenoon Isaac Hoover and I were quarrying stones and in the afternoon we were filling lime kiln.*

7. *Today Father and Mother and grandmother and Nancy Stoltzfus were in ... with two horses. Isaac and I were filling lime kiln.*

160

8. Isaac and I were filling lime kiln. And Father and Mother were visiting in Conestoga.

9. Today we made done filling lime kiln and Father and Mother came home. And this evening Christ King's came and stayed overnight.

10. This forenoon Father and Mother were with Christ's over to John Zook's. And I fetched a load of coal at Stauffer's Coal and Lumberyard.

11. Today I dunged the stables and cleaned the cistern out. And father and Moses and John went in Farmersville. This evening Daniel Lapp was here.

12. Today Beckie and I and Christ were at Christ Stoltzfus's for dinner and for supper at Sarah Stoltzfus. This evening we were at the singing at John Fisher's. It was a good singing.

13. This forenoon we sold two cows to S Sensinig. One for 15 dollars and the other for 30 dollars. And Moses and I were ... stones in the ground. Father went out to Stauffer's to pay his coal bill.

14. Today we made done picking stones. And father and Aaron went to Farmersville.

15. Last night it rained and snowed and it's rough and cold weather.

16. This morning Eli Stoltzfus started hauling lime. And it's rough and stormy weather. This afternoon father took a hog to Sensenig that weighed 299 pounds at 8 cents a pound.

17. This forenoon they made done hauling lime. We got 1012 bushels at 8 cents a bushel. Amount $80.96. This afternoon we were hauling coal. And Beckie helped to bake pies at John Zook's.

18. Today I dunged the stables and father went in Farmersville. This evening I was at the auction in Mechanicsburg. Aaron went away too.

19. Today we were at the meeting at John Zook's. This afternoon Aaron went to Aaron Glick's. I was at home and Father and Mother went with Simon Zook's. And in the evening we were at the singing at John Glick's. And it's cold and stormy weather.

20. Today Aaron and I were quarrying stones. And this afternoon father took a load of chickens to Jay Stoltzfus. Had $15.30 worth of chickens. From there he went to grandmother.

21. Last night Christ came home. And today Christ and Aaron were quarrying stones. And I worked around the barn. And this afternoon it commenced to snow. And it's rough and stormy weather. We have dull times but plenty to eat.

22. Today Christ and Aaron were quarrying stones.

23. Today I helped to thresh at John Zook's and father took a hog to S Sensinig for 8 cents a pound. It weighted 294 pounds. Christ and Aaron were quarrying stones.

24. Today Christ and I were quarrying stones and Aaron was filling lime kilns.

25. This forenoon I dunged the stables and Christ and Aaron were filling lime kilns and this evening Aaron and I were in Farmersville.

26. Today Aaron went away. And I was at home. This evening we had a singing at Stephen Stoltzfus's.

27. This forenoon father went in Lancaster on the train and I fetched two loads of coal and so on.

28. Today we worked at the stone. And this evening we worked at the auctions at Mechanicsburg.

29. Today we were filling lime kiln.

30. Today was Thanksgiving Day. And Christ and Aaron were at Jacob Glick's. And Father and Mother were at grandmother's. And this evening we were at the singing at John P Fisher's. Always speak the truth.

December 1. This forenoon Christ and Isaac Hoover were quarrying stones. And this afternoon it rained.

2. This forenoon they were quarrying stones. And Father and Mother went in Farmersville. Christ and Aaron went in Lancaster and I worked.

3. Today we were at the meeting at Daniel Stoltzfus and it rained the whole day. And it rained this whole day. In the evening we had a good singing.

4. Today Christ went to grandmothers and we worked around the barn. And this afternoon father took a load of turkeys to JP Stoltzfus. He had $20.34 worth of turkeys.

5. Today John Allgyer and Becky Glick married.

6. Today they were hauling lime. And we have a pretty decent snow. And this afternoon I took a sleigh ride and we have cold weather.

7. Today Samuel Esh and Annie Stoltzfus married. And Christian Lapp and Leah Zook married. And we were at the wedding and it was an excellent wedding. But it's cold weather just now.

8. This morning we came home from the wedding. And we didn't work much on any account.

9. This forenoon I dunged the stables and this afternoon Christ and Aaron were at the auction at Meyer's Store in Mechanicsburg. I was at home.

10. Today I was at the meeting at Black Jacob Stoltzfus. And this afternoon we had some visitors. They were Gideon Beiler, Isaac Glick, Aaron Glick, Joshua Lapp, Mollie Blank, Annie Beiler. It was a pleasant day. And tonight we were at the singing of Jacob Stoltzfus.

11. This morning Christ went down to Jacob Smoker's. And I was at Wenger's Mill. And in the afternoon I fetched a load of cinder ash at this mill. This evening

Aaron and Beckie went in Farmersville. And our dam is all frozen over. And we have cold weather. Love one another.

12. Today John King and Beckie Lapp married. And David Blank and Beckie Beiler married. And Samuel Lapp and Katie Stoltzfus married. And Christ and Aaron were at John King's wedding. And father visited old Johnny Stoltzfus.

13. Today father went over to grandmother. And Aaron and I were hauling dung. And it's rough weather.

14. [This date was left empty]

15. Today is cold and stormy weather

16. Today we worked around the barns and so on.

17. Today we were at the meeting at Benuel Stoltzfus. This evening we were at home.

18. This forenoon I was at Wenger's Mill. And this afternoon Christ and ... and I went in Conestoga.

19. Today Isaac Glick and Annie Yoder married and we were at the wedding. And it was an excellent wedding. And tonight we were at Isaac Stoltzfus's. And it's very warm and pleasant weather.

20. This forenoon we came home. And this afternoon I fetched a load of chopping. And this afternoon Christ went into Mechanicsburg.

21. Today Christian Beiler and Fannie King married. And we were at the wedding and it's very warm and pleasant weather. Father made ready to thresh.

22. Today we made done threshing. We got 340 bushels from the four stacks. And we sold $4.60 worth of turkeys to Meyers.

23. Today we started stripping tobacco. And Aaron went in Brownstown. This evening we were at the auctions at ... This afternoon it rained a little.

24. Today Simon Zook's were here. And we were at home. This evening we were at the singing at John Smoker's. This morning David Glick died. We leave muddy rags.

25. This forenoon I was with Samuel Stoltzfus. Afternoon I was at Black Jacob Stoltzfus. Christ and Aaron's were at Joel Fisher's. And it's warm Christmas weather but bad and muddy roads.

26. This forenoon Christ and Aaron came home. And David Glick was buried. He was 53 years, 4 months and 20 days old. And father went in Farmersville. It's rough weather.

27. Today Christ and Aaron's were filling lime kiln. And father and I butchered a bull. And it's warm and pleasant weather. Wheat is worth 60 cents. Chickens are worth 6 cents a pound.

28. This forenoon Isaac Hoover helped to fill the lime kilns. And this afternoon it rained. And we butchered a hog. And it's warm weather. This evening Christ went down to David Smoker's.

29. Today we were stripping tobacco and I fetched a load of chopping at Wenger's Mill. And Beckie helped to bake at Simon Zook's.

30. Today it snowed the whole day but the ground ain't frozen. And we were stripping tobacco.

31. Today we were at the meeting at Simon Zook's. And we had some visitors. They were Daniel and Molly Lapp, Aaron and Fannie Glick, Benuel and Katie Stoltzfus, Amos, Elam and Katie Stoltzfus, Daniel and Susan Zook, Benjamin and Annie Umble, Jacob, Katie and Susan Yoder, Daniel Fisher, Danny Beiler, Barbara Glick, Lydia and Annie Beiler, and Joseph and Jonathan Yoder from Mifflin County. This evening we were at the singing at Simon Zook's.

January 1, 1894 Today the crowd was at John Glick's for dinner. And for supper at black Jacob Stoltzfus. And this evening in the singing at Jacob Stoltzfus. And it's warm and pleasant weather. And today Samuel Beiler was buried he was sixty eight years, four months and twenty three days.

2. Today we were stripping tobacco. And Christ went down to David Smoker's. And it's warm and pleasant weather. Wheat was down to 58 cts.

3. Today I was stripping tobacco. And father went in Farmersville. Aaron was telling the 1894 funeral for Lizzie Stoltzfus. We have pleasant weather.

4. Today Aaron and I were stripping tobacco. And we had a warm winter so far yet.

5. Today Lizzie Stoltzfus was buried. She was seventy-seven years, two months and twenty-eight days old. The funeral was at Jacob Stoltzfus. And it's damp and sunny the whole day. And Moses and I were stripping tobacco.

6. Today we were stripping tobacco. And I dunged the stables. This afternoon I took a load (of) corn to Wenger's. This eve Aaron and Aaron Glick went away. A. King.

7. Today I was at home. And Abram Beiler's and Jacob Esch were here. And it's warm and pleasant weather.

8. This forenoon we were stripping tobacco. In the afternoon we were filling limekiln. Isaac Hoover helped us. And it's warm and pleasant weather....

9. This forenoon I fetched a load of coal. And today we made done filling limekiln. This evening Father and Mother went over to Grandmothers.

10. This morning I took Aaron over to Jacob Stoltzfus to work there. And this afternoon I was stripping tobacco. And it's cloudy weather.

11. Today father and I were stripping tobacco.

12. Today was the stormiest day that we had for a long time. And I was stripping tobacco.

13. Today I was hauling wheat at Wenger's mill at 73 cts. And it's warm and pleasant weather.

14. Today we were at the meeting at Jacob Stoltzfus. And this afternoon Jacob Esch was here. And it's warm and pleasant weather. And this evening we were at the singing at Gideon Deiner's.

15. Today I hauled some wheat. And stripped tobacco. And so it went on with blue Monday.

16. Today David Smoker started hauling lime. And I loaded the lime for him. And it's warm and terrible slushy and muddy roads.

17. Today I was loading lime for David Smoker. And we have terrible roads. And we sold 8.00 dollars worth of chickens to Sam Carpenter's. 1894. Dare to be honest, good and true. Dare to do right. And you'll find your way through.

18. Today David Smoker stopped hauling lime. The roads are too bad. This forenoon Aaron was at home. And Father and Mother went to Barbara Zook. And I fetched a load of chopping at Wenger's Mill.

19. Today. This forenoon we were stripping tobacco. And this afternoon I helped to thresh at Joseph Hoover's. And it's nice and pleasant weather...

20. This afternoon father went in Farmersville. And I dunged the stable. And it's warm and pleasant weather. Remember me when this you see.

21. Today Beckie and I were at John Lapp's. And Father and Mother were at Menno Stoltzfus. And it's damp and rainy the whole day.

22. Today father and I were stripping tobacco. And it cleared and it's warm and pleasant weather.

23. This forenoon I was stripping tobacco. And this afternoon I fetched a load of chopping.

24. Today I was stripping tobacco. And it's nice and pleasant weather. In 1492 Chistopher Columbus discovered America. I think it must have been a hopeless journey. Then I went home.

167

25. This afternoon Father and Mother went to Snaderville to a Doctor. And Isaac Glick's were here. And it's cold and stormy weather. 1894.

26. Today we made done stripping tobacco. And it snowed pretty near the whole day. But no snow at all. We hadn't any sleighing this winter yet.

27. Today we sold 14.87 worth of chickens to S. Sensenig. And I hauled a load of wheat to Wenger's Mill. At .60 cts a bus. And brought along a load of chopping. And it's cold and rough weather.

28. Today we were at the meeting at Esther Ebersole. And this evening we were at the singing at same place.

29. Today it rained and stormed the whole day. And we didn't work much of anything. Jesus came into this world to save sinners from sin. Do unto others as you would like to have unto you. Life is real. Life is earnest. And the grave is not its goal. Dust thou art. To dust returnest was not spoken of the soul.

30. Today it snowed and stormed. Today Noah Beiler and Mary King married. And this ground is covered with snow now.

31. Today we took a cow to S. Sensenig for $13.00. And I was in Brownstown. It's warm weather.

Feb. 1. Today I didn't work much of anything. And it's warm and pleasant weather. 1894.

2. Today I handed a load of wheat to Wenger's Mill. We sold two hundred and five bus. Now at .61 cts a bus. And I took a load of corn to Joel Wenger's Mill. And the ground is covered with snow just now.

3. This forenoon I dunged the stables. And I fetched a load of chopping. And this afternoon we were at the sale at Mr. Mc. Gallighers. And it's damp and wet weather. This evening Christ, Aaron and Samuel Stoltzfus. Christ was here over night. And so on...And Father and Mother were with Grandmother.

4. Today it snowed the whole day. And Christ was here all day. But the snow melted pretty fast. This evening I was at home. Eggs are worth 14 cts a dozen.

5. Today is cold and stormy weather. And we don't work much of anything just now.

6. This forenoon I fetched a load of coal at H. M. Staugger's Warehouse. At $4.70 cts. a ton. And it's warm and pleasant weather. 1894.

7. Today David Smoker was hauling lime. And I loaded the lime for him. And father went in Brownstown. And we have solid roads.

8. Today David Smoker was hauling lime. And it's cloudy weather.

9. Today it rained the whole day. And I made ready for the meeting. And the women baked the pies for the meeting. Amos King born Sept. 6 1874. And we have terrible muddy and slushy roads. Don't matter which way you turn, You always find in the Book of Life, Some Lesson you have to learn.

10. This forenoon I dunged the stables. And it's warm and pleasant weather. And I took a load of corn to Wenger's Mill. And fetched eleven loaves of bread at Brownstown for the meeting. Thou shalt not steal.

11. Today the meeting was at our place. And it's warm and pleasant weather. This afternoon David Blank's were here. This evening we were at home.

12. Today it snowed the whole day. And it's cold and stormy weather. I fetched a load of chopping.

13. Today I was at the sale at John Glick's. And it's cloudy weather. This evening we had a...

14. Last night we had some visitors. They were Christ and Jacob Kauffman. Annie and Beckie Kauffman, Mattie Esch and Alice Neuhauser. And some say it's sleighing. And some don't.. This afternoon I was in Farmersville. 1894.

15. Today it snowed the whole day. And we have lots of snow. And we have excellent sleighing. And I was at the sale at Reuben Getz. 1894.

16. Today Father, John and Moses went to Grandmothers. And it's terrible cold and stormy. And I didn't work much of anything One hundred years one century.

17. This forenoon I dunged the stables. And this afternoon I went in Farmersville. And it's good sleighing. And this evening I took a sleigh ride.

18. This forenoon we were at home. And last night it rained. And the sleighing is fast. This afternoon we were at John Stoltzfus. This evening they had a singing. And we have terrible muddy roads.

19. Today it's pleasant weather. And I took a load of corn to Wenger's Mill. Columbus discovered America in 1492.

20. This forenoon I fetched a load of chopping. And this afternoon I was at the sale at Christian Lapp's. Arkansas, Missouri, Kansas. Iowa, Ohio, Texas, Wisconsin, Pennsylvania, Tennessee. 1894

21. Today we sold a bull to Mr. Dougherty. He weighed 1130 lbs. At 3 ½ cts a lb. We took him to…And a sheep for $4.00 dollars. This evening I went over to Aaron's awhile. Muddy roads.

22. Today Father and Mother went to Grandmothers. And I went to Brownstown and at Wenger's Mill.

23. Today it's cold and stormy weather. And Father and Mother went to John Zook's. And I was splitting wood. Think three times before you speak.

24. This forenoon I dunged the stables. And this afternoon I was at the sale at John King's. And it's pretty cold and stormy weather…1894.

25. Today Father and Mother and I were at the meeting at John Blank's. And this afternoon I was with Benuel Stoltzfus. And it commenced to snow terrible. This evening John Blank's had a singing.

26. Today it snowed the whole day. And the snow is about six inches deep and very solid.

27. This morning I fetched Grandmother and Nancy Stoltzfus. We had a turkey roast. Christ and Barbara Zook were here. And it's excellent sleighing. And wheat is as low down as .57 cts a bus.

28. Today was warm and pleasant weather. And this afternoon Beckie and I went in Farmersville. And the sleighing is pretty near gone. And I fetched a load of chopping. Eggs are worth .15 ct. a doz.

March .1. Today was warm and pleasant weather. And John got sick he has the "beast fever." 1894. And Simon Zook's were here with the sleigh…

2. Today I was at the horse sale at Weidler's Hotel. But horses are very cheap just now. Amos C. King

3. This forenoon we dunged the stables. And this afternoon Aaron came home from Jacob Stoltzfus. This evening Beckie and I went over to Grandmother's.

4. This forenoon we were at the meeting at Henry Fisher's. And this afternoon we were at Barb Fisher's place. This evening we were at the singing at Henry Fisher's. And the roads are terribly muddy.

5. This forenoon I helped Beckie to wash. And this afternoon I went in Farmersville with 30 doz eggs at only 13cts a doz. We have some snow yet…

6. This forenoon I was at the blacksmith shop…In the afternoon I was at the watch sale at Abram Beiler's And it's warm and pleasant weather.

7. Today I worked on the woodpile. And father worked in the shop. And John is pretty sick yet. Horses are very cheap just now. Love your neighbor as yourself.

8. Today Aaron and I were quarrying stones. And we have warm and pleasant weather. Never say I can't.

9. This forenoon we were quarrying stones. This afternoon Aaron was at the sale at Mr. …

10. *This forenoon we dunged the stables. And this afternoon we worked on the woodpile. A. C. King.*

11. *Today we were at the meeting at Moses Stoltzfus. And this afternoon we were with Aaron Glick. This evening we were at the singing at Miles Kauffman's. And it's warm and cloudy weather.*

12. *Today we were hauling dung. And it's nice and pleasant weather. Paddle your own canoe.*

13. *Today Aaron helped to thresh at Joe Hoovers. And I was spreading dung. And Father and Mother went to Dr. Widders at Snaderville. Pleasant weather.*

14. *Today we were hauling dung. And it's pretty cold and stormy weather. Honesty is the best policy.*

15. *This forenoon I sowed our clover seed. And Aaron was spreading dong. In the afternoon Aaron and I were at the sale at Abram Stoltzfus. And it's rainy weather. Try and speak good for anybody.*

16. *This forenoon we were hauling dung. In the afternoon we were spreading dung. And Father and Mother went to Grandmother. Eternity.*

17. *This forenoon we were hauling dung. And this afternoon I dunged the stables. And Aaron was spreading dung. We had a pleasant March.*

18. *This forenoon Christ Rheile and Grandmother were here. I was at the singing at David King's. And Aaron was at the singing at Joe Blank's.*

19. *This forenoon we were hauling dung. And this afternoon we were spreading dung. And we sold a calf to Mr. McCloud for $6.15. And it's very warm weather. Always do you best. And you will soon do better.*

20. *Today we started plowing in the corn stalks. And Aaron went down to Menno Stoltzfus's to work.*

21. This forenoon I was spreading dung. In the afternoon Aaron came home. It's damp and rainy weather.

22. Today we made done hauling dung. And it's unseasonable warm weather. Wheat is worth .57 cts.

23. Today is Good Friday. And Aaron, Beckie and I were at John King's. And it's cold and stormy weather.

24. Today Eli Stoltzfus was buried he was forty-seven years, ten months and seventeen days old. And Aaron was spreading dung. And I was plowing.

25. Today we were at the meeting at Stephen Stoltzfus. This afternoon we were at Moses Stoltzfus. This eve we were at John Glick's. And it's rainy weather.

26. Easter Monday. This forenoon Aaron and I took four sheep to Lititz. Amounted to $12.60 cts. And we had some visitors. They were David Fisher, Stephen Esch, Barbara Smoker, Ary Stoltzfus, Annie Lapp and Beckie Esch. This afternoon we were at black Jacob Stoltzfus playing ball. This evening we were at the party at Mike Kauffman. And it's unseasonable cold and stormy weather. Amos C. King.

27. This forenoon Aaron went to Menno Stoltzfus. And I took a horse to Samuel Carpenter for $15.00. And I took a load of corn to Wenger's Mill. And it's snowy and cold weather. And I fetched four bus. of lime at Givler's limekiln. At .20 a bus.

28. This forenoon I was in Bareville. And this afternoon I was plowing. And it's still cold weather.

29. Today it snowed pretty near the whole day. But the snow melted. This evening I fetched a load of chopping. And it's very unpleasant and wet weather.

30. Today father went down to Grandmother. And this afternoon I was plowing. Aaron worked at the stone.

31. Today Aaron and I were plowing. And it's cloudy weather. And eggs are worth .08 cts a doz. Potatoes .50 cts a bus.

April. 1. This forenoon Beckie and I went to Henry Zook's. And this afternoon at John Glick's. And Father and Mother went to Grandmother. And Christ was at home.

2. This forenoon Aaron went to Menno Stoltzfus. And we were plowing. And it's pretty cold weather. 1894. And father went to Lancaster on the train. A. C. King.

3. Today we were plowing. And it's chilly weather.

4. Today it rained for part of the time. And we cleaned our oats. This eve Aaron came home. 1894…

5. Today it rained pretty near the whole day. And Simon Zook got his hand crippled. He was quarrying stones. Father and Mother went to Snaderville. A. C. King.

6. This morning Aaron went to Menno Stoltzfus. And father and I were plowing. And last night David Smoker died from Typhoid Amonio. And it's cold and stormy weather. We have wet weather just now. This evening Beckie and I were at John Zook's. 1894.

7. This forenoon we were plowing. And this afternoon it rained a part of the time. And father went in Farmersville. Hard times and we get plenty of poor people. But farmers have plenty to eat. But no sale for nothing pretty near. But I can't make it better.

8. Today we were at the meeting at Christ Miller's. This afternoon Aaron was at Amos Stoltzfus. And today David Smoker was buried. He was twenty-four years, six months and twenty-five days old. And tonight I was at John Zook's. And it's cold weather.

9. Today I was plowing. And Aaron worked at the stones. And J. …fetched a sick steer. And we sold the rest of our steers today to David Weaver for $3.60 per hundred. And we have cold weather.

174

10. This morning we took our steers to Bareville to weigh and then to New Holland. They averaged twelve hundred and sixty lbs. Amount to $318.60. And I was harrowing. And this afternoon it snowed the whole afternoon. And it's cold weather.

11. Today it snowed the whole day. And this is the first time in my life that I saw such a snow in April. The snow is about twelve inches deep. And twelve inches melted about. And we worked in the shop. A terrible weather.

12. This forenoon it snowed a while yet. And we worked in the shop. This afternoon father and Aaron went in Farmersville. And its wet and slushy weather. And some sleighs were used to.

13. Today Father and Mother were at the funeral. David Blank's baby was buried. It was ten months old. And Aaron and I took ten bus. of potatoes to Ephrata. At .45 cts. a bus. And this evening Aaron were at John Zook's. And Simon Zook died from the Lock Jaw. And they Baptized him today. And the ground is still covered with snow. 1894.

14. This morning Father, Aaron and Beckie went to John Zook's. And the ground was frozen this morning. This afternoon Moses and I took ten bus. of potatoes to Ephrata. At .45 cts a bus. And Aaron was telling the funeral. And the roads are terrible muddy.

15. Today Aaron and I were at Joe Hoover's. This evening father and Beckie went to John Zook's. And we have warm and pleasant weather. 1894. But we have still some snow yet. In God we trust. This evening Christ King's came…

16. Today we were all at the funeral for Simon Zook. He was seventeen years, nine months and eighteen days old. And It's warm and pleasant weather. This evening I started sowing oats. The land is wet.

17 This forenoon I was plowing. And this afternoon I was sowing oats. Aaron went to Menno Stoltzfus.

18. Today I made done sowing oats. And Moses and I were plowing. Father went in Farmersville

19. *Today we made done plowing corn stubble. This evening Aaron came home. And it's cloudy weather.*

20. *This forenoon it rained a little. And this afternoon we started planting potatoes. And we sold twelve dollars worth of chickens and our tobacco for one and half cents to Isaac Myers. A. C. King*

21 *Last night it rained powerful. And today Aaron and I baled the tobacco. And this afternoon father and Beckie went in Lancaster. This evening Aaron went away. And the roads are terrible muddy.*

22. *Last night it rained. And today we were at the meeting at Amos Stoltzfus it was order meeting. This evening we were at home and it's dry times.*

23. *This forenoon I was plowing. And this afternoon we were planting potatoes. And father took the sheep to Aaron's. To Samuel Carpenter amount to $39.90*

24. *Today I was plowing. And we made down planting potatoes. And Father and Mother went to Snaderville. And it's unpleasant and cold weather. 1894.*

25. *Today I was plowing. And Moses and John were white washing. Father went to John Zook's.*

26. *Today I was plowing. And this week the Electric Rail Road surveyors went through here…1894*

27. *Today I worked at Claus Marven's. And Moses was harrowing. And it's warm weather. A. C. King.*

28. *Today I worked at Claus Marven…West Earl…*

29. *This forenoon we were with Grandmother. And this afternoon we had visitors. There were Eli Smoker's Aaron and Fannie Glick, Jacob Esch. Benuel Stoltzfus and Stephen Fisher. And we were at Mill Way. This evening Father and Mother went to Grandmother.*

30. *Today I worked at Claus Marven's. Amos C. King.*

May 1. Today I was plowing. And Moses was harrowing. And Aaron and Isaac Hoover were quarrying stones. And it's warm weather. 1894.

3. Today I made done plowing. And Aaron and Isaac were hauling stones. And it's pretty dry weather.

3. Today was a holiday. And Aaron went away. And Simon Zook's and Christ and Barbara Zook were here. This evening Beckie and I were at John Zook's. And tonight Christ and Daniel Lapp. John Beiler, Samuel Stoltzfus. Mary Stoltzfus and Mollie Lapp were here awhile. A yes by gone days…

4. Today old Christian Stoltzfus was buried. And father , mother and Beckie were at the funeral. He was seventy-two years, nine months, and twenty-one days old. And we started planting corn…

5. Today we were planting corn. And it's warm weather. Dare to be honest good and true.

6. Today we were at the meeting at John Beiler's. It was a large meeting. And it's warm weather.

7. Today we were planting corn. Pretty dry weather.

8. Today we were planting corn. Father was in Farmersville. Be kindhearted just and true. A. C. King.

9. Today we made done planting corn. And this afternoon I went to Claus Marvens. We charge him 2.75 a day. Aaron was making fences. And we took the colts to the meadow. By gone days.

11. Today we were white washing. And father was painting Aaron's buggy. And it's cloudy weather.

12 Today I was white washing. And Aaron was making fence. And this evening we went down to Samuel Lapp's. And it's dry and pleasant weather.

13. Today we were at John Beiler's for dinner. And at Samuel Esch's for supper. This evening we were at the singing at Christ Lapp's. And it's warm weather.

14. Today we were at Daniel Esch's for dinner. And this afternoon we went home. This evening Aaron and I went in Farmersville. We had pleasant times.

15. Today we were making fence. And we sold 8.60 cts. worth of chickens to I. Myers. A. C. King.

16. Today Aaron and I were making fences. And Moses was harrowing the tobacco patch. This evening it rained a nice shower. 1894. Our mind is a hive in which to store, Which we will need when youth is o'er.

17. This forenoon it rained. In the afternoon I made the tobacco land ready and we started planting tobacco. In God we trust. A. C. King

18. Today is damp and rainy weather. And we were planting tobacco. Amos C King born Sept 6 1874

19. This forenoon we were planting tobacco. And Christian Kanaegy and his wife and her sister were here. And this afternoon it rained. This evening Father and Mother went to John Fisher's. And Christ came home overnight. If you come into the religious circle, Come only with notion.

20. Today we were at the meeting at John Glick's. And it rained the whole day and it's stormy.

21. Today we didn't work much of anything. And it rained pretty near the whole day. We have powerful wet weather just now. The time is swiftly passing by. And we must bid adieu.

22. Today Aaron and I were making fence. And we have wet weather. And Father and Mother came home.

23. Today it rained a part of the time. And we didn't work much of anything. In the sweet by and by.

24. Today it rained a part of the time. And we have powerful wet and dirty weather.

25. Today we made done planting tobacco. And it rained again. And we were making wire fences.

26. Today we were making wire fence. Aaron was working at Menno Stoltzfus. And it rained again. And tonight I was at Menno Stoltzfus. 1894.

27. Today I was at home. And Mary and Beckie Stoltzfus, Mary Miller and Mary Yoder were here. And Father and Mother were with Barbara Zook. And tonight Aaron was at the singing at Ben Beilers. This evening father went over to Grandmother.

28. Today it rained a part of the time. And father fetched Grandmother and Aunt Susie.

29. Today I was shoveling potatoes. And we have very wet weather. And John Zook's were here.

30. Today I started shoveling corn. And old John Stoltzfus were here. And it's cloudy weather.

31. This morning it rained a little. And Joel King's were here. And Moses and I fixed the lane.

June 1. Today I was shoveling corn. And this evening Aaron came home. And it's wet weather.

2. Today Father and Mother went to see John King. And Aaron was shoveling potatoes. I was shoveling corn. This afternoon Aaron went in Lancaster.

3. Today Beckie and I were at the meeting at David Beilers. And it was a clear but not a pleasant day.

4. Today I was shoveling corn. And Aaron was shoveling potatoes. And father bought a cow at Eden for 24 dollars. And it's cloudy weather.

179

5. Today it rained a part of the time. And I fetched a load of posts at 22 cts. apiece. 1894.

6. Today I was shoveling corn. And it rained part of the time. We have very wet weather just now.

7. Today we started shoveling tobacco. And so on…

8. Today we were making fence. Unsettled weather.

9. Today I was shoveling corn. And Aaron was making fence. And it's pleasant weather. This evening Christ came home. Aaron was in Farmersville.

10. Today we were at home. And Jacob King and Jacob Fisher were here. And Francis and Beckie Hoover were here too. And it's a clear and pleasant day.

11. Today I was shoveling corn. And Aaron was shoveling potatoes. And we have warm weather.

12. Today I was shoveling corn. And Aaron was making. This evening Samuel Stoltzfus and Mollie Lapp and Isaac and Aaron Glick were here. And Beckie was at the quilting at Isaac Stoltzfus.

13. Last night it rained a nice shower. And Aaron and I were making fence. Father was in Farmersville.

14. Always do your best and you'll soon do better.

15. Today Aaron and I were making fence. 1894.

16. Today we were making fence. And so forth. And this evening Christ and Daniel Lapp and Mary Stoltzfus were here. And it's very warm weather.

17. Today we were at the meeting at Eli Smoker's. And this evening they had a singing.

18. Today I was shoveling corn. And Aaron was shoveling potatoes. And John King was here putting up a wire fence for us. And it's warm weather.

19. Today I was shoveling corn. And Aaron was scraping corn. And it's unreasonable warm weather.

20. Today we started hay making. And I was scraping corn. Aaron worked at the limekilns.

21. Today we hauled some hay in. And it's excellent hay weather. And this hay is fine. But we have very warm weather.

22. This morning Aaron took a two horse load of hay to Claus Marven for $10.00 dollars. And we were busy hauling in. But very warm. One by one we pass away, here on earth we cannot stay. Something we all should know.

23. Today we were busy hauling hay. And we have excellent weather to make hay. And so...

24. Today we were all at home the whole day. The thermometer reached 105 degrees and the air is warm. But this evening we had a heavy thunderstorm and a heavy rain. This evening Aaron Glick was here awhile.

25. Today Beckie and I went for cherries at David Beiler's. And Father, Moses and John went to Grandmother. And it's a warm day. And we sold a calf to Mr. Ludwig for $6.85.

26. Today Aaron worked at the limekiln. This evening we took some hay in. We have a fine hay crop. And it's warm weather.

27. This forenoon Moses, John and I were picking sour cherries. Aaron worked at the limekilns. This evening we made done haymaking.

28. This forenoon we were making fence. In the afternoon shoveling corn. And it's warm weather.

29. *Today we were shoveling corn. The crop looks good. And we have wet weather just now.*

30. *Today I made done shoveling corn. And this afternoon Father and Mother went to Samuel King's.*

July. 1. Today we were all at the meeting at David Smoker's. And Beckie and I stayed there in the afternoon. This evening they had a singing. And it's a very warm day. Here on earth we cannot stay.

2. *Today we started harvesting. And it's warm weather.*

3. *Today we were busy at … And it's excellent harvest weather. One by one we pass away.*

4. *Today we were busy harvesting. Our mind is a hive in which to store, which we will need when you is o'er.*

5. *This forenoon we made done … wheat. And this afternoon we started hauling wheat in.*

6. *Today it rained a part of the time. And we were…corn. And I picked some cherries.*

7. *This forenoon we worked at the corn. And this afternoon we were busy hauling wheat.*

8. *Today we were all at home. And Christ was here. And this evening Ben and Jacob Fisher, Jacob King, and David and Jonas Beiler were here. Amos C. King.*

9. *Today we were busy hauling wheat. And it's cold harvest weather. Harvest $1.25 and wheat .53 cts a bus. That looks good for farmers.*

10. *Today we were hauling wheat. Speak the truth.*

11. *Today we made done harvesting. We made six stacks and the barn is well filed. Mind your steps.*

12 Today we were ... corn. It's dry weather.

13. This afternoon we started hauling dung. And it's powerful warm weather. Idleness is a great sin.

14. This forenoon we were spreading dung. And the thermometer reached 100 degrees and it's little...

15. Today we were at the meeting at Abram Stoltzfus. And it's warm and dry weather. And this evening David Lapp and Lydia Fisher were here awhile.

16. Today Aaron worked at the limekilns. And I was painting a tin roof. And this evening we had a little shower. And it's excellent weather.

17. Today we didn't work much of anything.

18. Today, I reaped the oats. Aaron worked at the limekilns. Father worked something, too.

19. Today Aaron and I worked at the oats. And the thermometer reached 100 degrees. Think twice before you speak once. West Earl.

20. Today we threshed our oats. We got two hundred and thirty two bushels of oats. And we have pretty dry weather just now.

21. This forenoon Aaron took the engine home. And then we didn't work much anymore. This evening we had ice cream. And brothers Christ and Jacob Esch and Amos Stoltzfus were here.

22. This forenoon Father and Mother went to Joe Beilers. And Aaron, David and Fannie Glick were here. And it rained a little.

23. Today we were hauling dung. And it's cloudy weather. And wheat is worth .48 cts a bu. already.

24. Today we were spreading dung. And last night it rained a little. And today we had a quilting. This evening we had a thunder rain. Step by step.

25. Today we started plowing. And we have powerful warm weather this month through.

26. Today Aaron helped to thresh at Abram … And we made done hauling dung. And it's unreasonable warm weather.

27. Today I was plowing. And it's powerful warm. This evening Aaron and Beckie went to Grandmother.

28. Today Father and Mother went over to Grandmother. And we bought a cow from Isaac Myers for $35. This forenoon I was plowing. And it's remarkable warm weather. Here on earth we cannot stay.

29. Today we were all at the meeting at Eli Stoltzfus. This afternoon Aaron went with Aaron Glick. I was at home. And it'd warm yet.

30. This afternoon we cleaned our dams. And I plowed in the forenoon. And it's still warm weather.

31. Today we worked at the dams. And this evening it rained a nice shower. We had a quilting.

Aug. 1. Today I was plowing. And Aaron worked in the tobacco patch. Still warm weather.

2. Today Moses and I were plowing. And this evening we had a thunderrain and the ground is soaked. Our corn crop looks excellent. 1894.

3. Today Father and Aaron went in Lancaster. And Moses and I started putting away tobacco. And it's most too wet to plow today.

4. Today Moses and I were plowing. This evening Aaron and Beckie went to Jacob Stoltzfus. And Father and Mother went to Grandmother overnight. She is sick. And it's cooler and pleasant weather.

5. *Today Beckie and I were at John Glick's. And Simon Zook's and Menno Stoltzfus's were here. This evening we were at home.*

6. *Today Moses and I were plowing. And Father and Aaron worked in the tobacco patch.*

7. *Today we were plowing. And we need rain again. If you come into the religious circle, come only with one notion. And mind your steps.*

8. *Today we were plowing oats stubble ground. And John Fisher's and Joe Beiler's were here. And it's little cold and pleasant weather.*

9. *Today we were plowing. And Father went over to Grandmother. She is sick. In the year of our Lord.*

10. *This forenoon I was plowing. And in the afternoon Aaron and I helped to thresh at Joe Hoover's. The wheat crop is doing good. And we bought two steers and a bull. The steers weighed 1220 lbs at $2.70 per hundred. The bull 690 lbs at $2.60. And it's fair weather.*

11. *This forenoon we made done threshing at Hoover's. This afternoon we put some tobacco away.*

12. *Today we were at the meeting at Jonathan Stoltzfus. And it rained the whole forenoon. And this evening they had a singing.*

13. *Today I helped to thresh at Levi Hoover's. They had Mr. Shreiner's traction rig. They charge 3 ¾ cts a bus. Wages for threshing are $1.00 a day.*

14. *Today Solomon Stoltzfus and Leah Glick and Susie Beiler were here quilting. We were cutting tobacco. And Eli Stoltzfus started hauling lime. And it's warm weather. One by one we pass away.*

15. *This forenoon they made done hauling lime. He got 990 bushels. At 7 ½ cts a bushel. 1894.*

16. Today Moses was harrowing. And we were putting away tobacco. This corn crop looks good.

17. Today Moses was harrowing. And it's cloudy weather.

18. Today is a cloudy day. And we put some tobacco away. Here on earth we cannot stay. This evening Aaron went away. And Christ came home. And it's a pleasant evening.

19. This forenoon we were at Simon Zooks. And this afternoon we went down to Uncle Christ Stoltzfus. And in the evening they had a singing. And we had a thunderstorm and a good rain.

20. This forenoon it rained. And this afternoon we mowed the meadow. And it's still cloudy weather.

21. Today we made done cutting tobacco. And Father and Aaron went to the horse sale at Ephrata. And it's not so warm and pleasant weather. Evil habits are gathered by unseen degrees, as brooks make rivers and rivers run to seas. He who hides the wrong he did. Does the wrong thing ever. Think twice before you speak once.

22. Today Moses was harrowing. And Father and Mother went to Grandmother. Aaron painted our buggy. I worked at the run.

23. Today we didn't work much of anything.

24. Today we were plowing. And we sold $3.21 worth of chickens to Isaac Hoover.

25. Today I was plowing. Father and Mother went to Grandmother. And it's warm weather.

26. Today the meeting was at Christian Stoltzfus. And this afternoon Aaron was at Jacob Stoltzfus. And we were at home.

27. Today Father and Mother, Grandmother and Nancy Stoltzfus went down to Uncle Elias Stoltzfus. And Beckie went to David Beiler's quilting. And Moses and I worked around the barns. Aaron ain't well he don't work anything.

28. Today Father made ready for threshing. And we started making out potatoes. The potato crop ain't so well. Plenty of them but too small. But that's better than not at all. We have smoky and unclear weather.

29. Today we started threshing. We have John and Simon Zook's engine. Life is real life is earnest. And the grave is not its goal. Dust thou art, to dust though returnest, was not spoken of the soul. Men are but children. But of a larger growth.

30. Today we made done threshing. We got five hundred and forty four bus. The wheat crop is pretty good. But wheat is worth .52 cts a bus. Example sheds a genial ray. Of light that men are apt to borrow. So first improve yourself today.. And then improve your friends tomorrow.

31. Today we were making out potatoes. And it's still smoky weather. I got my wealth by saving. I always worked my way. And I never cared a shaving. For "luck" in wages or in play.

Sept. 1. Today we were making out potatoes. And it's warm and smoky weather. Our mind is a hive in which to store. Which we will need when youth is o'er. Mind your steps.

2. Today was a warm day. And Father and Mother went to Barbara Zook. This eve Aaron and I were at Joe Hoover's. 1894.

3. Today we were making out potatoes. And Aaron went to Grandmother. The crop is middling. Father went over to Henry Fisher's for wheat winter five wheat. At .65 cts a bus.

4. Today we made done making out potatoes. And we took a load of straw to Grandmother. And we have very dry and smoky weather.

5. Today Isaac Hoover and I were quarrying stones. And grandmother was here. And it's warm weather. Father sowed some barley.

6. Today Isaac and I were quarrying stone. And Father made sixty gallons of cider.

7. Today Moses and I were hectoring apples, cider and potatoes. For cider we got .10 cts a gal.

8. This forenoon Aaron came home. He was over at Grandmother. And this evening we had the heaviest thunder rain that we had for a long time. And the corn is badly blown down. And tonight Father and Mother went to Grandmother. And Christ King's barn burned down.

9. Today we were at the meeting at Menno Stoltzfus. And it's very warm weather. Aaron went down to Christ overnight. This evening we had a heavy rain again.

10. This forenoon we were making fence. And we bought eight steers at $3.10 per hundred. They weight 7500 hundred. And we started cutting corn. And it's very wet weather.

11. Today Isaac Hoover and I were quarrying stones. And Father was making wire fence.

12. Today we were at the funeral for Mary Stoltzfus. She died from the Lockjaw. She was nineteen years, four months and twenty-seven days old. It's clear and pleasant weather. And Father and Mother were there over night. Mary Stoltzfus is here this week helping to sow.

13. Today we were cutting corn. Father was making fence. The corn crop is heavy and tangled.

14. Today we were cutting corn. And Aaron made some cider. Here on earth we cannot stay.

15. This forenoon we were hauling stones. And cutting corn in the afternoon. One by one we pass away. The time is swiftly passing by. And we must bid adieu. Think before you speak.

16. Today Aaron Glick and I were at the meeting house meeting. The folks were baptized. This afternoon e were at John's... This evening we were at Jacob Glick's awhile. And we had as heavy thunder rains. And John Zook's and Stephen Stoltzfus were here. Aaron went away too.

17. This forenoon Father went in Farmersville. And we have wet weather just now. This afternoon Moses and I were cutting corn. And so further.

18. This forenoon we were cutting corn. And Father took fourteen bus. of potatoes to J Hard at .50 cts a bus. This afternoon it rained again. Mind your steps.

19. Today it rained the whole day.

20. Today we were busy cutting corn. Aaron don't work much of anything. Warm weather.

21. Today we were cutting corn. But the corn is heavy and badly tangled.

22. This forenoon we were cutting corn. And this afternoon Beckie and I were at Isaac Stoltzfus. And it's clear weather.

23. Today the meeting was at Jonas Stoltzfus. The young folks were baptized. It was me and Aaron Glick, Noah Stoltzfus, Jacob Zook, Jonas Ebersol, Susie Zook, Fannie Glick, sisters Beckie and Fannie Stoltzfus, Katie Stoltzfus, Barbara Glick, Barbara Zook, Katie Petersheim, and Lydia Miller. It was a larger meeting. This afternoon Christ King and Jonas Fisher were here. It was a warm and pleasant day.

24. Today we were cutting corn. And Aaron made some cider. Moses was harrowing.

25. Today we were cutting corn. And we started sowing. And we bought three pigs from Isaac Myers at $4.25 a head. And it's colder and a great change in the weather.

26. Today Isaac and I were cutting corn. This morning we had a frost. Father and Moses were sowing. And it's cold weather. Aaron was picking apples. And so forth.

27-29 Today Isaac and I were husking corn. The corn is excellent. And we bought two steers from David Weaver. They weighted 1754 bls. At $3.10 per hundred. This afternoon Aaron went to a land sale near Heller's Station.

189

28 30 Last night I was with Christ at David Smoker's. This forenoon he went along home. And Jacob and Menno Esch were here.

28. Today we made done cutting corn. And husked some corn. Plenty corn to cut yet.

*** [The previous dates were crossed out and not in order. I have transcribed them as they appear.]

Oct. 1. Today Father was plowing corn stubble. And we hauled the fodder off. Stormy weather. Aaron fetched six bus. of sow wheat at D. Groff.

2. Today Father and Aaron were at the funeral for John Lapp. He was seventy-two years, nine months and twenty-three days old. We made done plowing corn stubble. And Aaron was at the sale at Lizzie Stoltzfus property. Amos C King born Sept 6, 1874. And I was bred and born and raised in West Earl Township, On the old stony farm. And stumbled over many a stone.

3. Today we made done sowing wheat.

4. Today Uncle Samuel King's were here. And Moses and I worked the corn … away and cleaned the wagon shed. And Aaron went to Ephrata with apples and potatoes. Apples are 20 cts a piece. Potatoes 45 cts a bus.

5. Today Moses and I were husking corn. And Aaron bought Lizzie Stoltzfus property for $900. And it's warm weather.

6. Last night Aaron was at Jacob Stoltzfus. Today Moses and I were husking corn. Father was hauling ground in the wagon.

7. Today we were at the orders meeting at Samuel Stoltzfus. Father and Mother were at Uncle Christ Stoltzfus for supper. 1894. And it was a very pleasant day.

8. Today Father and I were in Lancaster. Aaron took a load of potatoes to Ephrata at 45 cts a bu. This afternoon I picked some apples.

9. I was too lazy to write. And so I didn't write. Now you see how lazy I am.

27. *Today we were husking corn. And we have an excellent corn crop. This evening Aaron and I went away. Yes we did, too.*

28. *This forenoon we were at John Glick's. This afternoon the crowd was here. They were Aaron and Fannie Glick. Daniel and Susan Zook, Brother Christ, Mary and Barb Stoltzfus and Jacob Esch and Michael Smoker and Emma Fisher. This evening we were at the singing at Lydia Beiler's.*

29. *Today we made done husking corn.*

30. *This forenoon Aaron and I were hauling corn fodder. This afternoon it rained.*

31. *This forenoon it rained a part of the time. And this afternoon Father and Moses went in Farmersville. And I was splitting wood.*

Nov. 1. This afternoon we were hauling corn fodder. This afternoon Father went down to grandmother.

2. *Today we were hauling corn fodder.*

3. *This forenoon it rained. And this afternoon I was hauling wheat to Wenger's mill. At .54 cts a bushel. Yes, that's the way it goes in these days.*

4. *Today we were at the meeting at Jacob Beiler's. And Christ and Aaron were at Joshua Lapp. This evening we were at the singing at Jacob Stoltzfus.*

5. *Today it rained pretty near all day. And we worked at the corn husk. And so further. And Uncle John King's were here.*

6. *Today Aaron and I were filling lime.*

7. *Today Aaron and I fetched a load of posts down at Compassville. And Grandmother, Nancy Stoltzfus and Katie Stoltzfus were here.*

8. *Today it rained pretty near the whole day. And Aaron and I worked at the corn husk.*

9. Today we made done hauling corn fodder. This afternoon we were filling limekiln.

10. Today we were filling lime kiln. And this afternoon Christ came home. This evening Aaron Glick was here awhile. And it's pretty cold and stormy weather.

11. This forenoon Aunt Barbara and Christ Zook were here. This afternoon Christ, Aaron, Beckie and I were at Jacob Stoltzfus. This evening we went home. And it's cold weather.

12. Today Aaron was hauling coal to burn lime at H. M. Stauffer's Coal and Lumber yard. The cost is $2.75 a ton. Christ and Isaac Hoover were quarrying stones. And Father and I were making fence. This morning the ground was frozen hard this morning!

13. We have nice and pleasant weather. And we are busy working in the stones.

14. Today we hauled in a wheat stack. And the boys worked at the stones.

15. We are still working at the stones. And it's nice and pleasant weather and warm too.

16. Today was a very pleasant day. And we hauled in two stacks. And quarrying stones.

17. Today it rained pretty near the whole day. And this forenoon Beckie and I went in Conestoga. This afternoon Christ and Aaron came down too. It's unpleasant weather.

18. Today we were at the meeting at Jacob Kurtz. This afternoon we were at John Stoltzfus's. And this evening at the singing. And it's a nice day but it's little cold weather. And it's nice weather.

19. This forenoon we went home. And Stephen Stoltzfus started hauling lime. And I was hauling ground. And it's cold weather.

20. Today they made done hauling lime it gave 850 bus. And we were hauling ground.

192

21. Today it rained a part of the time. And I fetched a load of cinder ashes at Mill Way Oil works.

22. Today Christ and Aaron were filling limekiln. And I fetched a load of Cinder Ash at Mill Way.

23. Today it's damp weather. And we worked at the limekiln. No cold weather just now.

24. Today we made done filling lime kiln. And I fetched a ... of coal at Leacock Station. And Uncle Christ ... were here for supper. This evening I went away. Stormy weather.

25. Today Father and Mother went to John Zook's. And Christ and Aaron went to Jacob Stoltzfus. And it's cold and stormy weather. They were at the singing at Stephen Stoltzfus. 1894.

26. Today we were hauling dung. And it's cold.

27. Today we were hauling dung. And this afternoon Uncle Jonathan Kauffman and Uncle Jonathan King were here for supper. Christ went over to Grandmother. He got a sore hand. And it's pretty cold weather.

28. Today we made done hauling dung. And this afternoon Father went in Lancaster. And it's cold and stormy weather.

29. Today is a cold weather. So we said. And it is Thanksgiving day. And Christ and Aaron went to Uncle Christ Stoltzfus. If you come into the religious circle, come only with one notion. Honesty is a good Policy.

30. Today it rained a part of the time. And we butchered a hog. I was hauling wheat to Wenger's mill. At .54 cts a bu. Wonderful world.

Dec. 1. Today it rained a part of the time. And Christ and Beckie went in Lancaster. This forenoon I dunged the stables. And so forth.

2. Today we were at the meeting at Jacob Zooks. And this forenoon it rained. And this afternoon we were at Amos Stoltzfus place. And this evening we were driving around in the mud. And got nothing but dirty buggies and dirty clothing.

3. Today the boys and Isaac were quarrying stones. This afternoon Aaron took a load of lime on his property. And I worked so what I wanted. And it's a very pleasant and warm day.

4. Today David Smoker started hauling lime. And we hauled lime on Aaron's property. And hauled some coal. But the roads are muddy.

5. Today David Smoker and Eli Smoker were hauling lime. I worked on the woodpile.

6. Today they were hauling lime. And we were quarrying stones. And Father and John Zook went down to Christ King's.

7. Today they made done hauling lime. And we were filling limekilns. And the roads are terrible muddy. But it's warm and pleasant weather. In God we trust.

8. This forenoon we dunged the stables. And this afternoon it rained. And we worked in the shop. He who seeks me early shall find me. Love one another. 1894.

9. This forenoon Father and Christ were at the Dunker meeting. And Henry and John Stoltzfus and Isaac Walker were here. And this afternoon we were at Daniel Stoltzfus. And this ever awhile too. And the roads are muddy.

10. Today Christ and Aaron were filling lime kiln. And I took a load of corn to Wenger's mill. And Father went in Farmersville. Eggs are .24 cts a doz.

11. Today Isaac Glick and Malinda Stoltzfus married. And Esra ... and Rachel Petersheim married. And it's a rainy day. We sold a steer to Moses Butza for $3.50 per hundred. He Weighed 820 lbs. And a hog to Isaac Myers for $18.00. And we started stripping tobacco.

12. Today we were busy stripping tobacco. And it's damp and rainy weather. This evening Aaron went to John Zook. And we have muddy roads.

13. Today Christ and Aaron were filling limekiln. And we sold a steer to Mr. Butza for $3.70 per hundred. He weighed 880 lbs. This evening we were at Jacob Stoltzfus awhile. And muddy roads.

14. Today Christ and Aaron were filling limekiln. And Father went to the pump fixer. And I worked on the wood pile and what I wanted.

15. Today I dunged the stables. Christ and Aaron were filling limekiln. This afternoon I went to Wenger's mill. And it's very nice and pleasant weather. This eve Aaron went away.

16. Today we were at the meeting at Feronia Beiler's place. This afternoon Father and Mother went to Uncle Christ Stoltzfus. And to Grandmothers overnight. And we went home. And Ben Fisher and Jacob Esch were here. And this eve we had a large singing at Beiler's.

17. Today Uncle Elias Stoltzfus, Grandmother and Nancy Stoltzfus were here. Christ and Aaron went down to Aaron's property. And this is a warm and pleasant winter so far yet. We have our cows on the pasture. I worked at the wood.

18. Today Amos Floyd and Leah Umble married. And we butchered a bull. Aaron took a load of shingles to his property. At $4.50 per thousand.

19. Today I was stripping tobacco. And the rest were putting a new roof on Aaron's house. And it's a warm and pleasant day. 1894.

20. Today Godeon Beiler and Mollie Blank married. And I stripped tobacco. And they worked at Aaron's house. And we bought five steers from D. Weaver. They weighed 2910 pounds. At $2.90 per hundred. And it's a very warm and pleasant day.

21. Today we were stripping tobacco. And Aaron and Beckie went to Grandmother. And Christ and I fetched two loads of cinder at Mill Way. And it's nice and pleasant weather.

22. *This forenoon I dunged the stables. And Father and Christ were at the sale at Mechanicsburg. And Christ King, Katie Yoder, and Annie Kauffman were here overnight. And it's cloudy weather.*

23. *This forenoon we were at Aunt Barbara Zook's. And at John Zook's for supper. And it's nice and pleasant weather. This eve Christ went away.*

24. *Today we were stripping tobacco. And Aaron was in Lancaster. This evening Christ Rheil's were here. And it's nice and pleasant weather.*

25. *Today Daniel Lapp and Mary Stoltzfus married. And we were at the wedding. And it was an excellent wedding. Father and Mother and the boys were at Grandmother's. And it's pleasant weather.*

26. *Today we slept a part of the time. This afternoon Christ and I were at Jacob Stoltzfus. This evening it commenced to snow.*

27. *Today we were stripping tobacco. And it snowed on some account. And it's cold weather.*

28. *Today we were stripping tobacco. And it's dandy sleighing. The first snow we had this winter yet. And not much cold weather yet.*

29. *This forenoon I dunged the stables. And took a load of corn to Wenger's Mill. And it's excellent sleighing.*

30. *Today we were at the meeting at Daniel Stoltzfus. And it's pretty cold weather. This afternoon Aaron Glick and I were with Samuel Stoltzfus. And this evening we were in the singing at Stephen Stoltzfus. In Conestoga, Christ was at the singing at Christian Esch's. And it's pretty good sleighing yet.*

31. *Today I fetched a load of chopping. And the others worked in the shops. And it's cold weather. And it's dandy sleighing.*

New Year Jan.1. Benjamin Fisher and Katie Stoltzfus married. And Christ and Beckie went to Isaac Glick's

196

2. *Today Father and Mother, Moses and John, started for the wedding. And Esra and Mary Zook were here to keep house. And I didn't work much of anything. And it's cold weather.*

3. *Today brother Aaron and Lydia Fisher married. And we were all at the wedding. And it was an excellent wedding. And it's dandy sleighing.*

4. *This forenoon we went home. And Father and Mother, Moses and John went to Chester Co. And it's cold weather. And it's dandy sleighing. This evening Jacob Esch was here awhile. 1895.*

5. *This forenoon we dunged the stables. This afternoon I was in Brownstown. And this evening they came home from Chester County. And it's cold weather. And it's good sleighing.*

6. *Today we were all at home. And it rained the whole day. And we had twelve days sleighing so far. Great wide beautiful wonderful world.*

7. *Today we took some tobacco down. And it's damp and rainy weather. Christ was with Grandmother. And I took a load of corn to Wenger's Mill. Aaron brought the sleigh home. And fetched his buggy. And Samuel Glick and Malinda Mast married.*

8. *Today Father worked in the shop. And Christ and I took some tobacco down. And stripped some tobacco. And I fetched a load of chopping. And it rained and snowed the whole day. And the sleighing is fast.*

9. *Today Aaron came home. And it's wet and slushy weather. We were stripping tobacco.*

10. *Today Jonathan Beiler and Katie Fisher married. And Aaron's went visiting And we were stripping tobacco. The tobacco crop is excellent.*

11. *Today we were stripping tobacco. And Beckie helped to bake pies at Simon Zook's. Amos C. King.*

12. *Today I dunged the stables. And stripped tobacco. This evening Aaron's came home. And David Lapp's and Jacob Esch's, John Ebersol, Joel Keim, and Moses*

Erb from Holmes Co were here over night. And it's cold weather. Christ came into this world to save us poor sinners. Evil habits are gathered by unseen degrees. As brooks make rivers and rivers run to seas.

13. Today we were at the meeting at Simon Zook's. This afternoon I was with Aaron Glick. This evening we were at the singing at Henry Zook's. And it's cold weather. Honesty is the best policy.

14. Today Christ and I were stripping tobacco. And Aaron has the grip. And it's cold weather.

15. Today we butchered two hogs. This evening I went over to Menno Stoltzfus. To work there, he is sick.

16. Today it rained and snowed the whole day. And I dunged the stables for Menno Stoltzfus. This evening I went home. Honor your Father and Mother.

17. Today we were stripping tobacco. And we have still some snow. And not so cold weather. An ounce of prevention is worth more than a lb of cure. Wheat is worth .55 cts a bus.

18. Today I was stripping tobacco. And Christ and Aaron has the grip. And it's cloudy weather. And we sold some sausage at .09 cts. a lb.

19. Today I dunged the stables. And took a load of corn to Wenger's Mill. And it's nice and pleasant weather. Chopping costs .10 cts. ...

20. Today Joseph Beiler's were here. And I was at David Smoker's. And it's pleasant weather. This evening I was driving around. He who sows thistles cannot reap wheat.

21. Today Christ and I were stripping tobacco. And it's damp and rainy weather. And I fetched a load of chopping.

22. This forenoon we took our tobacco all down. And Lydia and Father were washing. And it cleared off and got pretty rough.

23. Today Aaron's were visiting at John and Simon Zook's. And Father and Mother went along. And Christ and I were stripping tobacco. This evening Aaron and Fannie Glick and Stephen and Emma Fisher were here.

24. This morning Aaron's came home. And this afternoon they went to Grandmother. And Father went in Farmersville. Christ was stripping tobacco. And I have the grip.

25. Today they were stripping tobacco. And it's clear but cold weather. Always do your best.

26. This forenoon they dunged the stables. This afternoon they stripped tobacco. And it's wet and damp weather. Wonderful world. This afternoon Uncle Christ Stoltzfus were here. And this evening Christ went away.

27. Today Christ was at the meeting at Christ Petersheim's. And the rest were at home. This afternoon Christ was at David Smoker's. Cold weather.

28. Today Christ fetched a load of chopping. And it's nice and pleasant weather. And they stripped some tobacco. I have the grip.

29. Last night fell a pretty decent snow. And Christ and I were stripping tobacco. And Father worked at Christ's sleigh. And it's pretty cold weather. He who sows thistles cannot expect to reap wheat. It's nothing about a little sin. But it won't stay little.

30. Today we made done stripping tobacco. And Father went to the carpet weavers at Akron. And it's cloudy and unpleasant weather. 1895.

31. Today Christ and I baled our tobacco. And Father went over to Grandmother. And it's about half sleighing. And it's cold weather.

Feb. 1. Today we took our tobacco in Farmersville. To S.M.Seldomridges. We had 1841 lbs. of wrappers, 270 lbs. seconds and 100 lbs fillers. Amount to $126 dollars. And it's cold weather. Christ was at the sale at Bareville.

2. Last night it snowed. And this forenoon, too. And Christ dunged the stables. I ain't well. This afternoon Father and Christ were at the sale at Brownstown. And it's dandy sleighing. Dare to be honest, just and true. Dare to do right. And you'll find your way through.

3. Today Joseph Blank and Mary Reno married. And Christ, Beckie and I were with Grandmother. And Father and Mother were at Joe and Levi Hoover's. This morning the mercury was 10 degrees below zero. And it's excellent sleighing. This evening Christ took a sleigh ride. 1895.

4. Today Christ and Father went in Lancaster. Christ got his teeth filled. And it's cold weather. We have plenty snow this winter and sleighing just now.

5. Today Father and Mother were at Grandmother and at Uncle Abram Stoltzfus for supper. And Christ took a bag of flour and a crock of lard and a crock pudding to Brownstown. They sent it out to the Kansas and Nebraska sufferers. And it's cold and stormy weather.

6. This forenoon Aaron's came home. And we don't work much of anything just now. This afternoon Christ was in Brownstown. This morning the mercury was 4 degrees below zero. This evening Aaron's went to Uncle Samuel King.

7. Today John Ebersol and Laura Miller married. And it snowed terrible the whole day. And Christ took a load of corn to Wenger's. We have cold weather. Eggs are 24 cts. a doz.

8. Today we didn't work much of anything. And we have a terrible snowstorm. It's not fit for dog to be out. The snow is pretty deep. We had snow from the 27th December and lots of it now. Just as the tree is planted it is apt to grow.

9. This forenoon Christ and I dunged the stables. This afternoon we went to Wenger's Mill. And it's terrible stormy weather. And the roads are bad drifted, more than they were for many years. The railroads and everything is blockaded.

10. Today the meeting was at John Miller's. But we didn't go. On account of the drifted roads. And it's still cold and stormy weather. A. C. King.

11. Today Christ and I opened some roads. And fetched a load of chopping at Wenger's Mill. Wheat is worth .54 cts. a bu. Horses are cheap.

12. This afternoon Christ and Beckie went in Farmersville. And I was sewing carpet rags. And we have sleighing right along just now.

13. This forenoon we didn't work anything. And this afternoon Christ and I went to Akron. And the roads are terrible drifted. And we have cold weather. And Samuel Beiler's wife was buried. She was thirty-eight years, ten months and twenty-six days old. And it's cold and stormy weather.

14. This forenoon I was at the mill. And Aunt Barbara and Christ Zook and John's Zook's were here. And Christ and I were at the sale at Jonathan Beiler's. And it's a warm and pleasant day. 1895.

15. This forenoon we opened roads. And Christ went to Grandmother. This afternoon we were at the sale at George Yost. And it's a pleasant day.

16. This forenoon we dunged the stables. This afternoon I was in Brownstown. And we have still sleighing. This evening Christ went away.

17. This forenoon Beckie and I were at John Glick's. And for supper at Henry Zook's. And we had some visitors. They were Jonas and Christ Stoltzfus and Katie Stoltzfus and Sallie Blank. And this evening we were at the singing at Moses Stoltzfus. And it's pleasant weather.

18. This forenoon I took a load of corn to Wenger's Mill. And this afternoon we were at the sale at Daniel Esch's. This evening Aaron came home. And it was a pleasant day. 1895.

19. Today we worked in the shop. And Christ was shoveling snow for Daniel Stoltzfus. And the sleighing is poor but plenty of snow at some places.

20. Today we worked in the shop. And this afternoon I took a load of corn to Wenger's. And Father and Aaron were at the sale at Brownstown. And we have muddy and slushy weather.

21. This forenoon Christ and Aaron went to Akron. And last night it snowed a little. This afternoon we were at the sale at John Nolt.

22. This morning Christ went to Grandmother's. And brought a load of coal along. And we worked in the shop. This afternoon we were at the sale at John Royer's. And it's cold weather.

23. This forenoon I dunged the stables. And Christ and Aaron went to the sale at John's … And they brought Lydia along up. And we have plenty of snow drifts yet.

24. Today we were at the meeting at John's Zook's. And this afternoon Aaron and Fannie Glick and Jacob Esch were Here. And this eve we were at the singing at John Zook's.

25. Today we were cutting wood. This afternoon we opened the lane. And I took a load of corn to Wenger's Mill. This evening Father and Mother went over to Grandmother. It's warm weather.

26. Today we worked at the wood. And this evening Aaron's went to John Glick's. And Father and Mother came home. And it's rough and stormy weather.

27. This forenoon we worked in the shop. This afternoon Father went in Farmersville. Christ went in Ephrata. And I was in Brownstown. And it's a warm and pleasant day.

28. This morning I took tow hogs to J. L. … They weighed 490 lbs at .05 cts a lb. $24.50. And I was opening the lane and the road. And last night it rained and the snow is going. Eggs are worth 23 cts a doz. Wheat 55 cts a bu.

March. 1. Today I fetched a load of coal. Christ was at the sale at Bareville. Fathers worked in the shop. This evening Jacob Esch and I were with Aaron Glick. And so on.

2. This forenoon we dunged the stables. And it rained and snowed. And it's terrible muddy.

202

3. This afternoon I went in Farmersville. And Beckie and I went in Lower Pequea at Gideon Fisher's And the roads are muddy.

3. Today we were at the meeting at Joel Fisher. This evening we were at the singing at Daniel Stoltzfus. And over night at Joshua Lapp's. And this afternoon we went home. And it's pleasant weather.

4. This forenoon we went home. This afternoon I took a load of corn to Wenger's. And Father went in Farmersville with eggs. They are worth .20 cts. And we sold nine steers to D. Weaver for $4.60 per hundred.

5. This forenoon we took our steers to Bareville. They averaged 1267 lbs. And this afternoon Christ and I were in Lan. And I bought a harness for $14.50. And it's cold weather. This evening Aaron came home. Muddy roads.

6. This forenoon we butchered a hog. And I was hauling wood. And Christ and I went in Brownstown. Father was in Farmersville.

7. Today we worked at the wood. And it's cloudy weather. This evening it rained. The black cow got a calf. Pigeons are .35 cts a pair.

8. Today we worked in the shops. And its' muddy and unpleasant weather. 1895. And Christ and I were in Brownstown

9. This forenoon it snowed. And we dunged the stables. This afternoon Aaron went to John Fisher's. And Christ and Beckie went to Grandmother. And the roads are terrible muddy. And Father and I worked in the shop. A. C. King.

10. Today we were at the meeting at Esther Ebersol. And it's a pleasant day. But muddy roads. This evening we were at home. 1895.

11. Today it snowed nearly the whole day. And this forenoon we worked in the shops. This afternoon Christ and I went to Farmersville. And it's unpleasant and wet weather. Eggs .14 cts.

12. Today we worked in the shop. And it's cloudy and damp weather. And the ground is covered with snow again. Avoid evil companions.

13. This forenoon Christ went to Brownstowns. And we worked in the shop. And this evening it rained. And this evening Aaron's came home.

14. This forenoon Aaron and I took a load of stuff to his home. And this afternoon we were at the sale at Mr. Stauffer. And it's a pleasant day. But we have terrible muddy roads.

15. Last night fell about three inches of snow. And today Beckie and I were at the funeral for Fannie Beiler's daughter of David Beiler. 1895. She was seven years, six months and three days old And it rained and snowed the whole day. Aaron was at the sale at Rothsville. And Father and Christ worked in the shop.

16. This forenoon it rained and snowed. And I took a load of corn to Wenger's Mill. And brought Aaron's furniture along from J. L. Muma. And Aaron took a load of corn fodder to his home. And Christ fetched 50 yds of carpet at Akron. From Mr. Getz carpet weavers. At 32 cts a yard. And it's cold and stormy weather.

17. This afternoon Aaron went to Grandmother. And the rest were all at home the whole day. And it's unpleasant cold and stormy weather.

18. This forenoon Aaron took a load of hay down. And this afternoon a load straw to his home. And Christ and I hauled some wood. And Father went to Lancaster he bought some mechanic tools for Aaron. The ground is nearly covered with snow yet. And we have terrible roads now.

19. This forenoon Christ helped to thresh at Joe Hoover's. And Aaron and Father went down to Aaron's home. This afternoon Christ was at the sale at Jacob Stoltzfus. And it's pleasant weather.

20. Today we were hauling goods to Aaron's home. And Father was in Farmersville. Eggs are 11. And it's unpleasant and cold weather this month.

21. Today Aaron's moved to Monterey. And it's a nice and pleasant day. And we were all there. 1895.

22. Today Father and Christ worked at Aaron's. And I was hauling wheat to Leacock at .54 cts a bu. And worked around the barn. And it's little cold.

23. This forenoon we were hauling dung. This afternoon we dunged the stables. And hauled a load of wheat to H. M. Stauffer. At 55 cts a bu. This evening I went away. And the roads are muddy.

24. Today we were at the meeting at Jacob Stoltzfus. And it's rainy and damp weather just now. And this evening we were at the singing at same place.

25. This forenoon we worked around the barn. This afternoon Christ and I threshed at Joe Hoover's.

26. Today we were hauling wheat to H. M. Stauffer's. At 55 cts a bu. And it's cold and stormy weather. And this evening Aaron's came home. A. C. King. And we had snow from the 27 Dec. and some yet.

27. Today I didn't work much of anything. Mother and I got the … Christ and Moses were hauling dung. This afternoon I went down to Aaron's. And it's cloudy and stormy weather. Let now your heart be troubled; ye believe in God. Believe also in me. If ye love me, keep my commandment. But that's the trouble with many people.

28. Today Andrew 1895 Petersheim was buried son of Christian Petersheim. He was seventeen years, three months and twenty-four days old. And Christ and I made ready for threshing. Moses was rolling the grass field. And it's unpleasant stormy weather. And Father was in Farmersville. Eggs are .10 cts.

29. Today we were threshing. We got one hundred and eighty three bu. Wheat. And we sawed some wood. And it's pleasant weather.

30. Today we were hauling dung. And Father and Christ Zook went down to Grandmother. And Father bought 8 pigs from Isaac Myers for $14.00. This evening Christ went away.

31. This afternoon Christ and I were at Daniel Lapp's and Jacob Stoltzfus were here. And it's very pleasant and clear weather. Thou shalt not steal.

April 1. Today Father went in Lancaster. And I sowed the clover seed. And started plowing. And Christ was spreading dung. And it's cloudy weather. And Spring is coming again.

2. Today I worked around the barn. And Christ and Henry Leipol were quarrying stone. We sold 5 bu. Potatoes to Mr. Leicy at .60 cts a bu. This evening it rained. And this is a late spring. We have some snow banks yet. 1895.

3. Today Father worked at Aaron's. And I was hauling dung this forenoon. Christ and Henry Leipold were quarrying stones. And it's cold and stormy weather.

4. Today Father worked at Aaron's again. This forenoon we were hauling dung. And last night pet got a colt. This afternoon I was plowing. 1895.

5. This forenoon Christ and I were hauling stones. And we sold a calf to Isaac Myers for $6.89 cts. This afternoon I was plowing. And Father and Moses were at the sale at Akron. And this evening Christ and Beckie went down to Aaron's.

6. Today Christ and I were plowing. And it's cloudy and stormy weather. Be kind to each other.

7. Today we were at the meeting at Isaac Stoltzfus. And this afternoon we were at Aaron's. A. C. King.

8. Today it rained nearly the whole day. And Father and Christ went in Lancaster. And Moses and I went to Farmersville. And it's stormy weather.

9. This forenoon I took a load of dung to Aaron's. And Christ went in Farmersville. And I was oiling harness. This evening Father Christ took a cow to Akron for $31. Mind your own business.

10. Today Father worked at Aaron's. And Christ hauled some wood to Grandmother. And I started plowing in the sod. And it's stormy weather. Do unto others as you would like to have done unto you.

11. Today Christ was making fence for Abram Stoltzfus. And this forenoon we were hauling logs to the sawmill. This afternoon I was plowing. This morning the ground was frozen.

12. Today was Good Friday. And this afternoon Father and Mother went to Barbara Zook. And Christ and I went to Brownstown. And it's cloudy weather.

13. Today it rained nearly the whole day. And we dunged the stables. And I fetched a load of chopping. This evening Christ went away. 1895.

14. Today is Easter. And we were at the meeting at Jacob Stoltzfus. And this evening they had a large singing. And we have a late spring.

15. This forenoon I was at Jacob Glick's. And this afternoon at Samuel Esch's. And overnight at Aaron's. And Christ was making wire fence. And it's rough weather. And we sold $10.00 worth of chickens to I Myers.

16. Today I was plowing. And Moses was harrowing. And it's cold and stormy weather.

17. Today we sowed our oats. And it's cold weather. This morning we had a frost. 1895.

18. Today we started planting potatoes. And it's a pleasant day. Evil habits are gathered by unseen degrees. As brooks make rivers and rivers run to seas. Here on earth we cannot stay.

19. This forenoon we made done planting potatoes. And Eli Stoltzfus started hauling lime. And I was plowing sod. This morning we had a frost.

20. Today Eli Stoltzfus made done hauling lime. He got eight hundred and forty three bus. And I was plowing. And it's pleasant weather.

21. Today we were at the order meeting at Moses Stoltzfus. And it's a very pleasant day. This evening we were at Simon Zook's. Dare to be Honest. 1895.

22. *Today we were plowing. And it rained a little. And Father and Mother went to Bareville. A. C. King. And Christ was making wire fence for Abram Stoltzfus.*

23. *Today we were hauling dung. And Father bought a cow from Christ Stoltzfus for $25. And it's clear and stormy weather. This morning we had a frost.*

24. *Today we made done hauling dung. And Father worked at Aaron's. And it's cloudy and warm weather.*

25. *Today Moses and I were plowing. And Christ was spreading dung. Father and Mother went in Farmersville. And it's warm and pleasant weather.*

26. *Today we were plowing. Christ made done spreading dung. And Father was trimming apple trees. And this afternoon it rained and so on.*

27. *Today it rained the whole day. And we didn't work much of anything. West Earl.*

28. *This forenoon Father and Mother went to Aaron's. And it's damp and rainy weather. This afternoon Christ and I were with Jacob Esch. And this eve we went away. 1895.*

29. *This forenoon I went to Wenger's Mill. And Christ went to Farmersville. And it's still rainy and cold and unpleasant weather.*

30. *This forenoon Christ was hauling wood for Grandmother. And we worked around the barn. And steers were as high as 6.25 per hundred.*

May. 1. Today Christ was splitting wood for Grandmother. And Father went to Aaron's. This evening I was plowing. And it's wet weather. Modes and John were white washing. In God we trust.

2. *Today Christ and I were plowing. And it's clear weather. Our mind is a hive in which to store. What we will need when youth is o'er.*

3. *Today Christ and I were plowing. And it's clear and very warm weather.*

4. Today Christ plowed the tobacco patch. And I was plowing too. And it's very warm weather.

5. Today we were at the meeting at Christ Miller's. And it's a clear and pleasant day.1895.

6. Today we started planting corn. And Lydia worked here today. And it's clear and warm weather.

7. Today we were harrowing. And this evening we planted some corn. And we had a thunder rain. The time is swiftly passing by. And must bid adieu.

8. This forenoon Moses and I were whitewashing. And Christ helped to thresh at Joe Hoover's. This afternoon we planted corn. And last night it rained. And it's very warm weather.

9. This forenoon we were whitewashing. And thing afternoon we were planting corn. Always do your best.

10. Today we made done planting corn. And Father worked at Aaron's. And I took a load of hay to H. K. Duck. At $12 dollars a ton. 1895.

11. This forenoon we dunged the stables. And Christ was planting corn for Levi Hoover. And Father fetched a load of posts at Leacock at .22 cts.

12. Today we were at Isaac Stoltzfus for dinner. And at David Smoker's for supper. And this evening at Aaron's. And it's cold and wet weather.

13. Today we were hauling ground in the lawn. And it's cold and stormy weather. A. C. King.

14. This forenoon it rained. And it's cold and unpleasant weather. Christ hauled a cord of wood for Mr. Lund. And all the time busy.

15. Today Christ was making post fence. And Father and I worked at the lawn. And it's wet and unpleasant weather. 1895.

16. Today Christ and I were making post fence. And this morning we had a frost.

17. This morning we had a frost again. And I fetched Lydia. And the women's baked the pies for the meeting. And we worked around the barn. This evening I fetched my new buggy. From Mr. Dillman for $50.00.

18. Today we cleaned the stables. And Christ was shoveling potatoes. And we have cloudy weather. Father was at the wood sale at cedar hill.

19. Today the meeting was at our place. And it's still damp and cold weather. This evening we had a singing. We had a good time.

20. Today Father went down to Grandmother. And Christ made some fence. And this evening we planted some tobacco. And it's cold weather.

21. Today Father, Christ and John went down to Aaron's. And it rained nearly the whole day. This evening I fetched a load of chopping.

22. Today they worked at Aaron's. And Moses and I were cutting down locust trees. A. C. King.

23. Today I was with Benuel Stoltzfus. And Christ went away to. And David Blank's and Aunt Barbara and Christ Zook were here. And it's a very pleasant day. Honesty is the best policy.

24. Today Father, Christ and Moses worked at Aaron's. And I made the tobacco land ready. And we have cold nights so far yet. Christ came in this world to save us poor sinners.

25. Today Father worked at Aaron's. And we were planting tobacco. This evening Christ and I went away. And it rained a little. In God we trust.

26. Today Father and Mother were visiting. This afternoon Christ went to Henry Zook's. And Beckie was at John Zook's. And I was at home the whole day. And it's damp and rainy the whole day. 1895.

27. Today Father worked at Aaron's. And we planted a lot tobacco. And it rained a part of the time.

28. Today we planted some tobacco. And it's cloudy weather. This evening Beckie and I went down to Aaron's. Father fetched a load of posts at H. M. Stauffer at 22 cts a piece. Lanc. Co.

29. Today I started shoveling corn. And Christ was shoveling potatoes. And it's warm weather.

30. Today we were digging in posts for a wire fence. This forenoon I was in Brownstown. And it's powerful warm weather. 90 degrees.

31. This forenoon we took a steer to Bareville. He weighed 1205 lbs. at $5.00 per hundred. And Father worked at Aaron's. And Christ and I made some fence. This evening we planted some tobacco. And it's remarkable warm weather. And the red cow got a calf. Wheat is .80 cts a bu.

June. 1. This forenoon we were digging in posts. This afternoon Father and Christ went in Lanc. And I went to Farmersville. The thermometer reached 104 degrees. And we sold our mare pet to Samuel Wenger for $60 dollars. This evening we planted some tobacco.

2. Today we were at the meeting at John Beiler's in Middle Pequea. And at Uncle Elias Stoltzfus for supper. And at the singing at Daniel Lapp's. And it's a powerful warm day. 1895.

3. This forenoon we were at Jacob Glick's. And this afternoon we went home. This evening we made done planting tobacco. And it's warm weather.

4. Today we were planting tobacco for Aaron. And it's cloudy and warm weather.

5. Today I was shoveling corn. And Christ was shoveling tobacco. And this evening we had a nice rain. And Aaron's mare got a colt.

6. This forenoon we planted some tobacco over. This afternoon I was shoveling corn. And Christ was hoeing tobacco. And it's colder weather again. It's nothing about a little sin. But it won't stay little. The time is swiftly passing by. 1895.

7. Today I was shoveling corn. And Christ was hoeing tobacco. And Father fetched a hay load from Rebman and Son for $47. And it's pleasant weather.

8. Today I was shoveling corn and potatoes. This afternoon John Zook's were here. And this evening Aaron's and Lephenia Fisher were here. And we had ice cream. And we have pleasant weather.

9. This forenoon Father and Christ went to the Mennonite meeting. And this afternoon Christ and I were with John Beiler. And Father and Mother went down to Grandmother. And this evening Beckie and I were at the singing at Jonas Lantz. 1895.

10. Today we were shoveling and hoeing. And Father and Mother came home. And it's cloudy and warm weather. Always do your best and you will soon do better.

11. Today Christ and I were quarrying stones. This forenoon Father and Mother were at Aaron's. And Amos Lapp's and Eli Stoltzfus were here. A. C. King.

12. Today Father worked at Aaron's. And Christ went with Jacob Stoltzfus to Black Horse. And I hauled 103 bus. wheat to Wenger's Mill at .80 cts a bus. And I took a load of hay to Isaac Myer's at $9 dollars a ton. And it's warm and cloudy weather.

13. Today I was shoveling corn. And Christ was shoveling potatoes. And it's pretty dry weather.

14. Today I was shoveling corn. And Christ was making fence. And we bought a cow from Isaac Myers for $30 dollars. And it's cloudy weather.

15. Today I was shoveling corn. And Father and Mother went to Grandmother over night. And Christ went away too. And we have warm weather.

212

16. Today we were at the meeting at Amos Stoltzfus. This afternoon we were at home. And it's a pleasant day. This evening we were at the singing at Amos's. These are by gone days.

17. This evening Father and Mother came home. And Christ and I worked at the corn. This evening Aaron's were here. It's dry weather.

18. Today I was hauling hay to Brownstown at $6 dollars a load. Christ scraped corn and potatoes. And it's dry and warm weather. 1895.

19. Today I was shoveling corn. And we sold our steers to Moses Butza for $4.50 per hundred. He took one today. He weighed 970 lbs.

20. Today we started making hay. This forenoon I was shoveling corn. And it's dry and warm weather.

21. Today we were busy hauling hay. And it's dry and good hay weather. Mind your steps.

22. Today we made done scraping corn. And it's damp weather. This evening we fetched a load of hay. This evening Jacob and Katie King came overnight.

23. This forenoon we were at Simon Zook's. And this afternoon at John Zook. And this evening we were at Aaron's. And it's a clear and warm day. In God we trust.

24. Today we were making hay. And we have wonderful warm and dry weather.

25. Today we were busy making hay. And it's excellent hay weather. And this morning I took a load of hay to Hiram Duck for $8.

26. Today we made done making hay. And we have an excellent hay crop again. And we have dry and warm weather. Wheat is .75 cts. 27. This morning I took a load hay to Aaron's. And Christ was shoveling tobacco. And we took two steers to Moses Butza at 4.50. And they weighed 1750 lbs. This evening we had a heavy thunder rain. 1895.

28. This forenoon we were thivering corn. And this afternoon we were shoveling corn. And we sold two calves to Isaac Myers for $14 dollars.

29. Today we started bindering. And Christ was making wire fence. And we have wet weather.

30. Today we were at the meeting at Stephen Stoltzfus's. And it rained this forenoon. This afternoon Joel Fisher's., Aaron's and Christ and Aunt Barbara Zook were here. And Aaron Glick. This evening we were at the singing at same place.

July. 1. This evening we were bindering. And Christ and I were shocking. And the ground is wet.

2. Today we were busy bindering. And it's not so warm weather. And it's cloudy weather.

3. Today we made done bindering and shocking wheat.

4. Today we started hauling in wheat. And we took tow steers to Moses Butza for $4.50 a hundred. They weighted 1930 lbs.

5. Last night it rained nearly the whole night. And this forenoon, too. This afternoon Father and Mother went to John Zook's. And Bekie, Moses and I went for cherries at Jacob Stoltzfus. And we have wet weather now.

6. Today we were...corn. And Father was raking. Christ was weeding potatoes. And Beckie and Mary Zook went to Aaron's. This evening I went away. And it's cloudy and damp weather.

7. Today we were all at home. And Joseph Hoover's were here. And it's a very warm day. This evening Christ and Beckie went to Daniel Stoltzfus. 1895.

8. This forenoon we were shoveling tobacco. And this afternoon we were hauling wheat. But we have plenty damp and wet weather just now.

9. Today we were busy hauling wheat.

214

10. Today we made done harvesting. And Moses and John were picking black cherries. Dare to be honest.

11. Today we were shoveling and hoeing tobacco. And this afternoon Father and Mother, Grandmother and Nancy Stoltzfus went to Aaron's. And it's cloudy and damp weather. This evening Christ went in Farmersville.

12. Today Christ and I were shoveling corn. Always do your best and you will soon do better.

13. Today Father and mother, Grandmother and Nancy Stoltzfus went to Katie Stoltzfus. And we made done shoveling corn. This afternoon Beckie and I went in Farmersville. This evening we had ice cream. And we have smoky weather now.

14. Today we were at the meeting at John Glick's. This afternoon we went over to Uncle Christ King's. And this evening at the singing at John Glick.

15. Today we were hauling dung. And it's cloudy and not so warm weather just now.

16. Today Christ, John and Christ Zook and I went down to Christ Fisher's. And Father and Mother went in to Conestoga. Whatever you do, think at the hour you have to die.

17. Today Father and Mother were visiting in Conestoga. And we worked a little of anything. And it's smoky and dry weather just now.

18. Today we worked around the barn. And this evening Father and Mother came home.

19. Today we started plowing. But the ground is pretty hard. And we have warm weather.

20. This forenoon I was plowing. And this afternoon Father and Mother went to Pequea. The thermometer reached 100 degrees. This evening we had a thunder rain. And Christ went away.

21. Today Father and Mother were at the meeting at Uncle Christ King's. And Christ and I went away too. This evening we were at the singing at Joshua Lapp's. And we have warm weather.

22. Today I was plowing. And the rest worked what they wanted. And it's very warm weather.

23. Today I was plowing. And Christ was reaping oats. And we have plenty cloudy weather.

24. Today we made done reaping oats. And John Neuhauser's, Grandmother and Nancy Stoltzfus were here. And I was plowing. Whatever you do, Think at the hour you have to die. 1895.

25. Today I was plowing. And we turned the oats. No matter which way you turn, you always find in the book of life. Some lessons you have to learn. Wheat is worth .55 cts a bu. just now.

26. Today I was plowing. And this afternoon we took some oats in. And it's warm weather.

27. Today we threshed our oats. We got two hundred and forty bus. And we bought five springers for $61 dollars. This evening we had a thunder rain. And Christ and I went away.

28. Today we were at meetings at David Beiler's. And this afternoon Jacob Esch, Joshua Lapp and David Beiler were here. And we were at the camp meeting.

29. Today we made done plowing in the wheat stubble. And we hauled some dung. And we sold Aaron's mare to Wayne Kulp for $75 dollars. What good examples do I find. Written in the book of truth. Of children that begin to mind, Religion in their youth. Amos C. King br Sept "6" 1874.

30. Today we made done hauling dung. And Father and Beckie were in Lanc. And we have pretty dry and cloudy weather. Days of the past.

31. Today we made done spreading dung. And worked the tobacco. And it's little cold weather.

Aug. 1. Today I was plowing. And Christ was quarrying stones. And Father and John were at the horse sale at Vogansville. Still cold weather.

2. Today Christ and I helped to thresh at Jacob Pfantz. And Father went down to Aaron. And it's getting pretty dry again. If you come into the religious circle. Come only with one notion. Great, Wide beautiful wonderful world.

3. This forenoon I was plowing. And this afternoon we worked in the tobacco. And Father and Mother went to Aunt Barbara Zook. And it's dry weather.

4. This forenoon Simon Zook's and Barbara and Christ Zook were here. And this afternoon we were at Aaron's. This evening we had a nice rain. And we were all at home. Here on earth we cannot stay.

5. Today I was plowing. And Christ was quarrying stones. And we have warm weather.

6. Today I was plowing. And Uncle Christ King, Aunt Susie Petersheim and Christ and Barbara Zook and Lydia were here. Christ was quarrying stones. And it's warm weather. 1895.

7. Today Father and John worked at Aaron's. And Christ and I were quarrying stones. A. C. King.

8. Today we started cutting tobacco. This evening Father went in Farmersville. And we have warm and dry weather. The tobacco crop is middling.

9. Today we were putting away tobacco. One by one we pass away. Here on earth we cannot stay.

10. This forenoon I fetched a load of coal at H. M. Stauffer for $4 dollars a ton. And this afternoon Father and Mother went to Amos Stoltzfus. And this evening Beckie and I went to Conestoga. And it's wonderful hot weather. 1895.

11. Last night we were at Christ Rheil's. This forenoon in the meeting. And at Uncle Aaron's for dinner. And at Jonas Stoltzfus for supper. This evening at the singing at John Stoltzfus. And tonight Jonas Stoltzfus barn burned down. It was struck by lightning. We had a heavy thunder rain. And tonight we were at David Yoder's. And Daniel Stoltzfus were here over night. 1895.

12. This forenoon we went home. And Father and Mother went with Uncle Dan's down to John Stoltzfus. And we worked a little what we wanted. A. C. King

13. This forenoon I and Christ were quarrying stones. This afternoon we worked at the tobacco. And we have very warm weather this month.

14. This forenoon I was plowing. And Grandmother and Nancy Stoltzfus were here. And Christ helped to Thresh at Daniel Stoltzfus. This afternoon we started harrowing. And I was suckering tobacco. And it's very warm weather.

15. Today Christ helped to thresh at Daniel Stoltzfus. And this forenoon I was plowing. This afternoon we were putting away tobacco. And this evening we had a thunder rain. 1895.

16. Today Christ and I helped to thresh at Abram Rupp. And we sold a calf to Isaac Myers for $8.25. And it's remarkable hot weather now. And the tobacco crop is nearly extra.

17. Today Christ and I were putting away tobacco. And this afternoon Father and John were at the cow sale at Bareville. And he bought two cows one for $42 and the other $34 dollars. And Aaron's were here overnight. This evening I went away. And it's still warm weather.

18. This afternoon Christ and I went to Joe Hoover's. And it's a great change in the weather. And this evening we were at home. In God we trust.

19. Today we were suckering tobacco. And Father bought a little pig from Moses Stoltzfus for $3 dollars. And it's not so warm weather.

20. Today Christ, Moses and I helped putting away tobacco at Aaron's. And Father worked a little, too. And it's pleasant and not so warm.

21. Today Aaron's were here. And Aaron's helped putting away tobacco. This afternoon Father was at the wood sale at Abram Bupp's woods. One by one we pass away. Here on earth we cannot stay.

22. Today Father went down to Grandmother's. And we were putting away tobacco. The old cow got away.

23. This forenoon we started making out potatoes. And this afternoon Christ and I helped to thresh at Joe Hoover's. And Father was at the horse sale at Weidler's Hotel. And we have warm weather.

24. This forenoon we threshed at Joe Hoover's. And this afternoon we were putting away tobacco. And this evening Christ went away. And we have so pretty dry weather now. And warm too.

25. Today we were at the meeting at David Smoker's. And this afternoon we were at Jona Lantz. And this evening we were at the singing at Amos Stoltzfus. And it was a warm and pleasant day.

26. Today Christ and I helped to thresh at Levi Hoover's. And the wheat cop ain't so good. And on the "24" we bought 8 steers from David Weaver for $2.90 cts per hundred. They averaged 560 lbs. And we have warm and dry weather.

27. Today we had a good rain. And Christ made 32 gallons of cider. And the cider and apples are plenty. Well indeed everything is plenty.

28. Today we were putting away tobacco. And it's a warm day. This evening Christ, Beckie and I went to Aaron's help to peal pears.

29. Today we were putting away tobacco. And this evening we had a shower. Days of the past.

30. This forenoon we were making out potatoes. And this afternoon we were putting away tobacco.

31. Today we were making out potatoes. And this afternoon Aaron bought a horse for $75 dollars. And we have still warm and close weather.

Sept. 1. This forenoon Beckie and I were at John's Glick's. And Christ was at David Smoker's. This afternoon we were at Noah Smoker's. And this evening we were at the singing at Benuel Fisher's. And it's a pleasant day and cool air going.

2. This forenoon we were making out potatoes. In the afternoon worked at the tobacco. And this evening Christ and I went down to Aaron's.

3. Today Christ and I helped to thresh at Jacob Stoltzfus. And it's a cool and pleasant day.

4. Today we made done threshing. And Grandmother and Nancy Stoltzfus were here. A. C. King.

5. Today we made done making out potatoes. And the crop is pretty fair. And Father and Mother went down to Grandmother. And we bought some peaches at .75 cts a bushel.

6. Today we made done putting away tobacco. And I was plowing the tobacco patch. And Christ was hauling coal from H. M. Stauffer. This evening it commenced to rain. Lancaster Co.

7. Today it rained a part of the time. And I was plowing. Christ was at Aaron's. This evening I went away. And it's damp weather.

8. Today they were all at the meeting at Abram Stoltzfus. And I was at home. This afternoon Father and Mother were at Aaron's. And we had some visitors. They were Jacob and Katie King, David, Sarah and Mary Beiler, Jonas and Susan Beiler, Jacob and Fannie Fisher, Aaron Glick, Ary Peachy, Katie Stoltzfus and Annie Beiler. And this evening we were at the singing at Abram Stoltzfus. And Christ Stoltzfus died. And it was a warm day.

9. Today Christ and I helped to thresh at Menno Stoltzfus. And Moses was plowing the potato patch. And we have still warm weather.

10. Today we made done threshing at Menno Stoltzfus. And Father and Mother and Beckie were at funeral for Christian Stoltzfus. He was thirty-one years, four months and Six days old. And Moses was plowing. And it's very warm.

11. This forenoon Christ and I were hauling stones. And this afternoon we worked at Aaron's. 1895.

12. This forenoon we were quarrying stones. And this afternoon we cut down a tree. And Father went in Farmersville. And Christ made 47 gallons of cider. And Moses was harrowing. And so on.

13. This forenoon we started cutting corn. And this afternoon Christ and I helped to thresh at John Zook's. And it's cold and stormy weather.

14. Today we made done threshing at Zook's. This evening Father went to Brownstown. And it's cold weather.

15. This morning we had a heavy frost. And Christ and I went to the Lower Millcreek meeting at Jacob Beiler's. The young folks were baptized. This afternoon we were with Abram Beiler. And this evening at Jacob Stoltzfus. And Christ and Barbara Zook were here.

16. Today we were busy cutting corn. And it's cloudy and warm weather. This evening it rained. A little thinker is always a big talker.

17. Today we were busy cutting corn. And it's warm weather. This evening Christ and Beckie went to Aaron's. Wheat is worth .58 cts a bus.

18. Today it rained a part of the time. And we were picking apples. And this evening we cut some corn. And we have warm weather.

19. Today we were busy cutting corn. And we sold a calf to Moses Butza for $7.76. They are worth $5.75 cts. a hundred. And we cooked apple butter.

20. Today we were threshing. WE got three hundred and thirty eight bushels. And it was a very warm day. Wages are $1.00 a day.

21. Today we were cutting corn a part of the time. The thermometer reached 98 degrees. This evening Christ went away.

22. Today Beckie and I were in the Middle Pequea meeting at Jacob Glick's. The young folks were baptized. And Daniel Peachey was their preacher from Illinois. This evening we went home. We had a warm Sept. so far.

23. This forenoon we were hunting cattle. And this afternoon cutting corn. And it's warm weather.

24. Today we were busy cutting corn. And Moses and John were harrowing. And we sold some chickens to Myers at .10 cts a lb. This evening I made some cider. And Christ went in Farmersville.

25. Today we started sowing wheat. And we sold ten bushels of Lebanon Valley wheat to Milton Royer at .62 cts a bu. And Christ and I were cutting corn.

26. This forenoon we were cutting corn. This afternoon I was sowing. And Christ made fence for Abram Stoltzfus. This is the land which God hath given us for our dwelling place.

27. Today we made done cutting corn. And it's dry and stormy weather. Christ was picking apples. Here on earth we cannot stay. One by one we pass away.

28. Today Christ and I went in Lancaster. And it's nearly cold weather. This evening I was at Aaron's. These are days of the feast.

29. Today Daniel and Susan Zook were here. And Father and Mother went away. This evening it commenced to rain. Evil habits are gathered by unseen degrees. As brooks make rivers. And rivers run to seas.

30. Today we started husking corn. And I was sowing wheat. And it's rough and stormy weather. This evening Christ and I went to the husking at John Beiler's. Dust thou art. To dust returnest.

Oct. 1. This morning we had a heavy frost. And I was picking apples. And Christ was husking corn. Moses was hauling wheat to Wenger's Mill at .65 cts a bus. Beckie was with Grandmother.

2. Today we were busy husking corn. And this morning we had a frost. We have dry weather.

3. Today we were at the order meeting at Jonas Stoltzfus. And it was a clear and pleasant day. This evening Father went to Grandmother's overnight. And Christ and I went to Jacob Stoltzfus.

4. Today we were busy husking corn. And Father made 48 gallons of cider. The corn crop is excellent.

5. Today we were husking corn. And we have very dry weather. This evening Christ went away. And we got our steers dehorned. In God we trust.

6. This forenoon we were at home. And this afternoon Christ, Beckie and I were at Ben Beiler's. And it's a warm and pleasant day. And this evening they had a large singing. And Uncle Abram Stoltzfus's were here for supper.

7. Today we were busy husking corn. A. C. King

8. This forenoon it rained a little. And we were shelling corn. And this afternoon we were husking corn. And we have dry weather.

9. Today we were busy husking corn. A good name is rather to be chosen than great riches.

10. Today we were husking corn. And it's dry and stormy weather. O what joy! O what bliss! When we can meet where Jesus is. Sorrow and death shall be no more. When we have reached that heavenly shore. Never forget that God is ruling.

11. Today we were at the funeral for John Beiler's wife. She was eighty-two years, two months and four days old. And we bought six steers from David Weaver. At $2.90 cts a hundred. They averaged 5 hundred and some. And it's dry and stormy weather. 1895.

12. Today Christ and I went in Lancaster with potatoes. At 25 cts a bu. And it rained the whole forenoon. And Christ bought a goat…And this afternoon Father and Mother went to Aaron's. And this evening they went to Grandmother's. This evening we had some visitors. Dare to be honest.

13. Last night it rained a part of the time. And this whole forenoon. This afternoon Christ and Beckie went to Daniel Lapp's. And this evening Aaron's came overnight. And I was at home the whole day.

14. Today we were busy husking corn.

15. Today we were husking corn. And Father was in Farmersville and in Snaderville. And it's damp and cloudy weather. Always do your best. And you will soon do better. Honor Father and Mother.

16. This morning we had a heavy frost. And we were busy husking corn. And Father took a load of corn cobs to Hiram Duck at .03 cts a bus.

17. Today we were husking corn. And it's stormy weather. This afternoon Christ worked at Grandmother's. This evening Christ went to the husking at John Stoltzfus.

18. Today we were husking corn. And we had cold and rough weather this month yet.

19. Today we were husking corn. And this afternoon Father and Beckie went to the Auction at Brownstown. This evening Christ went away.

20. Today we were at the meeting at Christian Stoltzfus. We had a large meeting. It was a cold day.

21. Today we were busy husking corn. And the corn cop is excellent. And we have cold weather.

22. Today we were husking corn. And Father and Beckie went in Lancaster. Beckie got a set of teeth for $10 dollars. And we have dry weather.

23. Today we were husking corn.

24. Today we were husking corn. Days of the past

25. Today we made done husking corn. And we have an excellent crop. And it's rough and cold weather. And potatoes are worth .25 cts a bu.

26. Today we worked the potatoes in the cellar. And dunged the stables. This afternoon Father and John were at the Auction at Brownstown. And this evening Christ and I went away.

27. Today Father and Mother were at Joe Beiler's and at Grandmother's. And Uncle Christ Stoltzfus and Grandmother were here. And we were at home the whole day. And this evening we were at the singing at Daniel Beiler's.

28. This forenoon we worked AT the potatoes. And this afternoon at the wood. And so forth.

29. Today Father, mother, Grandmother and Nancy Stoltzfus were visiting in the Mill Creek. And Christ was hauling coal. And we worked a little of anything. And it's cold weather.

30. Today Christ worked at Grandmother's. And Moses and I worked at the wood. And Father and Mother went to Farmersville and to Snaderville. And we had cold weather the whole month.

31. This forenoon Christ and I were filling lime kiln. And this afternoon it rained. 1895.

Nov. 1. Today we hauled some corn fodder.

2. Today we dunged the stables. And Christ went in Lancaster. And this afternoon it snowed the whole afternoon. This evening I was at the Auctions.

3. Today was a clear and pleasant day. And we were at he meeting at Eli Stoltzfus. And three strange preachers were here. They were David Miller and two that I can't name. This afternoon David and Fannie Glick were here. And this evening at the singing at Eli's.

4. This forenoon we hauled some corn fodder. And this afternoon we butchered a hog. And it's a warm and pleasant day. Honor your Father and Mother that thou livest long in the promised land.

5. Today Christ and I were hauling corn fodder. This afternoon Father went in Brownstown. And it's damp and warm weather just now.

6. Today we made done hauling corn fodder. Thou shalt not take the name of God thy Lord in vain. This evening Christ was in Farmersville.

7. Today Christ and I helped to Thresh at Simon Zook's. Thou shalt not go up and down as a talebearer among the people. Blessed are the poor in spirit. For theirs is the kingdom of heaven. And where your treasure is there your heart will be also. A false witness shall perish.

8. This forenoon we were filling limekiln. And this afternoon it rained. And we put some tobacco down. This evening Beckie and I were at Aaron's.

9. This forenoon Christ and I were filling limekiln. And this afternoon Christ and Beckie went away. And it was a damp and wet week.

10. This forenoon it rained. And this afternoon Beckie and I went away. And this evening we were at the singing at Samuel Esch's. Don't matter which way you turn, you always find the book of Life, Some lessons you have learn. The time is swiftly passing by.

11. Today we were filling lime kiln. Aaron is helping us. And Uncle John King's and Christ and Barbara Zook were here. And it's cloudy weather.

12. Today we made done filing limekiln. And this evening Christ and I went in Farmersville.

13. Today we were hauling in wheat stacks. And it's cold weather. Butter is worth .25 cts a lb. Here on earth we cannot stay. Pigeons are .30 cts.

226

14. Today Aaron's were here. And it rained nearly the whole day. And we worked at the corn husk. What good examples do I find, written in the book of truth., of children that begin to mind religion in their youth. This evening Christ went away.

15. Today we started stripping tobacco. And we have plenty damp and wet weather. And Father went in Farmersville. Think at the hour you have to die.

16. This afternoon Father and Mother went to Aaron Nolt's. And I took a load of corn fodder to Aaron's. And it's a warm and pleasant day. And this evening Christ and I went away.1895.

17. Today we were at the meeting at Jacob Beiler's. And this afternoon mother, Beckie and John went to Grandmother. This evening we were at home. Christ came into this world to save sinners from sin.

18. This forenoon Christ and I were cutting wood. And this afternoon I hauled a log to Pinetown. And we have warm and pleasant weather. A good name is rather to be chosen than great riches.

19. This forenoon I was in Brownstown. And Father and Mother were at the funeral for John Beiler's child. It was five years, four months and fifteen days old. And Stephen Stoltzfus started hauling lime. This evening we were at Aaron's. A little thinker is always a big talker.

20. Today it rained a part of the time. And Aaron was here. And we were stripping tobacco. Dare to be honest, just and true.

21. Today they made done hauling lime. And it's cold and stormy weather. And we sold a hog to Moses Butza at .05 cts a lb. He weighed …Always do right, and you'll find your way through.

22. Today I hauled a log to Pinetown. And it's a pleasant day. Example sheds a genial ray, of light that men are apt to follow. So first improve yourself today, and then improve your friends tomorrow. Every generation is getting weaker and wiser.

23. Today we hauled a wheat stack in. And we dunged the stables. This forenoon Christ was in Brownstown.

24. This forenoon Simon Zook's were here. And this afternoon I was with Aaron Glick. And it's damp and rainy the whole day. And this evening I was at the singing at John Algyer's. 1895.

25. Today it rained nearly the whole day. And Aaron's were here. Mother has the ...

26. Today Aaron and I were in Lancaster with apples. And it's damp and rainy the whole day. And Christ came home. Do as you would like to have done to you.

27. Today Christ and I were stripping tobacco. And we have nice and pleasant weather. This is the land which God hath given us for our dwelling place. And this is a wonderful world. And the sun shines over wicked people as well as over good people. And the good are always happy.

28. Today is Thanksgiving day. And Aunt Barbara and Christ Zook were here. And I was with Jacob Esch. And it's a pleasant day. 1895. Thou shalt not commit adultery. Thou shalt not steal.

29. Today we were hauling dung. Aaron helped. Christ went away. And it's a pleasant day.

30. This forenoon we were hauling dung. This afternoon we dunged the stables. We have pleasant weather.

Dec. 1. Today we were at the meeting at Jonas Stoltzfus. And this afternoon I was with Ben Esch. And this evening at the singing at Aaron's. And we have cloudy and rainy weather. 1895.

2. Today I worked around the barns. And made ready for the wedding. And it rained nearly the whole day. And this evening Beckie, Moses, John and I went to Uncle Elias Stoltzfus overnight.

3. Today brother Christian and Mollie Lapp married. And we were at the wedding. And it was a cold and pleasant day. It was a large wedding.

4. This forenoon we came home. And Father was in Farmersville. And we have cold weather.

5. Today David Beiler and Lydia Stoltzfus married. And I was at the mill. This evening I was at Aaron's. Honor your Father and Mother that thou livest long in the promised land.

6. Today we worked a little of anything. And this afternoon Father went over to Grandmother. 1895.

7. This forenoon we dunged the stables. And this afternoon I took a load of straw to Grandmother. And Christ and Aaron's were here over night. And it's cloudy and cold weather. 1895.

8. Today we were at home the whole day.

9. This forenoon I was in Farmersville. And Christ came home. And we butchered a bull. And last night it snowed a little.

10. Today John Stoltzfus and Lephenia Kauffman married. And we butchered a hog. And we have cold and cloudy weather. The time is swiftly passing.

11. Today Christ , Aunt Barbara Zook, Aunt Susie Petersheim, and Susie Lapp were here. And I fetched a load of lumber at Pinetown. And it's a pleasant day.

12. Today Stephen Lapp and Katie Fisher married. And this morning it snowed a little. And Father and Mother were with Grandmother. This evening Beckie and I were at Aaron's. And it's cold weather.

13. Today we were stripping tobacco a part of the time. And it's nice and pleasant weather. And Father and Mother went to John Zook's. One by one we pass away.

14. This forenoon we dunged the stables. And this afternoon Christ's, Aaron's, and Beckie and I were with Grandmother. And it's pleasant weather. 1895.

15. Today we were at the meeting at Henry Zook's. And this evening at the singing at same place.

16. Today I was a the mill. And this afternoon I hauled some wood. And we have pleasant weather.

17. Today Jacob King and Fannie Fisher married. And Beckie and I were at the wedding. 1895. And Solomon Stoltzfus and Sarah Petersheim married. And it's a very pleasant day.

18. Today I was stripping tobacco. And so forth.

19. Today John Zook and Beckie King married. And we were hauling dung. And the roads are solid and pleasant weather. Here on earth we cannot stay.

20. Today we made done hauling dung. And Aaron helped us. And it's cloudy but pleasant weather.

21. Today we dunged the stables. And spread some dung. And this afternoon it rained a little. A. C. King.

22. Today Father and Mother were at Aaron's. And we were at home. And this evening I went away. And it's clear and pleasant weather. This evening Christ's came home. Think at the hour you have to die.

23. Today we were stripping tobacco. And Father went in Farmersville. And this evening Christ's and Beckie and I were at Joe Hoover's. And it's pleasant weather.

24. Today we stripped some tobacco. This evening Christ's went away. Corn is worth .35 cts a bu. 1895. O what joy, O what bliss, when we can meet where Jesus is. Sorrow and death shall be no more, When we have reached that heavenly shore.

25. Christmas. Today we were at the meeting at Joel Zook's. And this afternoon Beckie and I were at Isaac Glick's. This evening at the singing at Zook's. And it's very pleasant and warm weather. And Samuel Kauffman's child was buried, he was eleven years, eleven months and twenty-two day's old.

230

26. This forenoon I took Amos and Elam Stoltzfus and Jacob Yoder to Lancaster. And Father and Mother were with Aunt Barbara Zook. This evening I was at the singing at Jacob Glick's. And tonight it rained and stormed powerful. One by one we pass away.

27. This forenoon Christ's came home. And we were stripping tobacco. And we had no snow so far yet. But pleasant and not much cold weather.

28. Today I dunged the stables. And we stripped some tobacco. And this evening Christ's and Beckie went to Uncle Samuel King's. And I went to Menno Stoltzfus to keep house. And it's cloudy weather.

29. Today we were at Uncle John King's. And this evening we were at Aaron's. And Father and Mother were with Grandmother. Evil habits are gathered by unseen degrees. As brooks make rivers, and rivers turn to seas. And we have damp and cloudy weather.

30. Today it rained nearly the whole day. And we were stripping tobacco. And Uncle Elias Stoltzfus's were here. Here on earth we cannot stay. A. C. King.

31. Today we took a lot tobacco down. And stripping tobacco. And it cleared off. And it's stormy and cold.

New Year. Jan. 1. Today Aaron's, Jacob King's and Grandmother and Uncle Christ Stoltzfus were here. And this afternoon we were with Aunt Barbara Zook. What good examples do I find, written in the book of truth. Of children that begin to mind religion in their youth. A good name is better than great riches.

2. Today we were busy stripping tobacco. And Father went to Snaderville. This evening Christ's went to Grandmother's.

3. Today we were stripping tobacco. Life is real. Ife is earnest. And the grave is not its goal. Dust thou art, to dust returnest was not spoken of the soul. Whatever you do, think before you do it.

4. Today we stripped some tobacco. And this afternoon Christ's went away. And we dunged the stables. And I went to Brownstown. And it's cold and stormy weather.

5. Today we were visiting in Mill Creek. This evening we were at Aaron's awhile. And Uncle David Yoder's were here overnight. And we have cold weather. But no snow so far yet. Mind your steps.

6. Today I worked a little of anything. And Father went to Zook's. This evening Christ came home.

7. Today we butchered two hogs for Christ. And it's cloudy and cold weather. This is the land which God hath given us for our dwelling place. But not for a long time. 1896.

8. Today Christ and I were stripping tobacco. And this afternoon Father and Mother went on a visit to Pequea. And it's a clear and pleasant day. But we have plenty of ice this winter so far.

9. Today we stripped some tobacco. And this evening Father and Mother came home.

10. Today I was in Farmersville. And we stripped some tobacco. And it's warm and pleasant weather.

11. Today we dunged the stables. And I took a load of corn to Wenger's. And Aaron's were here for supper. And this evening I went away. 1896. And we have dusty roads this winter.

12. Today we were at the greeting at Feronia Beiler's place. And it's little colder. And this evening we were at the singing at same place.

13. Today we worked a little of anything. And I was in Brownstown. And this evening Jacob, Daniel and Ben Esch were here. And we had no snow on any account this winter. But dandy roads.

14. Today Christ was stripping tobacco. And I took Daniel Esch to John Glick's. And John Zook's were here for dinner. And this evening we were at Aaron's. And it's little rougher and cold weather.

232

15. Today Christ and I were cutting and hauling wood. And Father and Beckie went in Farmersville.

16. Today we worked a little of anything. This evening Christ was in Farmersville. And it's clear and pleasant weather. 1896.

17. Today Christ was hauling wood for Grandmother. At $3.50 a cord. And I helped to thresh at Joe Hoover's. This evening Christ and Beckie went to Grandmother. And Aaron Glick was here.

18. Today we dunged the stables. And worked around the barn. Father was in Mechanicsburg. This afternoon Christ went away. This evening Beckie and I went to Aaron's to keep house. And it's very warm and pleasant weather. And the roads are dusty and it's a dry winter.

19. This forenoon it snowed. And we were at Aaron's. And this afternoon we were at Gideon Beiler's. This evening we went home. And it's wet and slushy weather.

20. This morning I took two hogs to Theo Myer's. At .05 cts a lb. They weighed 441 lbs. Amount $22.64. And our road tax was $13.90 Well begun is half done.

21. Today I didn't work much any how. And it's cloudy weather. Life is real. Life is earnest. And the grave is not it's goal. Dust thou art. To dust returnest. Was not spoken of the soul. Every generation is getting weaker and wiser.

22. Today I hauled the milk to Leacock. And then went to Mechanicsburg. Bran is $14.50 a ton. And we took some tobacco down. It's damp weather.

23. Today it's damp and rainy. And we were stripping and taking down tobacco. 1896. And we had no snow on any account this winter.

24. Today it rained nearly the whole day. And Father and I worked at the tobacco. Think how you live.

25. Today I dunged the stables. And fetched a load of chopping. And Beckie was at Aaron's. This evening I was driving around in the mud.

26. Today we were at the meeting at Menno Stoltzfus. This afternoon Father and Mother were with Grandmother. And David Glick and Christ Zook were here. 1896. This evening I was at Aaron's. And it's cloudy weather.

27. This forenoon I was stripping tobacco. And this afternoon we made ready to thresh. And I fetched the engine at Zook's. And it's little rough and cold. And Moses and John got the …Chickenpox.

28. This forenoon we made ready to thresh. And this afternoon I was at the sale at … And it's very pleasant and clear weather.

29. Today we were threshing. We got two hundred and fifty four bu. And it's a very pleasant day. This evening Christ came home. Dare to be honest.

30. This forenoon I took two cows to Landis Valley for $35 dollars. And Father and Christ made ready to saw wood. This afternoon we were sawing wood. And it's a clear and pleasant day. And Ben Lapp was here over night.

31. Today I was stripping tobacco. And Christ was hauling wood for Grandmother. And Father was in Farmersville. Eggs are worth .16 cts a doz. This evening Christ, Beckie and I were at Aaron's. Pigeons are worth .30 cts a pair. Wheat .67 cts a bus.

Feb.1. Today we dunged the stables. And Christ was stripping tobacco. And I took a load of corn to Wenger's Mill. And fetched a load of chopping. And it's damp and rainy the whole day. Here on earth we cannot stay. One by one we pass away.

The following are from loose pages found in the back of the journal:

June, 1896
16. Today it rained nearly the whole day. And this evening Samuel Fisher's and Christian Lapp's came overnight. This forenoon we planted some tobacco over. And we were in Farmersville. 1896.

17. Today we were shoveling corn. And we have warm weather. Never forget that God is ruling.

18. Today we were shoveling corn. And Father is making a new porch. One by one we pass away.

19. Today I made done shoveling corn. And this afternoon we were fixing the lanes.

20. Today was a powerful long day. And we patched the barn roof. And we have warm and dry weather. This afternoon I was in Brownstown.

21. This forenoon Beckie and I were at Simon Zook's. And this afternoon we had some visitors. And it's a very warm day. This evening I was at the singing at Bab Fisher's place. Mind you steps.

22. Today we started making hay. And we have warm and dry weather. Mind your own business.

23. Today we were busy hauling hay in. And it's cloudy weather.

24. Today it's cloudy and rainy the whole day. And this afternoon Father and John went over to Grandmother. And we worked a little of anything.

25. Today it rained nearly the whole day. And this afternoon Aaron's were here for supper. Youth and aged alike must go. Fade degrees it shall be so. Love your neighbor as yourself.

26. Today it's cloudy and damp weather. And this afternoon I took a load of hay to Aaron's.

27. Today we made done hay making. We got a fair crop again. What good examples do I find, written in the book of truth, of children that begin to mind religion in their youth. A stitch in time saves nine.

28. This forenoon it rained. And we were at the meeting at John Blank's. And this evening I went away. Remember well and bear in mind. A constant friend is hard to find. And if you find one just and true, change not the old ones for the new. Think before you speak.

29. Today we started bindering. And we have warm and dry weather. One by one we pass away.

30. Today we were busy bindering. And it ain't so warm now. Life is real, life is earnest. And the grave is not it's goal. Dust thou art, to dust returnest was not spoke of the soul. O the good are always happy cheerful and delight. Think not to live long. But to live well on earth.

July 1. Today we made done bindering wheat. And was shocking. And Father and Mother were at Grandmother's.

2. Today we started hauling in wheat. And this evening Christ's and Jacob Esch were here. And we have warm and dry weather. Days of the past.

3. Today we were busy hauling wheat. And the mercury was at 100 degrees. Wheat crop is pretty well.

4. Today we were busy hauling wheat. And this evening we had a heavy thunder rain.

Nov. 17. 1896 Levi King and Barbara Fisher married

Nov. 19. 1896 John Smoker and ... Stoltzfus married

Nov. 24. 1896 Jacob Fisher and Ary Stoltzfus married

Nov. 26. 1896 Today was a double wedding. It was Daniel Fisher and Barbara Fisher. And Stephen Esch and Sallie Fisher married.

Jan. 12. 1897. Jacob Kauffman and Katie King married.

Dec. 2 1897 John Lapp and Beckie Stoltzfus married.

Dec. 7. 1897. John Lapp and Emma Kauffman Married.

Dec. 9. 1897 Henry Lapp and Katie Yoder Married.

Dec. 14. 1897 Benjamin Lantz and Mary Lapp Married.

Dec. 14. 1897 Levi Zook and Sarah Zook Married.

Dec. 16. 1897 Isaac Zook and Sarah Lapp Married.

Dec. 16. 1897 Enos Stoltzfus and Salina King Married.

Dec. 21. 1897 Samuel Smucker and Beckie Smoker Married.

Dec 21. 1897. Jacob Zook and Lydia Beiler Married.

Dec. 23 1897. Jonathan Smucker and Katie Lapp

Jan. 6. 1898. Jefferson Stoltzfus and Malinda Smoker

Jan. 11. 1898 Christian Stoltzfus and Levina Fisher

Feb. 17. 1898 Isaac Glick and Rebecca Beiler

APPENDIX B
"Life and Changes of Grandpa's Days"
Chapter 1
1898 – 1999
Memories written sometime in the
1990s, by John S Lapp
94 Glenbrook Rd, Leola, PA

To my ancestors, or to whom it may concern,

My parents were Samuel and Katie (Stoltzfus) Lapp. I was born September 27th, 1898. Born in Intercourse where in later years Dan E. Stoltzfus lived. (My brother in law). My father was a son of Christian and Nancy (Stoltzfus) Lapp. A family of eleven children, three died at eleven years old or younger, and three infants, died. My mother was the daughter of Benjamin and Sarah (Mast) Stoltzfus, a family of seven children. Aunt Lovina was one of them. As a child she had disease and her mind was somewhat shattered after that. She stayed single and after her brothers and sisters were no longer capable of taking care of her she then went to the nieces and nephews. She sang a lot and we have many memories of her.

My father died when I was three months old. He died during an appendix operation performed at home on the kitchen table. In those

238

days there was not much heard of going to the hospital, nor of appendix operations. Even a rush matter or emergency would have had to be with a horse and wagon. His age was twenty-six. Mother was left a widow with three children. My sister Annie was four and brother Benjamin was two. I was three months old. Father was buried at Gordonville Cemetery, Lancaster Co.

On the day of Samuel Lapp's funeral (my dad), his good friend Sammie Stoltzfus was sick and couldn't come to the funeral. So on the way to the cemetery the funeral wagon stopped in front of Sammie Stoltzfus house. They put the coffin with Samuel Lapp outside the window so Sammie could view him. They were about the same age. He was also married.

Soon after the funeral we moved to my grandparents in a double house, with Bishop Benjamin Stoltzfus, on the east side of the bridge near Morgantown. This was my Grandfather that became very close to me because I had no father. I well remember him. I often walked with him around the mill. He died in 1902. I was four years old then, so his presence was keenly felt. My mother did some sewing for other people when she was a widow, and she had her garden that she took care of.

I started school when I was six years old, in a three room school house, in Morgantown. Moss McGandrew was my teacher. Annie and Benjamin were also there, Benjamin did not go while I did. He was hired out to my Uncle Sammie J Stoltzfus near Weavertown school.

In about 1905, after my Grandfather died, my grandmother and my mother and Annie and I moved to the west side of the bridge. Just about 150 feet away from the other place. That same year my mother married again, to Amos C. King. She had been a widow seven years. My stepfather was a widower for three years and had two children by his first marriage. Lizzie was five years old and Jonas was three years old. My stepfather's house keeper was a single girl, (Susan, a daughter of Menno Beiler) until he remarried. Susan later married to Morris Zook, of Talmage. Jonas worked for the neighbors till 1908. Then they bought a farm just about one fourth mile east of Churchtown. The old order Mennonites built a church on that farm at the time we lived there. Benjamin then came home to help on the farm. Now there were five children together. Jonas had been taken in at the home of Levi Fishers when his mother died. They kept him till his father and my mother married. Jonas was four months old when his mother died.

In the Spring of 1911 we moved from Churchtown to Upper Millcreek where Elam King's now live. While we lived in Churchtown I went to Churchtown High School, in Intermediate classes 4th, 5th, and 6th. My teacher was Ella Sensenig, a good teacher and seemingly no problems while she taught. She taught my three years, then she took ill and died. She was a young girl about 22 years old.

The first day of my new teacher everything seemed to go havoc disorder. We soon moved then maybe things went better after I went out???

When moving took place we loaded our household goods the day before and we hauled everything by horse and wagons. I was sick that day and made the trip with dads in the carriage. Everyone had open carriages then. Emanuel Stoltzfus took the horses on foot, riding one of them. Benjamin and some others drove the cows up. About sixteen miles. The previous winter Benjamin and I made numerous trips back and forth with sideboard wagons loaded with implements etc. There were no paved roads then.

My dad sold the farm in Conestoga to old order Mennonites. He bought the farm in upper Mills Creek for twelve thousand dollars, a ninety acre farm. It had a stone barn. Some years later the gable end was blasted down by dynamite, to rebuild, in the year 1915. Batteries were used to set the dynamite off. The wall fell straight down. The work was done by Ike Fisher of Paradise.

School wasn't yet over when we moved so Benjamin, Lizzie and I went a while that spring yet, at Sunnyside school. The only other Amish there were our cousins, Joshua, Ben and Elsie King. I went to school two years then yet. At that time the scholars or the parents could have a choice as to how long they would go to school. Most boys went longer than the girls. It was not that important for the girls to learn mathematics as it was for the boys then. Girls stayed around the home then.

In school we played baseball and sometimes we went to the neighbors to play corner ball. That was a real treat for us. Mr. Clopp was a good teacher. I remember, once in school a young pupil raised his hand and wanted to correct another one. The teacher had a smirk on his face

240

when he asked him what he wanted. The young lad said, he said, Mike said de for dat, meaning this for that. We had three miles for Sunnyside school.

When I was a grown boy Dad did not need me at home all the time. Sometimes I worked for the township with road work. Dad let us have the money we earned away from home. The road work included getting rocks ready for the road, crushing stones with a sledge hammer we pounded, up and down, whack, crunch, till they were small enough for the crusher. I used the dump wagon to haul stones and dump them on the road. These wagons were horse drawn and had an opening at the bottom. My wages were two dollars a day except, when I used dad's horses, then I got three dollars. Very few cars were on the road then but more were coming soon. There were no paved roads except the main road from Lancaster to Ephrata. Now 772. Many were just plain dirt roads.

Benjamin worked at home till he was about 18, then he was hired out at Amos Stoltzfus. (Ames)

Ben paid $60.00 for his buggy. I paid $80.00 a few years later. Probably about 1914. We had no lights on our buggies. There was very little traffic at night. There were no street lights.

My harness cost $20.00, and the buggy horse about $150.00. The young folks went far for supper get-togethers and Sunday night singings. Sometimes we lost our way in the darkness with no lights on the buggies and no street lights and the town dark except for lights in the houses. No wonder the stars seemed brighter and the moon fuller, the night more quiet, that the owl was heard screeching and the crickets heard singing as we headed home.

In summer when it was wet the roads were bad. It was hard pulling for the horses. Our buggies were black but sometimes about all you could see was reddish clay clinging on. Mud was sometimes so deep it came almost to the buggy box and would cling to the wheels. In the winter the ruts that were made in the mud in late fall would freeze. Then we'd go bumpety, bump over the hills and rills.

And what about the Sunday suits, that were not washable. Clothes were dry cleaned, at home, using naptha gas, then aired out good on the line and in the sun. Then put in the closet where moth balls were hanging. When Sunday came again we had sweet smelling and clean clothes again.

In winter time there was much snow. Winters were quite different hen. Many of the grandchildren don't know of much snow and snow blizzards when being kept at home for days. We had to shovel the roads open by hand. The neighborhood got together to do it and we had a lot of fun doing it. Children made snow forts and threw snow balls. There was lots of sledding and ice skating. Sleighs were used to go to town, to school, and to church. We went to the grocery store to deliver eggs and buy a few groceries or other articles, like boots etc.

Many times there were snowdrifts as high as the fences and roads were filled with the snow. Snow oft got so hard that we could go and stay on top of the snow with horse and sleigh, over field and a stream and fences. Many sleighs had bells and so were those chimes as we sailed along. What fun.

Going through the deep drifts, though we sometimes hit a soft spot and over went the sleigh and also the people who were riding in it. There was a lot of fun in the snow and a lot of work, but there wasn't much other work in the winter time. Our dairies were small.

I remember a period of six weeks sledding and ice skating. We had skating parties and played "shinny on the ice" something like ice hockey that is played now. In cold weather we wore leggings to school, or when working out doors. These were to keep the legs warm. Were made of stiff leather and worn over the pants legs, and closed with straps. Buckle artics also were worn. Now we have waterproof shoes and high tops.

In 1914 or 1915 it was an unusual summer. It was cool all summer, and sometimes cold. It was so cold in hay making time that the men wore their coats, (iver ruck) on the job. Had barn windows closed while unloading hay. We had frost every month that summer. And that summer we did not always work on the sweat of the brow.

My dad always had two fields of wheat, about thirty acres. After harvest we would plow one field for seeding wheat again. We had about five acres of tobacco, two acres of potatoes and some corn. We usually had only one crop of hay in a summer, red clover and timothy. Sometimes we made a little stubble hay. We had no engines on our grass mowers. To haul hay to the barn we used a hay loader which was hitched behind the two horse wagon. It picked up the hay, took it up like an elevator and dumped it on the wagon. Some areas they are still used. It was loose hay. Hay balers were not here yet. Wagon loads of hay were pulled into the barn and unloaded by big hay forks. The forks had a long sturdy handle with a leather line at one end, also a heavy rope attached that went through pulleys, a work horse hitched to the rope and "giddap" the horse pulled the fork load of hay to the top of the hay mow. "Whoa" the hay dumped into the hay mow. The horse and rider came back to the starting place again and followed the same procedure until it was all unloaded. Sometimes a well trained horse would do the job without a rider.

Hauling manure...We hauled manure twice a year. In the Spring and after harvest was done. In between those times we dunged the horse pens and cow stalls and dumped on a pile behind the barn. We used the wooden wheelbarrels in earlier years and then later a better wheelbarrel was used. (After I was married) Dad had no manure spreader. We hauled the manure to the fields on low skid bed wagons made of heavy wood planks with side boards. Most times we hauled manure with two wagons. We would load the wagon heaping full then raise the sideboards up about 6 or 8 inches and fill it up again. We had two horses hitched to these wagons, a little like a two horse tree, with two angle trees. We would hitch from one wagon to the other. One wagon was loaded while the other was being unloaded. We had a manure hook to pull the manure off. Small poles, 8-10 inches apart. We would take the one sideboard off to unload. It was more than a few days job. And it brought a good appetite, and we were eager to get to mothers hot food at the dinner table.

There were many tramps and road walkers around in those days. They would often come around for a job. Some would help to haul manure or split wood. Some were good workers and some were thinking more of the meal awaiting than their work. Sometimes there was more than one at the same place working or for a night's rest in the barn. Sometimes they would get into a quarrel. They were always asked to give their matches to the owner before retiring. When we farmed, a tramp's wages were about $1.00 a day. Older ones came to the house for a hand out. Those who worked were usually given a place at the table. Mother never shut the door to a hungry man.

No one was on welfare in those days, and if they wanted something to eat they had to work for it or beg. There were also those who came around with suitcase with things to sell, such as, tooth brushes, shoe strings, etc. There was always something there you could use if you browned around a little. Mother would always buy something, except for one I remember who got too bold and nasty. Leah said, she doesn't want anything, and he had some words with her until I showed myself from behind the door. He soon was on his way then. These tramps walked quite a distance in a day, as there were few houses between the farms.

There were no hammer mills in those days. So we went to the mill to get corn ground in Talmage. We took a two horse wagon load. They would unload it, taking a barrel attached to a rope on the third floor and would let it down. Then we would shovel it full of corn and they would pull it up again and let another barrel down to be filled up while the other one was going up to be unloaded. This was done on the outside of the mill.

At harvest time we used the wheat binder like it is still being used by our plain people. Most times the wheat bundles were put on shocks like the old time pictures of grain fields in the Bible story books. This is not being done so much any more but it takes the eye where it's done. There were threshing machines but not near everyone had one on the farm. Bishop Jacob Stoltzfus and D.M. Stoltzfus both had one in our area. Each threshing rig had their own crew of 4 or 5 hands, usually young boys. They went to one place and helped that farmer and when finished went to the next one. A group of 4 or 5 families helped each other besides the threshing crew. Sometimes they would come in the evenings and set up for the next day and most likely some of the boys would stay overnight. They slept in the barn on a bed of straw and a few blankets. In the morning they washed their hands and faces in the milk house or at the watering trough. Everybody was up early that morning and preparing for the days work, seeing that the belts and everything was alright. And mother remembered them at the breakfast table, too. There was a busy day ahead, not only for the men but for the women as well. There were about 15 to 20 men and little boys to come to the table, and they were hungry.

244

Pies and cakes were baked, sometimes chickens to be feathered and cooked, and vegctables to be gathered from the garden. Cold water and drinks had to be prepared and carried out to the barn and to the stubble fields, which was a little rough on bare feet. Some men went barefoot, too, at threshing time as well as any other time. A few women came to help when there were not enough girls to help.

Wheat threshing lasted about till December, or later if wet weather came in. Dad used to make a straw stack in the barn yard. Our small old barn would not hold all the straw. Sometimes 3 or 4 stacks were made. Like hay, straw too was all put up loose. It created quite a dust in the barn. The wheat was put in grain bins and later the wheat cleaner came in to clean the wheat. Some of this wheat was taken to the mill and was made into flour then taken home and used to bake bread and baked goods.

THE GOOD OLD DAYS..........

There is so much to take my mind over the good old days, things that I remember as a child and my growing up years. Childhood memories are precious. There was not such a rush and hurry all the time. Those were the days that I could master when the pace was slow and I was faster.

The stores were different. Here and there was al little country store. There was nothing like the IGA stores, etc, where you could pick all kinds of frozen food and boxes of quick cooking mixes etc TV dinners and such was unheard of. I think we used our first cake mix in 1955.

These little stores contained barrels of crackers. If you asked for crackers the store keeper knew what you wanted as there was just one kind that I recall, except the thick oyster crackers. There were barrels of flour and sugar to be scooped into a brown paper bags. There were no plastic bags. If you wanted molasses you took a kettle along and the store keeper filled it for you, out of the molasses barrel. You did not go along and fill a shopping cart. You stood up to the counter and asked for each item then the storekeeper got it for you. Mother often sent a list of things on a paper that she wanted. She did not need a big piece as there were not so many things to get. We had our own flour and corn meal that was ground at the mill. Our food was mostly off the land.

There was also the jars of candy at the little country store. This was weighted out on the scales he had hanging over the counter. There was also penny candy or two for a penny. There were nice size chocolate candy bars for five cents or even two for that money or less. I remember getting a chocolate bunny at Easter time when I was a preschool lad and when I unwrapped it I found a penny stuck to the bottom of it, put there by a merciful store keeper. It was at the time when mother was a widow.

When I was in first grade walking to school one morning some English boy came along with a two horse wagon and offered me a ride. I accepted. I was carrying an orange lunch that I was so proud of. The boy told me to put it on the tongue of the wagon which I did and that well loved lunch box got smashed. I felt he did it on purpose. We were the only Amish in that school.

After school my job often was chopping wood or stacking it in the wood shed for the cook stove and the kitchen range. There was no gas heaters or gas stoves then. Sometimes we used a kerosene burner cook stove in the summertime. The kitchen range had a handy pipe shelf that was to keep things hot, and also had a reservoir where we could keep water hot. We could keep about a supply of two gallons of water. Then we had the teakettles on top of the range. My parents did not have running water at the sink.

Butchering day was an event we looked forward to in the winter time. Family or neighbors got together for the job. Hogs were butchered, we made puddings and put them in crocks with plenty of lard on top for a sealer, then it was stored in the cold cellar. Hams and slabs of bacon were cured with a home mixed cure then put in heavy paper bags and hung in the attic. It would keep over the winter like that. We would always butcher a beef, too. Meats could not b e kept long that were not cured because there were no refrigerators. Sometimes a chicken would be beheaded on a Sunday when company came. Canning meat was not in at that time yet either.

There was no stainless steel cookware in those days. Heavy cast iron pans and kettles, and aluminum kettles were used. Mother would often be standing by the hot cook stove stirring hot mush in the iron kettle. Hot mush was often served at the supper table with butter and milk. Then it was left standing overnight and the next morning was set so that it could be sliced and fried. We had that for breakfast along with pork puddings and eggs.

There were outside pumps at the well where we got our drinking water. Some people had a pump at the sink where they could get cistern water, and some had a dry sink and all the water had to be carried from the outside pump, poured into dish pans and then the dirty water had to be carried outside again and dumped. So water was used more sparingly.

We had no bathrooms, no inside toilets. In summer time we used the wooden tub and took our baths in the wash house, carrying all our water. Sometimes two had to use the same water, to save both water and work. But we did not think of complaining because everybody else did it the same way. In winter time we took the bucket behind the stove filled with hot soapy water, and had our baths there, a blanket hung for privacy.

We had the outside toilets away from the house – out back. It was called the out-house, true to its name. It was there in the winter was well as in the summer time, in the dark as well as in the daylight. There were always a few willing to go together before going to bed in the evenings. There were imaginary dogs out there sometimes. There was no bought toilet paper. The outdated Sears Roebuck catalog was hung on the side of the outhouse. A bag of limestone was kept in the outhouse to keep it free of bad odors. And it got plenty of airing out, and got scrubbed down with mothers homemade lye soap.

The weekly wash was done by hand, on the little rivel washboards, with plenty of homemade soap and elbow grease. Hung out in the air and sunshine. Then mother had nice clean wash again to fold and put back into the drawers. Sunday clothes were not washed except the shirts, which usually were, maybe a broad cloth or something similar. There were no drip dry dacron and cottons, double knits etc. The men and the boys Sunday suits were dry cleaned and also aired out good before they were put on hangers ready for the closet, where moth balls were kept to keep everything sweet smelling and free of moths. Sunday dresses were done the same way. Most dresses were of fine batiste for Sunday wear. Can you imagine the chore we would have to get back into that groove.

There also was much ironing to be done. There were no drip dry materials for bed linens or any clothing. So if you did not want a lot of wrinkles, you had to iron and most everything was ironed. So the sad irons were heated on the kitchen range, also which brought more heat in the summertime than was necessary or for comfort.

Most people had fruit orchards or at least a few fruit trees, apricot, apples, pears and walnuts. There was no canning in the early days. Fruit was dried and stored in a dry place over the winter. There were no freezers.

About every family also had some laying hens on the farm, enough for their own use and some to sell to the store keeper, that he would sell again to the town folks. We had hens running loose around the barnyard and in the barns, so we not only gathered eggs, we also had to hunt them. They would make their nest anywhere in the hay and straw. Sometimes we would find a nest of eggs that had been missed before and had to be discarded, and sometimes a cluck was left to set on her eggs and a bunch of fluffy yellow chicks were found and added to the barnyard group.

People did not have as much lawn back then, so that was less work. What was left of the garden was sold or shared with the neighbors or to town folks.

When I was a boy, there around us the town people had a cow. They had cow bells tied to their neck and left them out in the pasture, sometimes just along the road (dirt roads). There was little traffic so it did not matter if one roamed on the road once in a while. Each person knew their cow by the sound of its bell, and every cow seemed to know its owner. In the evening they would round up their cows and put them up for the night in the barn. They could hear from afar off where the cow was grazing by the sound of the bell. Farmers who owned 6 to 8 cows hauled their milk to the creamery on wagons. There were no milk trucks to come to the farm, and of course all milking was done by hand.

Uncle Stephen Stoltzfus lived up the hill from granddads. Their boys, Stephen and Samuel, used to watch the cows along the road in the summer time and I was often with them. Some places there were fences along the road but not between the meadow and the fields or between the next farmers land. We always enjoyed these times together.

When there was illness in the family home remedies were used in the home as much as possible. If there was need of a doctor he came to the house by horse and buggy, daytime or night time. You would not have thought of taking a sick child out with a fever or bad illness. Sometimes the doctor had to come on horse back and many times had to go through snow drifts over fields. He always carried his black satchel with him. Many babies died in those days, the cause of their deaths unknown. In some families quite a few.

Where there happened to be a large family they would let one or more of their children go to a family who had only a few children or none. They raised them as their own and they worked for them. But they were still not so far away that they couldn't be with the family occasionally. When they got married these people helped them get started to house keeping. Young marrieds started off with much less than they do now.

In Churchtown fox chases would often take place. We enjoyed watching these riders chasing the foxes and holding on to the horses they were riding, going across fields and fences. This often took place on a Sunday afternoon. Festivals also were held in summer time close by.

In 1917 my brother Samuel, nearly three years old, died very suddenly of diphtheria. This happened on second Christmas Day. He also had croup with it, he was sick only one day. Then we were quarantined for about three weeks. One year later sister Rebecca, one year old, took sick also with the same and again we were quarantined for three weeks. No one was supposed to come into our house and we were not supposed to go away.

In the fall of 1913 my sister Annie married to John F. Stoltzfoos. Brother Benjamin married in 1917 to Lydia King. They moved into the house with brother-in-law John and Annie, in a double house. He worked one year for John. The next year they rented a farm south of Eden. They lived there three years. I worked for Benjamin two years.

In 1919 Dave Esh and I took a trip to Big Valley, Belleville. The evening before, I went to Hass hat store, in Lancaster, to get my hat fixed. I missed the trolley coming home so I walked home (probably 8 to 10 miles).

Leah and I went together two years before we married. November 17, 1921 was our wedding day. Our nava huckka (witnesses) were my sister Sarah and Leah's brother John, and Leah's sister Lizzie and my step brother Jonas. Weddings were small compared to now, we did not invite any of our buddies to the wedding. We were married by Leah's uncle, Bishop Henry Lapp. That winter we visited all our uncles and married cousins. We went in an open buggy as we likewise did the first few years we were married.

Brother Benj. wife and my wife were sisters. In the spring of 1922 Benj. rented a farm near Sunnyside school, from Nathan Rupp. It was a farm of 120 acres. We also moved there that spring. We lived in a double house. I worked for him there one year then the next year we started farming where Amos Stoltzfus's (Levis) now live, near Center Square.

Leah and I started farming with $2,000.00. We had six cows and four horses, one walking plow, a harrow, roller, disk, sprocket-arm grass mower and a manure spreader. We raised tobacco and that year tobacco prices went up. I sold mine for 19 cents a pound. That was considered a good price, but some sold for 20 cents the same year. For quite awhile before that the price was about 10 cents to 15 cents a pound. At that time most of the side roads still were dirt roads. I scraped the roads in the Spring when the weather got settled with a township drag, often after a rain. Then put crushed stones on the road.

In 1918 Leah's sister Fannie and Levi Stoltzfus were married. They moved near Center Square where he and his son John still live. (At this printing Levi is not living anymore).

In 1927 we rented the Isaac Zimmerman farm. Also in the area of Center Square. Joe Zimmermans now live there. Levi, Dave Horst, and I hauled our milk together to Mechanicsburg, now called Leola, to a dealer who delivered milk through town. In 1927 we shipped our milk to Scott Powell Dairies. We did that for a couple years. Molk price was around $2.00 to $2.50 a hundred pounds. Later they closed the cooling station, then we shipped to Philadelphia. They set up a milk shanty at the end of our lane and we hauled the milk out of the shanty. The milk was picked up in the mornings except Sundays. But instead of Sunday pickup they also picked up Saturday evening. We had to have it out early on Saturday eve. Monday mornings we had three milkings. Sometimes in summer the milk could not always be properly cooled. Sometimes we got more milk than the cooler could hold, if we had extra good milking. Then once in a while a can of milk would turn sour and would be rejected. Ben and I each built an ice box that held six cans of milk. Two doors above and two below. We could put 300 lbs of ice in the top part. We took turns to fetch ice from the New Holland ice plant. We wrapped the ice in blankets so it would not melt till we got home.

250

At Zimmermans the house was not in the best of shape. It was close to the creek. When heavy rains came we got water in the house, and we could not use the cellar because it most always had water in it. Sometimes we got water in the kitchen. There was a spring house there, across the creek where we kept our milk, butter and eggs or whatever we needed that had to be kept cool. There was a water trough in there which always had fresh spring water running through. This was the way we kept our things from spoiling before we had a refrigerator. (Imagine running out to the spring house every time you wanted one of those items). A few years later we got a small refrigerator, rather we called it an ice box. It was made of wood and insulated. We kept it in the wash house. The ice man came a few times a week and filled it with block ice. We thought this was quite an advance from our spring house, where we always had to walk a distance for a bottle of milk for the baby or for a few things we needed at meal time.

While we lived there our little three year old John once followed me when I walked across the creek and he fell in. But I was right there and got him out in good shape.

One day a man came in there with a truck load of mattresses. We bought our first ones then and enough for all the beds that we had in use. The spare beds were still with straw sacks. We paid about $15.00 a piece for these mattresses. Before that we used straw sacks or finely chopped corn fodder in the sacks. A few times a year we emptied them and filled them with fresh straw. We sank into these at night. They were warm or at least we could get warm. Except for where a stove pipe may have gone through the room, the rooms were cold in the winter time. With these straw sacks and feather ticks or woolen blankets we were quite comfortable. What an inviting bed to sleep in, and snuggle up in winter time. In very cold weather we used bricks or good sized stones that were heated in the baker, or bags of shelled corn also were used. This soon had the bed warmed up. Once we were warmed up in there it was not always easy for the children to get out again. But once you were out of bed you didn't waste time getting down to the stove. Before bedsprings came the beds had heavy ropes to put the straw sack on.

Trolleys were running the tracks when I was a boy and quit a while after we got married. I'm not sure when they were taken off but they were still running in 1942, if I'm not mistaken. The tracks went across the lane at the Zimmerman farm, also went through Ben's land. Many people rode the trolley cars, some going to work, some going shopping or just going from town to town. We sometimes rode the trolley to go to church when it was in the Brownstown area, or rather the children did. The trolleys went every hour and on Saturdays every half hour, also on holidays. Sometimes there were 4 or 5 trolleys in a row, filled, and sometimes some had to stand. Men gave up their seats for the ladies. Fare to Lancaster, as I first remember was 7 cents to Lancaster. The engineers wore blue or black uniforms and hats. In 1925 , or around there they closed the tracks at Zimmermans' where they formally went through and went on through Brownstown. We lived at the Zimmerman farm 'til 1935. When I was a boy, one time we went to an auction where Dad bought a heifer at Blue Ball. We went to fetch it in the spring wagon. At Goodville it got wild and tore loose and ran through peoples gardens and yards. I remember we chased it but I don't remember if we caught it or not.

One time when we lived in Millcreek Dad sent Ben and I to Talmage to fetch something., O don't remember what it was anymore but at that time you could not buy ice cream just anywhere like you can now. At Brownstown there was a restaurant and we got a notion to go by there to get some ice cream. When we got home Dad said, "What were you doing in Brownstown?" He didn't care, but he said he heard our horse coming through Brownstown, This horse was a pacer and he knew his gait.

In 1934 I bought the farm where I now live. A 64 acre farm for $11,500.00. I put an addition to the barn, built two chicken houses, and added 15 feet to the silo.

We farmed tobacco, wheat, corn, potatoes and some cabbage. I took potatoes and cabbage tot he Green Dragon Market, and we also peddled some. I tended market for 18 years. For a while we dressed chickens and made potato chips and took them along to the market. We also peddled through town (Mechanicsburg). We quit the chicken and chip business after the oldest girls were married, but I still went to Green Dragon.

Fridays was Green Dragon Market day, and Saturdays was the morning to peddle things through, (now Leola). We went through Leola and part of Bareville. The dressed chickens were put on ice in boxes, loaded in the market wagon and weighed out on the hanging scales as we sold them, out on the street. Chickens were probably about 60 cents a pound. Chips were 10 cents, 25 cents, and 35 cents. If mother had extra things in the garden we took that along too. Town people were always glad for fresh vegetables. Strawberries sold for 25 to 35 cents a quart. Oft times we had spring onions and radishes.

I had a faithful horse (Dewey) we could depend on. We left him standing on the street while we went from house to house to knock on the doors. He would obey the command of (giddap and whoa) just about every time. One of the school children went along. There was not much traffic on the road, but the trolley tracks were right on the road or along side of it. Some people could almost step out only several feet to the trolley from their house.

When we came to the upper end of town in Leola we could smell the bread, cakes and buns being baked at Cooper's Bakery. We often went to the bakery to buy bread or some other goodies.

We also peddled potatoes and cabbage to Reading and a few other towns over there. In late fall many stored up for their winter use. Sometimes 8 to 12 bushels at one place, also sold to stores. We carried them to the cellars. We usually loaded about 75 to 80 bushels. The boys went along to peddle potatoes.

One time our truck broke down. We were close to a motel and had about half of our load yet. We went in and asked if they wanted any. They looked at them and thought that they were nice potatoes and they took them all. Sometimes we peddled til dark and carried them to the cellars. Everyone seemed to be pleasant and respectful. Now it would hardly be safe anymore in the dark nor would it be done in day time. Usually two of the boys went along.

Harry Miller had a little country store out across the meadow from us. Saturday evenings he also had auctions. We could get pretty good bargains. We bought whole bunches like they are taken off of trees. We hung them in the tobacco cellar. One time I bought baby chicks for one half cent a piece, I guess no one wanted them on a Saturday night. I was not prepared for them but we soon made room for them. When they were ready for market the price went up, we sold them for 40 cents a pound.

Oft times our friends, brothers and sisters and families came to go to the auction. Most times the women stayed at our house with the children, sitting on the porch on summer evenings, listening to the auctioneers. The children also enjoyed their outdoor games or after dark catching fireflies, and enjoying fresh homemade rootbeer or home made soda water drink. Sometimes a popsicle from Miller's store. What precious memories.

After Harry Miller moved away from his store he moved along New Holland Pike. We walked out there sometimes, but later we got most of our groceries from Pete Dixon in Talmage. We sent him a list on a post card of what we needed, then later in the week he delivered the groceries to our home. Sometimes we had eggs to sell that he took along for his store customers. The blacksmith shop was also in Talmage. His name was Adam Biem.

In 1934 son Amos had an appendix operation in the hospital. The operation cost $50.00 and $6.00 for the room.

When we farmed where we now live we helped and worked together with Brother Ben and his boys and Brother Jonas and his boys. Bens Johnny lived on the Rupp farm and Amos lived on the home place. We helped together in wheat harvest, silo filling and in putting up hay and tobacco and diggin potatoes. But in later years we each had our own help at home and no longer got together in our work. Also and enjoyable time was when we got together at the end of summer to settle up for the by gone summer. There usually was an ice cream party. The women and children also went along.

Ben's Johnny moved to Lower Pequea in about the year of 1949 or 1950, not sure. More modern equipment was used when I farmed than what my dad had. A much greater advance. My dad never had a manure spreader. While I was farming the corn binder came into use, where before the corn was all cut with the hand corn chopper. Then the corn was put on shocks and later we went and tore the shocks down, knelt on the ground and husked the corn, threw the ears of corn on piles, then went along with the tow horse wagon and threw it on there. Then we hauled it in and threw it into the corn crib, unloading it by shovelful or the children by hand full. And then the elevator came along. Corn that was put in the silo was also first cut by hand, loaded on flatbed wagons, hauled in and put into the silo through the ensilage cutter. My step dad sat on top of the silo till he was a pretty old man when we were filling silo, to keep watch as the ensilage poured in. This was done by tractor power.

Until 1951, we milked by hand, had 15-18 cows. We also raised some of our own heifers. There were no milk tanks, no sputniks. We used little milk stools to sit on to milk the cows. Wish we had them yet. When one cow was milked the bucket of milk was carried to the milk house away from the barn and emptied into 80 lb. milk cans when full. It was put in through a strainer. We got three or four cans from one milking. When we were finished the cans were set in the watering trough to cool. Then later in the evening put into the icebox. If a can of milk turned sour, Leah made butter or cheese, and that too was always a treat. It was a loss not to sell the milk but enjoyed at the table. If we had saved those milk stools we would have a nice antique. We got the milking machine in 1951. We thought this was a great time saver. The boys would go to the field after supper and the girls and I did the milking, or the younger boys helped.

On the farm, it is get up and out early to the meadow to call the cows in. Out on the dewy grass with bare feet. A fresh feeling and a great "waker upper." We also had a few range shelters out in the meadow where we kept young pullets.

In 1959 I started working at Leola pallet shop. I carried a lunch, was picked up in the morning and dropped off in the afternoon by another worker. Some more men went along. I worked there for almost twelve years. When I started to work there I got paid $1.00 an hour. Later I could earn $1.50 an hour. Later wages went up a little. I worked at the saw after I had been there awhile. They had a big saw with four blades which cut four pieces at a time. Sam D. Stoltzfus was killed here at the shop while we were away on a trip.

1970, as I was working at the pallet shop at Leola, I happened to break my wrist. I was in the hospital overnight, they put a cast on. I was off work almost 6 weeks.

SON AARON'S DEATH . . .

October 20th was a beautiful Sabbath day. Aaron and Leah and a few friends went to Eli Beilers that morning to stay with the children that day while Eli's attend communion services. (Eli's, our son in law). (Leah, also our daughter). Elmer and Miriam Stoltzfus were their friends. That evening many noticed a very beautiful sunset. We were visiting at brother in law Ike Kings. Then someone came and told us the sad news, that our son died. It was a great shock and hard to believe. In the morning he left home healthy as far as we knew, and he was in a cheerful mood.

That evening Aaron and his friend Elmer (Sam D's) went to Elam Fishers. Aaron and Elam (Levis) decided to go for a little drive with their horse. They were soon on their way back again and were about at Levi Fishers, Aaron was driving and then put his hand up to his head and said he has a head ache. Then he dropped the lines and slumped over. Elam took the lines and drove in at Levi's and they saw that life had fled. It was sad and shocking news to the family and many young friends. We thought this could not be, but it was final. Most of the family gathered at Levi's before the undertaker took his body away. Also neighbors and young ones gathered. After they took his body away we went home and all the family gathered. Neighbors had already gathered at our home. Our hearts were bleeding. Some stayed overnight.

The following days, until the funeral was over, many church friends and neighbors came to help. Many friends came to the viewing and funeral. A lot of young ones. He had many friends. They came to view his body and pay their last respects. This was very touching and meant a lot to us.

Funeral services were held at the home on the 23rd of October, 1957. He was buried in Myers cemetery. He was greatly missed, and still is, but we would not wish him back in this world of struggle and strife. We think of him often, sweetly resting with Jesus. He was the first of the family to go. Gone but not forgotten. Twenty-four years later my dear wife, Leah, was buried beside him.

Aaron's age was 17 years. He was an active boy, worked at home and was ambitious at work. His last job was painting the barn. Now someone else had to take the work where he left off. It was not an easy task.

When Aaron was a baby he had a bad birth mark on his ear. It took a part of his lower ear off. That is how it healed. He was some times asked about his queer looking ear. He would kid about a mouse having gnawed at it. When he died our family doctor (Ralph Goldin) said he was not surprised at this happening, but rather that it had not happened sooner.

Because of the deep birth mark he thought there might be internal faults. And so it was a busted blood vessel which was weak, at the brain. The doctor had never told us that. He felt here was nothing to do for it and would only cause worrying. But he was with us this long for a purpose.

In the fall of Aaron's death my wife Leah had a bad case of the flue. The two together was very hard on her. She could not do much work for a while.

After this more changes were made. The following spring, 1958 we quite farming. We planned farm sale for beginning of February, but then we had a snow storm and the sale was postponed for two days later. We then had a nice day for the sale.

We then built the daughty end to the house. Son Samuel was carpentering at that time, so he along with the rest of the family and friends and I built and also remodeled the other end of the house. Samuel and Sarah then moved in at the farm end of the house, that spring.

I sold the farm to Samuel for $55,000.00 Then he made some changes. He built another addition to the barn and made room for 32 cows. He tore down the tile silo and built two others. He tore the old milk house away and built one adjoining to the barn, and put in a bulk tank.

Samuel's farmed here till 1982, then they built a house at the end of the lane and moved in there. Then my grandson (Samuel's) John and Ida Lapp moved in and lived double with me, and took over the farming. That was in the spring after my wife Leah died.

John no longer farms wheat. They plant corn twice as thick as we used to and get twice as much to the acre, and use about twice as much fertilizer. They no more cut the corn by hand and no more put it on shock. A corn picker is now used, loaded right on the wagon. Then hauled to the shed, put on the elevator and so is run into the corn crib. Less hands to do the work, easier on the man...

Corn that is put in the silo is cut by the corn binder and a loader is used to put it on the wagon. When I was farming we had about 4 to 6 men cutting with the corn choppers and used that many wagons. In the later years of my farming I also used the corn binder, but it was thrown on the ground then picked up by hand and loaded on the wagon.

1940 they had a horse sale at Bill Lebers in Ephrata. The boys used to lead the horses home instead of hauling them on the truck.

My dear wife passed away on a Tuesday morning, November 17th, 1981. Age 79 years and 23 days. On that same date, 60 years before was our wedding day. The day she died was also a wedding day for one of our grandsons: John son of Ben and Verna Lapp and Rosanna, daughter of Elmer and Naomi Stoltzfus, at the bride's home. I had planned to go to the wedding, and Leah's sisters, Malinda and Rachel, had planned to come and stay with Leah. They did come early that morning, but we saw that Leah was not so well, so I decided to stay home. She was lying on the couch and seemed to be sleeping while the rest of us sat there talking. Then one of the sisters said, "Well, I don't believe she's breathing anymore." So very quietly and peacefully she passed away. It was quite unexpected. Most of the children were already on their way to the wedding and some were there when they found out that mother died. They all came as soon as possible, except Ben's. It was hard to decide for everyone what they should do that day. Some got a driver from the wedding and came here then went back again for dinner, which we were encouraged to do, and also wanted to do for the sake of Ben's and the young couple. They stayed awhile to help with the singing then came up here again. It was a hard day for us all. We wished mother sweet rest, she was quite sickly those last few years, but we miss her.

ABOUT THE AUTHOR

Shawn Smucker lives in Paradise, Pennsylvania with his wife Maile and their four children. He is a co-writer, author and blogs daily at shawnsmucker.com

If you are interested in having him write your own family stories, you can contact him at shawnsmucker@yahoo.com

To order a copy of this book:

- go to http://shawnsmucker.com/store/

OR

- send a check for $15.00 written out to "Shawn Smucker" to the following address:

275 South Belmont Road
Paradise, PA 17562

Include your name, to whom you would like the book signed, and your return address. Shipping is included.

Orders of 10 or more books are available at a discount. Contact Shawn for more details.

Made in the USA
Columbia, SC
14 March 2019